D0515074

Fast Cars, Cool Rides

Fast Cars, Cool Rides

The Accelerating World of Youth and Their Cars

Amy L. Best

NEW YORK UNIVERSITY PRESS

New York and London

NEW YORK UNIVERSITY PRESS
New York and London
www.nyupress.org

© 2006 by New York University
All rights reserved

Library of Congress Cataloging-in-Publication Data
Best, Amy L., 1970–
Fast cars, cool rides : the accelerating world of youth and their cars /
Amy L. Best.
  p. cm.
Includes bibliographical references and index.
ISBN-13: 978-0-8147-9930-7 (cloth : alk. paper)
ISBN-10: 0-8147-9930-2 (cloth : alk. paper)
ISBN-13: 978-0-8147-9931-4 (pbk. : alk. paper)
ISBN-10: 0-8147-9931-0 (pbk. : alk. paper)
1. Youth—California—San Jose. 2. Automobiles—Social aspects—
California—San Jose. 3. Subculture—California—San Jose.
I. Title.
HQ796.B432 2005
305.235'09794'09045—dc22   2005019161

New York University Press books are printed on acid-free paper,
and their binding materials are chosen for strength and durability.

Manufactured in the United States of America

c 10 9 8 7 6 5 4 3 2 1
p 10 9 8 7 6 5 4 3 2 1

For my daughter Ella and her father Christopher

Contents

Acknowledgments

As ever, I feel an enormous sense of gratitude to my parents, Natalie Best and Gary Best, who taught me not only how to drive (a painful process for us all!) but how to live a full life. My sister Christine's strength and goodness, have always anchored me. A great many people helped with this book, among them family and friends. Thank you to Helene Holland, Allan Kushen, Ira Margulies, Kevin McCauley, Terry McCauley, Barbara Pettus, Linda Pincus, Jeff Rodgers, Jonathan and Sarah Rodgers, and Vivian Taylor for support shown in ways both big and small.

This book was completed because of the support I received from George Mason University, especially the Department of Sociology and Anthropology, and from San Jose State University. Without a number of grants awarded by San Jose State University, collecting data for this project would have been more difficult than it was. Carol Ray willingly read each of the chapters I wrote, providing extensive comments that meaningfully shaped its outcome. Susan Murray, A. G. Rud, Judith Barker, and Julian Keenan also provided welcomed comment. Other colleagues, including Peter Chua, Diane Myers-Lipton, Scott Myers-Lipton, Bob Gliner, Rona Halualani, and Elena Klaw, also provided a meaningful intellectual space for me to develop many of the ideas that appear in the pages that follow. I'd like to thank all the members of the Department of Sociology at San Jose State University for their genuine collegiality during my time there. I am beholden to my students from San Jose State University, who played a significant role in this project. The classroom served as an exhilarating intellectual space for me to share ideas as I moved through this project. A number of my students, most from Silicon Valley, provided valuable information, contacts, and suggestions for additional research directions as this project developed. I am especially grateful for the excellent work of Maria Flores, Carmen Garcia, Danette Garcia, Robert Trade, Jason Yates, Felicia Dolores,

Heidi Remmers, and Karen Ranier, who served as my research assistants. I am proud to have directed such a skilled and committed group of researchers. The exceptional editorial team at NYU Press helped bring this book to print. Ilene Kalish is an excellent editor if there ever was one.

My daughter and my husband are at the center of my life. I dedicate this book to them for their boundless love and understanding.

Introduction

Fasten Your Seatbelts

On a late summer Saturday night, I get in my car to head downtown to check out San José's car cruising scene, where hundreds of young adults from all over the Bay Area gather to cruise up and down a strip of street that extends over ten blocks, to see and be seen. Students at San Jose State University, where I am teaching, tell me it is a crazy scene, rowdy and raucous, something I must definitely scope out if I am going to write a book about youth in San Jose, California, and their cars. And so I head downtown for the first time, unsure of what I might find. I arrive at Santa Clara Street, greeting the bright lights and bustle of a city's nightlife played out in and around cars. Rows of cars consume the street. Sounds wash over me: the screech of tires peeling out after a red light, the rev of a heavily powered engine, the voice of Eminem traveling from some unidentified car, competing with the sounds from another car. The bass from the car next to me, a red Mustang, thumps as the car shivers to the beat. I make my way down the street alongside hundreds of other cars. I pass a shiny black Cadillac, new and expensive, with a young Anglo-looking kid, maybe eighteen and wearing a wooly cap on his head, sitting behind the wheel. I am struck by his posture perhaps more than anything else, as he is sunk deep within the seat, almost eye-level with the steering wheel. To my left is a Camry with an "OBC Team" sticker on the back window. I pull up to a stop light just as it turns red. I can see, off in the distance, a small group of young men, dressed in oversized khakis slung low on the hips and the thin white tank tops that the young colloquially call "wife beaters." They pace the sidewalk, and, as cars pass, they holler attempting to gain the attentions of those passing by. A carload of girls cruises by, and one of the young men hollers out, more forcefully this time, his voice reaching a crescendo as he yells, "Was'up babeee!" As the light turns green, I watch as a white Pontiac GTO begins to move in front of

1

me. It is loud as the barreling muffler roars and the tires screech, producing the gray smoke of burning rubber. The heads of three young women standing on the corner of the street look up as they watch the car's halting start before returning to their chatter. Farther up ahead, I spot a small army of cops standing in the middle of the road inspecting the various cars that pass within their view. As a rule of the street, where there are youth en masse, swarms of cops are sure to follow.

I witness two cars as they are pulled over. Both are silver and small; both are driven by young people, one young woman appearing Anglo, the other Latino. There seems almost a loose protocol to being pulled over here. In this instance, the cop's arm shoots up, and his finger directs the first young driver into the center lane. The young woman immediately pulls in, and I see she is without a front license plate, something I too am without. I cruise by a convenience store on the right side. The parking lot is filled with cars and trucks, most of which are shiny and nice. Young men move in and out of the store, lingering in the lot. An older model Ford Mustang, bright red with a white racing stripe, parked in the lot catches my attention as two young men lean casually against the side of the car. The music booms from the car stereo, and the car appears to shudder at the rage of the sound within. I hear in the distance an old-fashioned-sounding honk from an older VW bug as it zips away.

This scene takes place in 2000, and over the next five years I return to Santa Clara Street many times, seeing much the same scene as young folks inch their way up and down this strip of street in search of fun and freedom, to see and be seen and much more. Over time, a picture begins to emerge of the young people of San Jose and their cars, an image that looks much like a large mural, with various scenes blending at their edges, one that captures the life and times of an urban world. The scenes are drawn from five years of watching and listening, paying close attention as young people organize themselves and their worlds around cars. The backdrop is San Jose, California, a rapidly changing community, the center of the tech revolutions that created thousands of "paper millionaires" in the dot.com fury, where the cars are as numerous as the people, where life unfolds quickly and one's ability to participate in its unfolding is largely dependent on having a car. San Jose is the eleventh largest city in the United States, but it is sprawling, stretching across many miles, making the car indispensable to almost all who live here.

The idea to study youth and cars emerged from a project I completed in 2000 that focused on the high school prom. I became fascinated by the social realities young people create and confront and the things and spaces that are meaningful to them. I came to study the youth in San Jose specifically because I lived there. At the time, I was teaching sociology at San Jose State University, its campus consuming several blocks in San Jose's downtown, not far from Santa Clara Street, where youth come to cruise. Sociologists often study those things they are close to; puzzles from their own lives inspire research and give rise to particular lines of investigation. That was not entirely the case here. The idea to study cars did not emerge out of any tangible interest in cars themselves on my part. I am not a car buff, nor do I have any nagging desire to have my dream car. I am concerned with the world's growing dependence on cars, but that apprehension did not inspire this research, either. Rather, that concern grew out of this research. I came to study cars because they provided a way into the worlds occupied by young people. Cars hold deep significance for the young, and thus studying cars meant studying a topic of great relevance to them. At the same time, an investigation of cars seemed to provide a way to explore, from the inside out, the meaningful shifts in the lives of young people, to trace the connections among the routines of everyday life for youth and the broader social forces of change, ones that have been coming for some time.

At the center of this project are the voices of some hundred young adults, an ethnically and economically diverse group, almost all from San Jose, who have shared with me their stories about driving and cars: stories about learning to drive, breaking curfew, encountering the law, and the far more routine aspects of simply existing in American car culture. Their stories chronicle time spent in the car, their attempts at brokering deals with parents to extend this time, and the lengths gone to to buy what is often seen as their ultimate ticket to freedom. Their stories are as varied as the youth themselves. While this is a book about these stories, it is what these stories reveal about the broader social issues that stand behind them that ultimately is of interest here: freedom and selfhood, place and space, visibility and respect, inequality and social distinction.

American Life and the Car

The American landscape was forever altered by the advent of the automobile. The significance of the car in organizing our lives is extraordinary, transforming our physical and symbolic worlds in unimaginable and unforeseen ways.[1] Few people give more than a passing consideration to their hold over us or to the ways cars operate as dynamic social forces in their own right. Perhaps this happens because it is difficult to imagine cars serving any purpose beyond their utility—they transport people simply and relatively easily, wherever and whenever they want to go: work, school, the grocery store. Or perhaps cars are so obviously markers of social distinction that we overlook precisely how they work as such.

Cars often serve as indicators of social and economic worth as well as key markers of identity. Marketers knew this long ago, even if we did not. On some very basic level, we understand that driving a particular kind of car has the power to transform how we feel about ourselves as individuals and as members of specific social groups. This may be explained in part because cars are important status symbols in American culture; in the language of sociology, cars are "status-conferring objects." Whether racing down the highway in a Mustang convertible, cruising down Main Street in a Lexus, or observing a Hummer parked in the driveway of a palatial home, we see cars as a way to announce one's material successes (or lack thereof) to the world, and many Americans, including this writer, have experienced a profound pleasure in that fact. But cars also speak to the ambiguity of class: poor people sometimes have expensive cars, and rich people sometimes have shabby cars. A fancy car does not always translate into a fancy life.

Of course, material success is not all that cars announce. Cars have what the French theorist Jean Baudrillard calls "identity value" in that they act as markers of social and cultural difference and thus communicate ideas about who we are in relation to who others are. Through this system of signs, cars also often serve as symbols of masculinity.[2] "Traditional notions of separate spheres and the control of technology ensured that the car came to be identified with masculinity," argues the cultural historian Sean O'Connell.[3] Car culture is often seen as a space where men can be men, and in many instances it provides one of the few opportunities for men to forge emotional ties with other men, often across generations. The car has long been a way for young working-class men to claim respect and dignity as men, to deflect the repeated assaults on their manhood staked elsewhere. But as much as the car and the culture that develops around it can bring men together, the car also creates and deepens divisions among men.

In 1930, there was one car for every 1.3 families in America.[4] Between 1969 and 1997, the number of households nationally with two or more cars doubled from 30 percent to 60 percent *despite* a decline in the size of American households.[5] Cars are firmly a part of the physical landscape of modern American life, an irreplaceable fact of our everyday worlds. Driving is often thought of as a leisure activity; consider the Sunday drive. We rely heavily on cars for leisure-related travel. Kids in the 1970s tuned in as the Brady Bunch visited the Grand Canyon in their family station wagon. Many of us have memories of long family caravans to various national parks. Indeed, this has been the subject of many a movie, the most classic being *National Lampoon's Vacation*, starring Chevy Chase. With rare exceptions, we rely on cars to travel between work and home. The fact that many Americans increasingly live in one community and work in another further compounds our dependence on cars. A commute of sixty miles or more each day is not in the least extraordinary in northern California's Silicon Valley or in many other cities marked by rapid and somewhat haphazard development, such as Dallas, Atlanta, and Los Angeles. Highway travel is part of daily life for most Americans as we tune in to morning radio traffic reports in the hope of avoiding being trapped in the very machine that once promised us our freedom.

Cars can be found everywhere, not just on the road. Young people are introduced to American car culture long before they are able to see beyond the steering wheel. A quick trip through Toys-R-Us will reveal a veritable windfall of plastic keys, gas pumps, colorful steering wheels, electric cars, match box cars, and so on. No doubt by the time a young person is legally eligible to drive, she has already spent countless hours behind the wheel, even if only in play. This is not to mention the incalculable hours kids spend as passengers in the car in carpools or running daily errands with a parent.

We are a car-dependent people, even if we hate to admit it. As Americans, we reject the idea of our dependence on anything, preferring to view the car in terms of our much-prized independence and freedom.[6] This is a more inspiring and guiltfree way to think of the car, but perhaps less honest. Paradoxically, the car is both a symbol of freedom, progress, and prosperity *and* a harbinger of the perils of rapid industrialization and the wreckage foisted on humanity by corporate capitalism.[7] After all, it was Henry Ford's assembly line that revolutionized the U.S. production process, catapulting U.S. industrial growth far beyond that of its competitors on the other side of the Atlantic.[8] Car proponents may revel in the triumphs of the automobile age, but one need not look too far to identify a host of problems related to the car. Endless waste (think about how we dispose of worn tires), the upset of ecological systems (think about roadkill), urban sprawl, the loss of open space, land erosion, global warming, spiraling traffic congestion, and a host of health-related problems such as the rise of obesity (think about the drive-thru) have all been linked to the automobile and our dependence on it for travel.[9] Fewer and fewer Americans today walk to work, and a majority of suburban communities are without bike lanes on their main roadways. The rise of the car, like the advent of television, is tied arguably to the decline in civic and public life, the fracturing of community, and an increasing sense of social isolation.[10]

Cars are a global phenomenon. The number of cars on the planet is increasing three times faster than the population itself.[11] America and western Europe have the lion's share, with 87 percent of all automobiles produced worldwide purchased by their populations.[12] Much like a revolving door, we replace our old cars with new cars and our new cars with newer cars, while people in other parts of the world mostly go it on foot. Theirs is a life without the barreling monster SUVs that represented 45 percent of the new car market in the United States in 2002. In this sense, cars reveal the vast economic gulf between the first and the third worlds. Cars and car use also reveal deep economic and social divisions between different sectors of U.S. society, since many are unable to afford a car and the voluminous car-related costs. Hostage to a failing public transit system, the elderly, the young, and the poor remain largely trapped, geographically (and often spiritually) disconnected from a life beyond their immediate social worlds, worlds often bereft of hope and meaning.[13]

Cars are caught in a complex web spun by the politically and economically powerful. Drawing attention to the political overtones of American car production in his book *Geography of Nowhere,* James Kunstler demonstrates the very calculated efforts of General Motors, in the 1930s, to dismantle public transportation by gaining financial control over bus, streetcar, and railway operations as the Great Depression threw many rail and bus companies into bankruptcy. GM's goal, which was ultimately realized, was to replace public transportation (specifically the efficient streetcar) with private transportation.[14] To talk about cars, then, is to talk about politics. Yet, the geopolitical considerations largely responsible for our everyday reliance on cars are usually set aside as people think of cars in terms of their likes and dislikes, as though the cars we drive were simply a matter of personal choice and preference. Ian Robert, a professor at the London School of Economics, argues, "Car-making is now the main industrial employer in the world, dominated by five major groups, of which General Motors is the largest. The livelihood and landscape of the United States and Canada were forged by carmakers. Motor vehicles are responsible for about one-third of oil use but for nearly two-thirds of U.S. oil use. The United States has paved itself into a corner. Its physical and economic infrastructure is so highly car-dependent that the country is pathologically addicted to oil. Without billions of barrels of precious black sludge being pumped into the veins of the economy every year, the United States would experience a painful and damaging withdrawal."[15] Endless pressures from the highway lobby have successfully thwarted the development and expansion of alternative public forms of transit, with consequences in real dollars.[16] For every dollar directed toward public transit, seven dollars go to the car, according to Jane Holtz Kay, author of *Asphalt Nation*. This is not the case in other industrialized nations, which boast far more comprehensive public transit systems than ours.[17] Yet, despite this stark reality, the car's ubiquity and its attendant problems remain outside our purview; the car escapes the critical scrutiny it warrants as we resign ourselves to wasted hours sitting in traffic.[18]

Kids and Cars

A handful of media images of kids and cars tell the prominent place cars have had in post–World War II American youth culture. The image of James Dean engaged in a perilous game of chicken while drag racing in *Rebel Without a Cause* is perhaps one of the most enduring. "Live fast, die young," Dean was rumored to have said before his untimely death, ironically the result of a car accident in which he was behind the wheel. The countercultural movements of the '60s are invoked by the single image of a handful of kids packed into a Volkswagen van (a microbus) in their pursuit of freedom from adult control, the oppressiveness of prevailing middle-class sexual mores, and the snare of suburban conformity. Youth disaffection is encapsulated in both images, serving as powerful reminders of the place of cars as young people articulate a distinctive politics and mobilize against a series of cultural "oughts" and "shoulds" as they confront a slippery cultural slope during their passage into adulthood.

Getting a driver's license is a milestone in American cultural life, carrying significance not only for parents and youth but also for the culture at large. It is one of the few widely shared rites of passage, beyond the high school prom or high school graduation, that signifies one's becoming an adult. Ideas about when one is legitimately an adult and about the degree of freedom to which a young person is entitled come to the fore as parents and their young adult children make decisions about the youths' getting a driver's license and, ultimately, a car. But the car is also an all-too-often contested terrain over which parental control is exercised, where parental anxiety and fear intensify and, sometimes, intergenerational tensions mount.[19] This was the case for nineteen-year-old Mike, one of the young men who participated in this study, whose car became his refuge when he was kicked out of his parents' home.

Kids use cars as templates to communicate ideas about who they are individually and socially. Consider, for example, the young woman who had written, with a bar of soap, on the rear window of her car, "I turned 18 today" or the young man I saw cruising one night who had painted "Self Made" in white script on the back window of his shiny black souped-up pickup truck. The car often serves as the centerpiece around which an entire night's activities unfold, largely because youth have few public places to spend a Friday night. I was struck by the amount of time young people spent in their cars, talking on the phone, listening to music, sleeping, studying, watching a DVD, or just talking. A recent study released by Teenage Research Unlimited, a market research outfit, found that 60 percent of teens spend at least four hours a week cruising in cars. A Saturday night drive down just about any busy roadway in just about any town or city where the bright lights of fast-food chains, convenience stores, and gas stations cast long shadows on seemingly empty parking lots is likely to reveal clusters of kids engaged in the curious activity adults too readily dismiss as "doing nothing."[20] Late-night street racing in empty business parks has become an increasingly popular activity among young men. These settings are often central to youth culture, serving as spaces where race, class, and gender identities materialize as kids negotiate the symbolic boundaries of place.

At the same time, as kids take to the streets, they often come up against a series of restrictions: town ordinances against cruising, state-wide driving curfews, zero-tolerance laws, and the recent graduated driver's licensing system.[21] These policy and legislative acts express how we have come to associate youth with risk and danger, often blaming them wholesale for a set of social circumstances that they had little role in creating. As Frank Furedi, author of *Culture of Fear*, insightfully remarked, "To be at risk is no longer about what you do but who you are."[22] These policies have tremendous consequences for how youth participate in their communities and can engage as citizens. Decisions made by legislators and policymakers that place restrictions on kids' driving, whether necessary or not, have the unfortunate outcome of limiting young people's full participation in public life, since many of these policies (e.g., anticruising ordinances) restrict or delay (as in the case of graduated licensing) kids' movements beyond school and home.[23] As young folks move in and out of public spaces, they struggle to remain visible in and against the concerted efforts by state legislators to render them invisible, positioned on the sidelines of public life through restrictive policies, and to create their own spaces in an age-segregated, adult-dominated world. Denied the traditional means of civic engagement, youth, many feeling increasingly marginalized and disenfranchised, struggle to exercise influence over the worlds they occupy in other ways. For some, policies that restrict young people's access to public space have inspired grass-root efforts to effect social change locally; for others, these policies are greeted with apathy on the one hand and in-your-face tactics of defiance on the other as in the case of some forms of street racing. At their worst, these policies magnify generational, racial, and class antagonisms between young folks, often of color, at whom many of these policies are directed, and adults, since they tend to criminalize what are otherwise commonplace activities, as anticruising ordinances so clearly illustrate.[24] For almost half a century, cars have been central to young people's efforts to gain visibility, to participate in community life, and to claim public space against a sweeping tide of organized efforts to preclude such possibilities.[25]

Kids face a world different from the one their parents faced, and this has consequences for understanding kids' use of cultural objects such as the car. At the dawn of a new century, kids confront a world of economic, political, and social uncertainty, and their personal worlds are increasingly organized by abstract systems of control.[26] While social movements that sought to redress enduring social inequalities, such as the civil rights and feminist movements, have created new opportunities thought impossible decades before, these changes have been tempered by dramatic economic and social changes often associated with what we call the global economy. Economic restructuring in the '70s and '80s has eroded the opportunity structures once available for a large percentage of youth, concentrating an overwhelming number at the lower end of the wage continuum in dead-end service jobs with little hope for improved prospects.[27] Countering public impressions of a world of bounty for a generation of the hyperindulged, in the mid-1990s, a mere one in five young men could expect to economically outpace his father, giving rise in some instances to disaffection and disillusionment as this generation faced a bleak economic future as a whole.[28] Yet, as youth encounter an adult world of emptying opportunity, they are also drawn into a culture of hyperconsumption, where desire runs over and the accumulation of endless objects is *the* measure of "having made it."[29] The specter of economic failure that has magnified the divisions between the haves and the have-nots, coupled with dramatic changes in patterns of consumption spurred by the unassailable pursuit of profit by consumer corporations, provides the backdrop for understanding the significant meanings young folks invest in cars today.

The Youth Car Market

The car stands as a symbol of the emergence of a distinct youth consumer culture, testifying to its spending power.[30] Social scientists talk about the colonization of youth markets by marketers as being analogous to the colonization of Africa by Great Britain. As mistaken a parallel as it may be, kids have considerable disposable income compared to generations before them; their influence over family spending is thought to be unmatched by that of any other generation.[31] The under-twenty-five set, the so-called "coddled, confident offspring of post–World War II baby boomers,"[32] has been termed "the millennials" and the "net generation" in marketing circles, and they are 71 million strong. In the eyes of marketers, their sheer size alone translates into a bonanza of untapped market share. This group of young consumers is often thought to be the inspiration behind the marketing renaissance of the late 1980s; its members are "the nation's dominant marketing force," surpassing their parents, the original band of youth consumers, in their ability to shape the direction of popular culture and consumer trends, according to some of the top marketing research firms, such as Teenage Research Unlimited, CNW Marketing Research, and Trends Research Institute, whose business it is to keep a close watch over consumer trends.

The auto giants were slow to realize the untapped potential of young consumers. As other industries, including sports and entertainment, recast their focus toward the younger set more than a decade ago, the auto industry, like the electronics industry, has only recently caught on. This is largely because youth (teens especially) were thought to be big consumers of small-ticket items—gum, hair accessories, lip gloss, CDs, comics, blue jeans, and so forth.[33] Yet, one could hardly say automakers overlooked young car buyers entirely. As early as the mid-1930s, American car companies began running ads for cars, usually low-priced and sportier versions of family sedans, that might appeal to younger drivers. But there are categorical differences between how youth are targeted by marketers today and how it was approached in earlier generations, in part because there are categorical differences between the consumer world young people occupy today and the world their parents faced at their age. This generation, unlike their baby-boomer parents, has come of age during a period when segmented marketing has prevailed over mass marketing, an age of competitive advertising that has spurred "a wave of brand mania."[34] Youth are becoming adults in the "age of accelerated meaning" where the image matters more than the product, in a "new branded world" of hypermarketing—endless corporate sponsorships and partnerships that are thought to have eroded the public sphere and civil society and created a crisis of democracy.[35]

The youth market for cars is rapidly expanding and will lead to "a phenomenal change in the way car companies will do business over the next decade," predicted Don Esmond, vice president and general manager of the Toyota Division, at the 1999 unveiling of the Echo, the first car by Toyota "designed for strong youth appeal." According to Teenage Research Unlimited, in 2002, 27 percent of teens ages 12–19 owned a used car, and 9 percent had a new one. This represents a significant slice of adolescents, given that the age minimum for legal licensing in most states is either sixteen or seventeen. By the time American teens enter college, 40 percent will have their own vehicle, and for a growing number these cars will be new. Car dealerships are far more likely to finance young car buyers than they were a few decades ago.[36] In 2004, buyers under twenty years of age accounted for almost 600,000 new car sales nationally.[37] Between 1998 and 2002, the percentage of thirteen-to seventeen-year-olds who could say that a car was "the newest thing bought" jumped from 4 percent to 10 percent.[38] In the spring of 2003, the *Wall Street Journal Weekly* declared that people ages 18–25 represented the largest car-buying market.[39]

Determined to capture its share of this expanding youth market, the auto giant Toyota recently formed a youth division, Scion, specifically designed to sell low-cost small sedans and SUVs to youth. To introduce its new concept car, the Scion division has sponsored concert tours, collaborated with hip-hop and youth-based magazines, and even used spotlights to flash the Scion image onto the exterior walls of large buildings to announce its arrival.[40] Others in the auto industry are only steps behind as they form teams of teen consultants to advise on car designs for the youth market. For some car companies, gaining the attention of young buyers has involved attempts to reinvent themselves. Oldsmobile began colloquially referring to itself as "youngsmobile" in the mid-1990s. The Plymouth minivan, a model that has typically been identified with suburban, middle-class housewives, repackaged itself as the ideal mode of transportation for extreme-sports enthusiasts—snowboarders and surfers, young white men in their teens and twenties—because of its extended cargo space. Tapping into a flourishing multibillion-dollar youth market of after-market accessories, the Saturn Corporation has signed licensing agreements with more than twenty after-market manufacturers to supply various add-on components for engine modifications and exterior and interior changes. Saturn is among a crop of car companies that are offering personalized and customized cars in an effort to entice young buyers, a group well known for its desire to express its individuality through its choice of cars and other consumer wares. Youth are also increasingly seen as a worthwhile market segment in the luxury car market; 1.5 million teens own what are called "near-luxury cars" (those priced between $28,000 and $35,000).[41] In the past few years, Lexus, BMW, and Mercedes-Benz have all introduced starter models, usually compact, sportier versions of their more expensive lines priced in the low $30,000 range, in the hope of gaining the brand loyalty of a younger set notorious for their brand disloyalty.

Since the late 1990s, the auto giants have come to play an ever-expanding role in the lives of youth, organizing their social spaces and social activities, as they forcefully attach themselves to signs that already register as repositories for youth culture and style.[42] Volkswagen joined forces with the computer company Gateway in its "Cram for College" campaign to "promote college graduation" by giving away ten Volkswagen Beetles, complete with Gateway's famous branded cow spots, in 1999.[43] More recently, VW paired with Apple Computer to give away free iPods (the world's best-selling digital music player) to VW Beetle buyers.[44] Volkswagen is not the only automaker to build market alliances with corporations that aren't in the business of selling cars. Toyota forged a three-year deal with Vivendi's Universal Studios, enabling Toyota to sponsor theme park attractions, place cars in Hollywood blockbusters, and distribute music CDs produced by Universal through Toyota dealerships, all as a part of its effort to gain greater youth market share.

These megacar companies regularly present themselves as youth advocates as they work to generate greater brand awareness among these "very savvy new car buyers."[45] To help deflect the rising cost of higher education, Toyota awarded $1.12 million in scholarships to high school seniors in 2002 as part of its "100 reasons to feel good about youth" campaign. Ford has sponsored football clinics for inner-city youth in Detroit. Volkswagen of America spearheaded a national safety belt initiative, Fasten Your Seat Belt . . . Go Far, with the educational book seller Scholastic Inc., in which teens designed public service announcements encouraging teens to buckle up. The PSAs' debut came during MTV's phenomenally popular television show *Total Request Live (TRL)*, which serves as an hourlong commercial promotion for pop superstars like Britney Spears, Justin Timberlake, Christina Aguilera, and Avaril Levine; the finalists and their schools were awarded a slew of gifts.

For many readers, this is a familiar tale about kids and the increase of commodification in their lives.[46] By examining the meanings youth assign to cars and by exploring how they use the car to navigate their present and future, I hope to show how they respond to the already encoded meanings that swirl around the car: freedom, success, and risk, among others.

Defining Car Culture

Where does a car culture begin and end? Traditionally "culture" has been loosely defined in terms of shared meanings and common practices. Culture was often thought to exist in connection to place and space, emerging out of specific locales. But, in an increasingly global economy with a steady stream of bodies crossing ever-changing borders, tying culture to a specific place proves difficult. In this sense, "culture" lacks permanence. At the heart of car culture is movement and flow; car culture is first and foremost a mobile one.[47] With this in mind, I take as my starting point an understanding of "culture" as a complex set of concrete social practices, symbols, artifacts, memories, and texts through which social meanings are expressed and created and social inequalities produced and reproduced. Culture is a terrain of loosely organized ideas and practices through which power works.[48]

To study cars and car culture is to investigate our material life and the maps of meaning upon which it relies.[49] Cars circulate on both material and symbolic planes.[50] In our culture, they are symbols, their changing and various meanings arising from our social encounters with them.[51] The pollution and waste cars emit testifies to their equally important material presence. Cars are concrete objects and signs, repositories of pleasure, yet hardly innocent.[52] In the words of Paul Gilroy, in his insightful essay, "Driving While Black," an investigation of cars and the cultural fields they cross must "encompass the alienated but nonetheless popular pleasures of auto freedom—mobility, power and speed—while appreciating their conspicuous civic, environmental, and political costs."[53] Car culture is forever bound to the historical relations of modern capitalist production and consumption. Quite simply, cars, unlike other material artifacts, have never existed apart from the economic logic of modern life; cars are first and foremost commodities. Car culture, then, should be understood as a culture inseparable from its market origins.[54] After all, cars are mass-produced and mass-consumed products, encoded by the auto industry, their meanings ascribed through production processes *and* consumption practices.

My understanding of car culture rests on such a framework. I use the term *car culture* in two specific ways. First, I use *car culture* in a broad sense to refer to modern American culture as shaped by the complexities of mass production and mass consumption. Today's American culture is increasingly mobile and frenetically paced. The ubiquity of cars and our culture's fascination with speed reflect this changing reality. In both material and symbolic ways, cars reveal the hegemony of a mobile life. Cars are key symbols of vertical and horizontal mobility, since they provide us with the means to move across place and space in ways that have dramatically altered our relationship to time and, also, though to a lesser degree, across social positions and symbolic status boundaries. Within American culture, we belong to different types of "car communities," as revealed by the price we're willing to pay for a car for ourselves or our teen children and the interpretive schemes we use to make sense of the car and its role in our lives.

I also use *car culture* to refer to various subcultural groups and spaces; by *subculture* I mean a loosely organized group of youth who share an appreciation for particular cultural styles and participate in a set of shared activities that revolve around the car. These distinct subcultural practices are formed by young car enthusiasts: young men and women who regularly participate in car-cruising or car-racing culture and whose activities are critical to the ongoing production of these cultural forms as both social practice and worldview.[55] Car cruising and car racing are two distinct car scenes that have momentary overlaps in San Jose, where this study was done. Car racers sometimes cruise San Jose's downtown streets, where car cruising is a popular weekend activity, and cruisers sometimes travel to the abandoned industrial zones and business parks outside San Jose's urban core to watch illegal street races. While the boundaries between these two groups are sometimes fluid, with some level of boundary crossing, when it comes to "identity talk," that is how these kids think of themselves and their peers; cruisers and racers draw distinct moral and aesthetic boundaries between their groups. Cruising is fundamentally communal as handfuls of kids pack into cars to make their way down the strip, while car racing is far more competitive. Both activities have solid ties to particular ethnic groups and are largely dominated by young men, serving as cultural spaces where masculinity plays out and where rigid gender distinctions are affirmed.

In the end, I am interested in grafting the connections between these two types of car cultures: the broader American car culture and the distinct subcultures, identifying their interrelatedness and investigating the ways young people travel in and across these different cultural fields as they make meanings, solidify their social identities, and negotiate a set of constraints that originate outside their everyday worlds. It is with this in mind that I also write with a particular understanding of youth culture. This culture is not something youth themselves create apart from or necessarily in opposition to the dominant culture. Many of the defining features of youth car cultures are not oppositional in the way other youth subcultures often are. Thus, I define youth culture as a set of practices and meanings organized by youth as they navigate increasingly abstract social forces that to this researcher often seemed to be beyond young people's immediate grasp, strangely in their worlds but also outside them.[56]

Our Cars, Our Selves

Young people attach ideas to cars about who they are. Thus, an investigation of their uses of cars provides occasions for examining the social and cultural contexts in which young people form their identities. These identities are made meaningful through a repertoire of *symbols* (dress, cars, bookbags, sneakers, hair extensions), *practices* (car cruising, car racing, body piercing, surfing, graffiti writing), and *sites* (streets, parking lots, proms, schools, skate parks, the arcade).[57] *Fast Cars, Cool Rides* zeroes in on the uses of cars by different youth, focusing on how cars operate as cultural objects through which kids make sense of what it means to be young in culture today and engage with the world around them. I examine the meanings youth attach to cars with a particular focus on the *practices, activities, symbols,* and *sites* that shape them in order to provide an understanding of how youth construct their identities within the overlapping spaces between commodity culture and youth culture, private life, and public life.[58] A study of cars provides an opportunity to map the messy cultural terrains where identities are formed, anchored, enacted, and transformed as youth are drawn into a complex of ideological, economic, social, and political processes through the uses of cultural objects.

Particular attention is given here to how these practices occur within a transforming social landscape, a posttraditional order where the traditional moorings for identity have been changed by globalization, the acceleration of production and consumption in late capitalism, the hypermobility of communications systems, and increasingly sophisticated media. Ours is a postindustrial world, where new forms of selfhood and social experiences have arisen that are tied less to traditional organizations and institutions than to cultural objects available in a commodity culture.[59] The sociologist Don Slater, in his book *Consumer Culture and Modernity,* explains, "In a posttraditional society, social identity must be constructed by individuals because it is no longer given or ascribed, but in the most bewildering of circumstance: not only is one's position in the status order no longer fixed but the order itself is unstable and changing and is represented through ever changing goods and images."[60] The consumer culture assumes critical importance as youth are called upon to craft their own identities. Young (and perhaps all) Americans increasingly rely on products to make statements about themselves as identities today are fashioned and refashioned out of the objects available to us in the commodity culture.[61]

The symbolic worlds of youth are enmeshed with the currents of a commodity culture such that youth speak a lingo that is peppered with the jargon of the market. Their references, inside jokes, monikers, and modes of address reflect their fluency in the language of the commodity market, its bewildering hold over them, and their ability to appropriate and rework that language in ways that speak as much to their realities outside the market as to those inside it. The brand of sneakers or jeans they wear, the music they listen to, the television they watch, the movies they go to see all provide clues to others about where they live, what they do, how they think about the world, and what they aspire to be. Little today is accidental. And though Americans may have an uneasy relationship to this fact because of its suggestion of calculated display, it draws our attention to the idea that identities today are made and remade endlessly, tried on and taken off, only to be discarded as new objects become available to us in the continual stream of commodities.

I think of identities as "projects," emergent features of ongoing social interaction, set within a set of structural relations, formed out of the discursive repertoires youth use to make sense of, interpret, and narrate their worlds. Identities materialize as young people occupy different interactional and discursive fields.[62] From this vantage point, identities might best be understood not as essential qualities of any individual but as historically contingent ritual enactments, so that even aspects of identity experienced as more or less fixed, such as sex and race, are fashioned differently across time and place.[63] In this sense, identities are not "attributes" that youth carry around with them in their backpacks but are realized in the practices they take up, the activities that occupy their time, the objects they use, and a complex of relations that organizes their everyday worlds, even if they do not originate in those worlds. As the educational scholar and cultural critic Henry Giroux has argued, youth "identities merge and shift rather than becoming more uniform and static. No longer associated with any one place or location, youth increasingly inhabit shifting cultural and social spheres marked by a plurality of languages, ideologies and cultures."[64]

The Study

To capture how cars figure in the everyday lives of youth and also to understand how a complex of social and economic forces mediates this relationship required the use of different research strategies: participant observation, in-depth interviewing, focus-group interviewing, and examination of archival and contemporary documents (e.g., films, print media, advertisements, bulletin boards, and personal Web sites maintained by car enthusiasts). As with most projects of this kind, my focus is not on drawing broad generalizations about all kids and their relationship to cars. Instead, this research is guided by an interest in excavating layers of social meanings and understanding the connection between the process of meaning making and youths' identity "projects." How social meanings are created, shared, contested, and reworked is loosely and sometimes haphazardly tied to distinct historical moments engendered by people as they respond to, interact with, and struggle against abstract social forces. *Fast Cars, Cool Rides* investigates how the messiness of history and historical processes, social acts, and social actors fit together to construct specific ways of being and becoming in a particular moment in time and space.

At the center of this project are in-depth and focus group interviews with just over one hundred young men and women, representing different economic locations, all between the ages of fifteen and twenty-three. They all reside in San Jose, California, and its surrounding suburbs, often called Silicon Valley. The locale provides an interesting setting for the study of cars and car culture; its boundaries are sprawling, and yet there is no real comprehensive public transportation system. Most residents rely on cars as their primary ground transportation, as evidenced by a 2000 U.S. Census report that a meager 4 percent of the city's residents regularly use public transportation.

San Jose bears visible markers of its increasing involvement in a postindustrial, global economy that has transformed the everyday life of the community. One such change has been the emergence of San Jose as a major immigrant-receiving city, with Santa Clara County now constituting a "majority-minority" county.[65] An estimated 60 percent of the county's residents are direct descendents of immigrants. Asian Americans and Latinos/as represent more than 55 percent of Silicon Valley's population.[66] San Jose comprises a number of ethnic enclaves across class groups. This ethnic segmentation is meaningful for the city's car culture, because it has given rise to ethnically segmented car scenes.

The youth who participated in this study represent the ethnic and racial diversity that characterizes the multicultural America that we have become as we move into the twenty-first century. A significant number of participants are first- or second-generation American. The voices of Filipino American, Indo-American, Southeast Asian, Chicana, Latino/a, black American, and European American youth fill these pages as they explore questions of culture and belonging, crisis and conflict, in a changing social and economic world.

As I began this project, I had originally planned to interview fifteen- to eighteen-years-olds only, but it became clear that I should also interview youth from nineteen to twenty-three years of age, since they make up a large portion of the youth car scene and share some similarities in life circumstances with this younger group. Like the fifteen- to eighteen-year-olds, many nineteen- to twenty-three-year-olds continue to live at home, and many hold the same kinds of jobs in the service economy as those in the younger group.

In total, forty-four semistructured and open-ended face-to face interviews were conducted with young men and women, ages 15–23, who represent widely different income and racial/ethnic groups. I conducted nineteen of those interviews. In 2003, I recruited three sociology students from San Jose State University who had completed a course in qualitative research methods with me to serve as my research assistants. Maria Flores, Danette Garcia, and Robert Trade together conducted twenty-five additional interviews, and these interviews are noted in the pages that follow. I conducted focus-group interviews because I was interested in documenting young adults' dialogues and exchanges; group interviews often enable the researcher to witness some of the same social dynamics that organize young people's lives outside research contexts.[67] Through focus groups, I interviewed fifty-two additional young women and men. I conducted five focus groups in total, each having between seven and fifteen participants. (See the methods appendix for further discussion of the group and in-depth interviewing.)

To contextualize the accounts collected through in-depth and focus-group interviews, I draw upon a series of observations conducted at a number of different car sites over a period of several years beginning in 2000. I attended car shows and visited car dealerships and various car washes around the San Jose community. I spent a number of afternoons walking around high school parking lots after school talking with kids and observing as they made their way out of school to their cars. I also spent time observing auto shop class at Freedom High School, a low-income school in Santa Clara County, attended primarily by Latino/a and Vietnamese students. I spent a portion of the 2004 spring semester observing four sections of auto shop class. The auto shop classes were dominated by young men of color. My presence as a white woman was carefully managed, though at times my being the lone woman was unnerving. Yet, the structure of the small, fluid working groups that made up the auto shop enabled me to move easily among them. Mr. O'Malley, the auto shop teacher, had a visible rapport with these young men, which facilitated my developing rapport. In a short period, I was able to break through fronts and participate freely in the group conversations, learning much about the mechanics of car upkeep and detailing.

Over several summers, I observed the cruising scene of San Jose. I cruised Santa Clara Street in San Jose's downtown alongside hundreds of kids.[68] Cruising Santa Clara Street is a widely popular social activity for many young adults who reside in Silicon Valley. Cruising is officially illegal in San Jose but is tolerated by city officials. On a typical Saturday night, a group of at least ten police officers assigned to the City of San Jose Cruise Management Division (CMD) can be seen standing in the middle of the main cruising strip directing traffic, inspecting cars, and issuing tickets. Several years ago, the city passed an anticruising ordinance. As a result, hefty fines and traffic-aversion strategies limit, though minimally, this social activity.

I visited Santa Clara Street several times each summer for five years to cruise. Each visit to Santa Clara Street lasted between one and three hours and typically included my cruising up and down the strip alongside other cars. My husband accompanied me on several of my first visits. He drove; I observed. As I gradually became more comfortable in the space, I visited the site alone. Because I was no longer able to write freely since I was now driving, I used a small tape recorder to log my observations. I spent most of the time observing from within my car. On a few occasions, I stopped at a convenience store to get something to drink or to get gas. Admittedly, as a woman I was reluctant to move far beyond my car, and in this sense my research was constrained and deeply gendered. Cruising is largely a male activity, and, on the surface of things, young men seem to run the show. As a woman, whether or not I am acting as a researcher, I am always careful when I occupy spaces where men appear to dominate. I was not, however, objectified as the young women were in this space. Consider the following reflections, written in my field notes:

> Few people are alone in cars and they seem to watch each other, zeroing in and then moving their eyes onward. Since I am a woman traveling in this scene I am aware of the risk of drawing unwanted attention. In a few instances I catch eyes moving over me and my car. In one instance I witness a guy check me out and my car (a station wagon) only to very quickly move on. Station wagons driven by women older than 30 garner little attention. Plus I am alone, which signals I am not of the scene but simply passing through. (May 2004)

There were clear instances when the young participants saw me as an obvious outsider to the space largely because of my age. In one instance, as I was turning off Santa Clara Street in my car, I was met by a group of young men trying to cross the street. One young man looked directly at me, saying, "Sorry, Mommy," as they continued across the street, now in complete hysterics.

In both meaningful and unexpected ways, this difference in age structured my encounters. The idea for this research project began when I was a graduate student working to complete my dissertation, which focused on the high school prom. At the time I was twenty-seven, single, and childless, living in New York City. When I conducted the ethnography on proms, I was able to more easily "pass" in the world of high school, since I looked a lot like many of them in terms of my style of dress. I wore overalls and jeans a lot more than I do now. The rapport I developed with kids as I studied the prom was easy and natural. Kids asked me to dance at the proms, girls asked me to help them with their hair, and I smoked cigarettes with some of the older kids. More than six years later, now in my thirties, married, and a mother who is settled into a tenure-track position that has enabled me to pay a mortgage, I find that my relationship to youth and their culture has changed considerably. My increasing immersion in the world of middle-class adulthood and the attendant shifts in lifestyle (I now drive a station wagon) and worldview resulted in a noticeable shift in the ways I conducted research, developed rapport, earned trust, and responded to comments offered up during interviews and observations. This shift has shaped the roles I assumed and those assigned to me while in the field.

Other matters were also at work. On a few occasions, I found myself having to work against what the sociologist Patricia Hill Collins has called "controlling images" of youth, young men of color in particular, while I was in the field. There were times when I suddenly felt uncomfortable cruising and struggled to make sense of why. My discomfort seemed to be not simply about age or gender. Consider my reflections, taken from my field notes:

> Directly in front of us is an older model car and convertible of some kind probably dating back to the 60s. It is occupied by four young men, all dark skinned. They appear to be Latino. They are driving down the middle lane of the road and for the first time I feel a little nervous about how the night will unfold. I notice that the several cop cars witnessed last week are not parked in the road. Are we too early, I ask myself? I start thinking about the image of four guys in a lowrider and what sort of other signifiers it conjures. I realize what a familiar image this is, played over and over in reel after reel in films depicting urban life. The value of this image is significant as it is often used as an image to convey danger, a foreshadowing of peril. And I also think how the presence of police officers makes me feel safe even though I know that these very officers make many of these kids feel vulnerable. (September 2001)

In that moment I was aware of the culture's hold over me. But I am also left with questions about my own ability to escape the narrow tunnel vision of a collective racial consciousness that aligns white with might and dark with danger. My feelings remain unresolved about the problems this presents in studying how young men of color occupy an urban landscape. Though I was often able to access aspects of my taken-for-granted world in the course of this research through sustained reflection, I continue to wonder about other moments where my own racial frameworks are more opaque and impenetrable. This is perhaps the limits of "researcher reflexivity," since it often presumes that we can make visible our prejudices and perspectives by accessing our inner world—a world whose doors sometimes remain closed.[69]

Reading the Book

This project sets out to extend the study of contemporary youth experience by investigating the relationships kids form in and around, with and without, the car. Each of the chapters zeroes in on a particular aspect of youth and car culture, but the book is divided into two parts. Part I focuses on the distinct car cultures in San Jose that are formed by youth. I focus my attention on the cruisers and the car racers. Chapters 1, 2, and 3 investigate the boundaries around which these youth car cultures are formed. In these first three chapters, I wrestle with difficult questions that kids face about the significance of gender, race, and ethnic identity in terms of the various senses of "belonging" in car culture. Chapters 1 and 2 examine car cruising and the varied meanings of this social practice. Chapter 1 focuses on young Chicanos'/as' attempts to construct a coherent narrative of ethnic identity and cultural belonging across generations through cruising, identifying the difficulties of this project as these young men and women are forced to confront changes to the Chicano community and changes to the downtown streets where other generations of Chicanos had once cruised. Highlighting the role gender plays in car cruising, chapter 2 investigates young women's participation in an activity that is heavily charged with sexual meaning. In chapter 3, I explore the illegal and organized car-racing scenes, focusing on the dynamics of race, risk, and masculinity. I examine the ways cars are defined racially and ethnically as young males struggle to find their place as men in a changing social world.

In Part II, I examine young adults' engagements with the broader American car culture. Chapters 4 and 5 explore the ways in which youth make sense of cars as they negotiate the everyday world of family, community, and a culture of consumption *as* youth. Chapter 4 revolves around the attempts of teens to manage the worlds of family, school, and beyond through the car. This chapter identifies the ways in which the car serves as a cultural object around which parents and kids negotiate family life, the demands of work, and the roles that gender and class play in these negotiations. Chapter 5 investigates the ways in which kids take up the car as a symbol of success as they imagine their lives as adults. This chapter focuses on how youth articulate their aspirations and expectations as they transition into adulthood by highlighting how they talk about cars. In the conclusion, I examine what a study of cars might reveal about the connections among youth culture, identity, public life, and consumer culture in today's world, where time is precious and mobility is highly valued. Finally, I explore whether cars in and of themselves can ever be linked to a transformative youth politics. The methods appendix examines the distinct methodological issues at stake in doing critical ethnography as they emerged in the course of working on this project.

On a basic level, this book is concerned with understanding the processes of growing up in American culture today as narrated by young adults themselves. I identify how kids actively participate in the ongoing production of cultural life and the meanings they attach to their participation. But, on another level, this book draws connections among youth culture and identity formation and the new cultural world order of hyperconsumption, economic uncertainty, and the resulting and often dramatic changes in how places and spaces are reorganized. As much as this is a book about youth and cars, it is also a book about contemporary American culture at the beginning of the twenty-first century. The analysis offered here asks how we should understand what are arguably monumental transformations in not only the lives of youth but the lives of us all.

Now, having finished the research, my thoughts turn to the young people this book is about. I wonder whether this will be a book *for* them or just a book written *about* them. I have tried to capture the complex facets of the lives of one group living in interesting times and to tell this story in a way that would be interesting to them. My hope is that I have told a good story, one that might inspire us, even in the smallest sense of the word, to think in new ways about our lives, about where we are going and whether cars are really going to get us there.

PART I

Cool Rides

1

Cruising Slow and Low
Young Chicanos/as Ride the Streets

The heart of Silicon Valley is downtown San Jose, a patch-work of streets on which a bustle of activity occurs day and night. In late evening on summer nights, hundreds of cars parade up and down Santa Clara Street, the center of San Jose's night life. Kids from all over Santa Clara County and neighboring counties come here to cruise. Dur-ing the several years I spent researching this project, I too visited this site a number of times, always in the late evening, always in the sum-mer, and always in my car. On one particularly warm August night, I head downtown to Santa Clara Street, arriving just as things are getting started. It is around 10:30. Booming bass trails the hundred or so cars that crowd the block as they slowly make their way down Santa Clara Street. Brake lights and shiny chrome stretch over several blocks. Cars line the street, moving at a slow pace. I, too, drive at a snail's pace down this jammed street. The sidewalks on either side are crowded with mostly young people dashing in and out of the side streets. Street lights overhang the five lanes, casting long shadows against the odd mix of upscale restaurants, crowded bars, clubs, and abandoned storefronts lining the sidewalk. Flanked by cars on either side, I pass a nearly empty grocery store parking lot on my left. There is a mix of traffic that clut-ters the street; surely not all are here to cruise. I inspect the cars within my immediate vicinity. I see an old Honda to my right, driven by a middle-aged man with two young kids in the back. He seems focused on the road before him, and his kids are nearly asleep.

An old Cadillac, faded brown, with three boys in the back and two in front pulls off the main drag, cutting the corner down a side street. I am struck by the strange sense of cool that hovers around the boys and their vehicle as they speed up at the turn and are suddenly out of sight. There is an excitement in the air, hanging heavy on this hot August night. I make my way down Santa Clara Street, passing two cop cars

and men in blue. Further on down the street, I see two more cops standing with two young women on the sidewalk, the four casually talking.
On my left I see a row of street bikes and a group of young men hover-
ing around them. A few sit on their bikes; another stands behind and
talks with a guy on the sidewalk. One yells across the street, "Hey
man." I spot a red 1960s-style Ford Mustang convertible just ahead of
me, sandwiched between the various cars, all at a standstill. Three girls,
all with dirty blond hair, sit in the car, giggling and talking over the
music that surrounds them. A little farther down, I notice another cop,
this time on foot, hanging out in the middle lane. To my right, I spot
an older model Honda Accord, stopped on the side of the street. Four
young men are crammed into the back seat. One sits talking on a cell
phone. A young woman stands just abreast of the passenger side door
before she hops into the car, and they start driving slowly down the
strip. Just behind me is another Honda filled with three young men.
One has a camcorder in his hand and is recording the cars as they
slowly pass; the other casually puffs on a cigar as he hangs his arm out
the opened car window and thumps his hand against the car's door in
time with the music that drifts from the car's interior. Farther on down
the stretch, three young women dance together on the sidewalk as they
wait in line to gain entry to Lava, a popular downtown night club. I can
faintly hear the dance music from inside the club.

As I near the intersection of Santa Clara and First Streets, a white
IROC zips across the intersection; a shiny black pickup with a lowered
suspension and shiny chrome rims follows only seconds behind. The
windows are dark on both cars, so I am unable to make out who is behind the wheel. A few cars ahead, I spot a light-green Chevy Impala riding slow and low. The license plate says "Impala, 1963." It is in mint
condition. Behind the wheel sits a young man, and, beside him, in the
middle of the seat, a young woman, presumably his girlfriend, to judge
from their proximity. I am not the only one to notice this car. Others
as they pass on foot and the drivers of other cars also check out this
nice ride.

Near the end of the strip, I turn down one of the side streets to turn
around. I spot a Ford Focus full of kids, the back of their heads illumi-
nated by the headlights from the cop car behind them that has just
pulled them over. All are still, waiting for the officer approaching the
car. I watch the police officer, hand gripping his billyclub as he radios
into dispatch through a small transmitter radio affixed to the collar of

his blue uniform. I slowly pass them as I turn back on to Santa Clara Street for another round.

It is difficult to imagine that these kids who come to cruise Santa Clara Street have anything in common with generations before them, since the scene seems so entirely modern. But car cruising has been a popular activity for American youth since the end of World War II.[1] And California has been its unofficial center. A series of shifts in economic and cultural life led to cruising's widespread popularity following the war, even though smaller groups of kids had cruised long before then. In postwar America, fuel was inexpensive and in abundance, and secondhand cars for the first time were widely available (since a growing number of Americans could afford and preferred new cars).[2] Increasing economic prosperity, the expansion of the middle classes, the emergence of a mass consumer market, and the development of sprawling suburban communities in the early 1950s meant that many families owned a car, and a small but growing number owned two. Though few youth owned their own cars immediately after the war, the surplus of secondhand cars in the 1950s meant that all was soon to change for these young drivers. Life was also changing on the family front in ways that transformed children's public and private lives. The growing affluence of families in postwar America and a shift in parenting styles toward a more permissive and democratic set of practices handed teenagers greater freedom and autonomy than teens had experienced in decades before.[3] As almost a harbinger of things to come, teenagers spent a growing amount of time away from parents; their lives were increasingly rooted in a peer-centered social world. Postwar teens enjoyed a world of "economic prosperity," "expanding opportunity," and "increased leisure time."[4]

A majority of this new leisure time was spent in and around the car. As teen enjoyed more free time and far greater disposable income, hot rodding, the customizing of stock cars, became a favorite pastime among teenagers, young Anglo men in particular, consuming endless hours of their free time. On weekend nights, these hot rods flooded the Main Streets of downtowns all across postwar America.[5] The historians K. Witzel and K. Bash write, "Main Street provided the primo place for people to show off their automobiles when moving. . . . After dark, when the stores closed and all the shoppers had gone home, the atmosphere for automotive carousing became electrified: Flashing lights, neon lights, blinking traffic signals, and glaring street lamps transformed the commercial corridor into a brightly lit automotive stage. . . . Everyone was there: greasers, gearheads, socialites, athletes, bookworms and trouble makers."[6] In many ways, cruising provided the occasion for young adults to participate in community life, since it drew large numbers of teenagers into public centers where the collective life of communities is played out. But many adults, failing to see this as an opportunity for young adults to affirm their membership in the larger community, expressed concern. This is hardly surprising; youth had been regarded largely as "a potential threat to a public order" ever since they had been recognized a distinct social group.[7]

By the early 1960s, leisure driving by youth down these Main Streets came to be seen as a nuisance. Their cars clogged the streets and obstructed local business, since many cruisers would park along curbside eateries for hours, often spending nothing while preventing would-be customers from shopping, and they were often loud and raucous as rock 'n' roll with a static overlay blared from the small radio speakers of their cars. Parental and policy concerns over the amount of time kids spent in and around their cars was also beginning to develop. Adult anxieties were inflamed as parents came to realize that kids used the car as a space for sexual activity, among other equally morally questionable activities, such as drinking, as well as for drag racing. Ultimately, alarm over the moral collapse of young adults (and concern over what was perceived as a threat to local commerce) led to a wave of anticruising ordinances. Adopted in many cities and towns in the 1960s, these anticruising ordinances gave rise to what arguably can be seen as the widespread criminalization of cruising and cruisers. These anticruising ordinances and curfews served to limit young people's engagement with the street and the public and the visible life the street afforded. But, in the end, they did not eliminate these engagements in public life.[8] Instead, they gave rise to a kind of cultural warfare waged between cops and kids over claims to these streets that continues to play itself out today. Cities across the United States have readopted anticruising ordinances in an attempt to keep youth off the streets. As we move forward into the twenty-first century, many youth continue to cruise up and down the Main Streets of America, despite the best (and worst) efforts of adults to prevent them from doing so.[9]

Like other leisure activities, cruising is a complicated social practice, rich in meaning and, for those youth who cruise, central to their sense of identity. Many readers will recall George Lucas's now-classic film

American Graffiti based loosely on his own coming of age in 1960s California. In making aimlessly "cruising the strip" the subject of a Hollywood feature film, Lucas helped to solidify the enduring link between cruising and youth sensibilities. Yet the youthful world of cruising captured in this Hollywood film is largely a white world, one without racial hostility or generational conflict or connection. There is little sense of the "moral panics" that have surrounded cruising or any notion of youth as "folk devils," which has served as the rallying cry for those seeking stricter policies on car cruising in communities across the United States but especially in California and the Southwest, where cruising has long been an important cultural activity for Chicanos/as.[10]

Cruising, and the public places where it occurs, is central for many Chicano/a youth. For a great number of young Chicanos/as in Silicon Valley, an area where Latinos/as represent more than 30 percent of the population, a large part of their sense of being Chicano is given expression through cars, cruising, and the streets where cruising occurs.

Lowriders and Brown Pride

Car cruising has had solid ties to Mexican youths' migration and settlement in the United States since World War II. At the same time that car cruising and hot rodding became popular among young middle- and working-class Anglos, Mexican American youth in California began organizing car clubs. They distinguished themselves from the hot rodders by the cars they drove and the style in which they drove them. Where Anglo hot rodders focused on muscle and speed, young Mexican Americans, mostly men, rode their cars "slow and low," since their purpose was to prolong the length of time on a main roadway and thus enhance their visibility.[11] The cars they drove were called lowriders, mostly 1930s and 1940s Chevys. These early lowriders were driven by the zoot-suiters, so-called Pachucos, young Mexican men from the 1940s southern California barrios.[12] Unlike many Anglo teens whose disposable income was appreciable, Mexican American youth, mostly children of immigrants or immigrants themselves, were poor. Since they did not have the resources to make the sort of car modifications done today, their cars, mostly restored jalopies, were typically lowered by sandbags, strategically placed in the cars' trunks. These young men created "something out of nothing" and, in doing so, established a car aesthetic that, fifty years later, would continue to have substantial appeal for young Chicanos, many of whose families struggle to remain above the poverty line.

Lowriders were not originally conceived of as the ethnic symbols they have become. The social meaning assigned to them by the dominant white society ultimately transformed them into ethnic objects.[13] The *New York Times* writer James Sterngold wrote, in an article featuring lowriders, "These in-your-face cars made a proud but almost invisible minority highly visible, in part because they were reviled by the white mainstream, especially the police here. They became irritating symbols of ethnic defiance, in effect giving young Chicanos a voice."[14] The young men who drove the lowriders were subject to sustained harassment by police officers and were generally regarded with suspicion as they, like the zoot-suiters themselves, were associated with petty crime, vagrancy, violence, and delinquency. But, while lowriders were often treated as "gangs on wheels" by mainstream America, in the collective imagination of Chicanos/as, lowriders and the young men who drove them were venerated for representing resistance to the Anglo conformity required of many immigrant groups in postwar America.[15]

In the 1960s, as the Chicano movement gained momentum, the lowrider, like the Afro and the zoot-suit, emerged as a potent signifier of past and present political and cultural struggle for Chicanos, serving as an important symbol of Chicano solidarity in the collective consciousness of young Chicanos/as. As strategic alliances between those who drove lowriders in Los Angeles and the Chicano movement at the public universities across California were forged in the name of La Raza,[16] the lowrider was mobilized as a symbol of democratic struggle against the demonization and criminalization of Chicano youth and the exclusion of these so-called folk devils from public life. Various public places— Santa Clara Street and Story and King Roads, in San Jose; Whittier Boulevard, in Los Angeles; and Valencia and South Van Ness Streets, in San Francisco's Mission district—emerged as key sites where these struggles were waged.

Modern lowriders, typically driven by older men because of the significant investment involved in restoring them, are quite elaborate. Most are restored Chevy Impalas, Regals, Monte Carlos, Cutlasses, and Bombas (old-style Chevy trucks), with lowered suspensions and customized paint jobs. Sometimes they are enhanced with complex hydraulic systems. Modern lowriders that compete in car shows often bear names like "Brown Sensation" or "Aztec Gold" to express cultural membership, and a number have distinct Mexican iconography, such as intricate murals of religious icons like the Virgin de Guadalupe or Aztlan imagery on the car's hood.

Cruising Slow and Low in San Jose

Today, cruising "slow and low" is a way some young Chicanos remain connected to this history of struggle. As they cruise, appropriating the distinctive style of their forebears, they create and maintain community, construct a coherent cultural identity, and symbolically struggle against the repeated assaults on the collective soul of their community.[17] In cities all over the United States, many Chicano youth embrace the lowrider as an object to "claim" an ethnic and national identity. They do so in a cultural context where the pressures to generate identity are intense, while the traditional anchors of identity are less secure as the vagaries of late capitalism threaten the dissolution of a shared identity tied to place.[18]

It is in this context that cruising and lowriding can be understood as social practices through which young Chicanos become involved in the active reinvention of ethnicity, whereby they produce alternative understandings of being Chicano against the images, mostly negative, that they confront elsewhere. Chicano/a youth write poetry about lowriding, produce creative photo essays about cruising, create pop art that captures life in the streets, and work on their cars and the cars of others in celebration of the lowrider and La Raza—all in an attempt to authentically "represent." Consider, for example, letters written by young Chicanos/as to *Lowrider* magazine, a major publication with a loyal and large readership. "As I read through the pages of *Lowrider* magazine and check out the *firme* rides, my heart fills with pride. It feels really good to see our *gente* doing something so positive and encouraging to all of the *Raza*," a seventeen-year-old Chicana writes. "My love for lowriders is unexplainable. . . . As time goes by, it seems as if Mexicanos are coming up stronger than ever." A young Mexicano living in Indiana writes,

I want to let it be known I am *Mexicano*, I also would like to send my respects to all the *gente* who have something positive to say about our *cultura.* . . . The reason I am writing this letter is to put in my two *centavos* about the *Raza.* Really, I think we need more *Raza* out here in Indiana. I have been living here in Indiana for three years and I am the only Mexican out where I live. I am proud to represent my *Raza* at school. . . . I miss cruising around with the *Raza.*[19]

A numbers of letters pay tribute to *Lowrider* magazine for promoting ethnic pride, ethnic attachment, and ethnic solidarity among Chicanos/as.[20] "Thanks again, *Lowrider* magazine, for keeping it real and reminding us all of the beautiful things that our culture contributes to the world, especially the beautiful cars and the beautiful women, but also the love that we all have for each other. You have helped keep my head up and my spirits strong! *Que Viva la Raza,*" one writer in his twenties, from Pennsylvania, offers. As they narrate both past and present as part of La Raza, these writers produce a cultural identity that hinges upon their connection to others through cruising and the car. These young Chicanas/os present a coherent narrative about who they are as they construct and reconstruct a shared sense of history, location and ethnicity.[21]

For the young Chicanos/as of San Jose, Santa Clara Street is ground zero.[22] Lowriding has long had a solid presence in the downtown area of San Jose, a city with well-established ties to the Chicano and lowrider social movements.[23] Today, however, few classic lowrider cars can be seen cruising "slow and low" down Santa Clara Street. The cars themselves have been "pushed almost entirely off the street" by sustained police enforcement and recent anticruising ordinances and can largely be found at organized car shows.[24] But, on the street, there remains a vibrant spirit of these early lowriders as they are collectively and individually celebrated by a large number of Chicano youth in San Jose. Many Chicano kids who cruise align themselves with the early lowriders, and some see themselves as "lowriders"[25] even though most don't own a car, let alone a coveted lowrider.[26] Many hold onto dreams of one day customizing an old Chevy Impala, passed down from an uncle or an older cousin. But, until then, they are content to just participate in the cruise. This was the case for Fernando, a Chicano student from Freedom High School who, when I asked if he had a car, replied, "I have an Impala, well, sort of." When my facial expression suggested that I didn't quite understand, he explained, "My uncle is going to give it to me if he doesn't sell it . . . this month I hope to get one."

Cruising itself is an inexpensive activity and thus widely available to youth. Being a part of the cruising scene doesn't require having one's own car. I regularly saw handfuls of young adults packed into the cars cruising along Santa Clara Street or traveling on foot up and down the street, checking out the cars and the people. Many of the Chicano boys from Freedom High School's auto shop cruised every weekend without a car. For those with nice rides, Santa Clara Street is a space for creative self-representation, displaying pride, and, in turn, gaining respect, as Augusto explains.

> *Augusto*: You feel the vibe . . . you can feel . . . everybody looking at you and see what you're driving and who's in the car with you and vice versa. You look away and some girls over here and over there and the kind of music and stuff like that. Everybody is watching.
>
> *Danette*: So is that the appeal—that people are watching?
>
> *Augusto*: You could say that. The attention . . . the attention you get. When you get a nice ride you feel proud of what you did. You feel proud of all those times you had to spend cleaning your car, waxing it. . . . Yeah, you take pride.

On the street, cruising a nice ride is a means for young Chicanos to gain a kind of honorable visibility largely denied them in other places and situations.[27] Young Chicanos' social experiences in education, employment, and the juvenile justice system are often embattled and demoralizing.[28]

Perhaps more than anything else, cruising offers a temporary semblance of belonging to what can feel like a coherent cultural community. "Cruising is all about community building. It's when the people of San Jo' come out and claim the streets. These are our neighborhoods," writes David Madrid in *DeBug: The Voice of the Young and Contemporary,* a local magazine that publishes articles written by San Jose youth. It is not always clear, however, how this group of young Chicanos/as operates as an actual community. Their lives outside the strip are largely disconnected, since they attend schools all over the city and often live in different neighborhoods and communities. Their social experiences are increasingly varied as a growing number of Chicanos move into the middle classes, while others face the demands of life in low-income areas; many are called up to claim membership in a street gang as they struggle to overcome a wide range of material deprivations.[29]

As they come of age in this changing social world, the traditional domains of social existence can seem increasingly precarious and their community life can be fractured and opaque. They struggle to anchor themselves somewhere, somehow. Middle-class Chicano kids, increasingly accused of ethnic betrayal, of "being whitewashed" as they move up and out of the *barrio*, struggle for authenticity and cultural legitimacy. Participating in the cruising scene provides them with a means of "keeping it real."[30] For many working-class and low-income Mexican American youth, taking part in the lowrider scene serves as an attractive alternative to life in a gang, since both operate as powerful sources of belonging and a means to gain visibility and respect. Many outside Chicano communities assume that lowriding is an extension of life in a gang, but, more often than not, it is a legitimate substitute.[31]

Knowing the ins and outs of the cruising scene and being able to display knowledge of how this world operates invests youth with significant cultural authority. Thus, being able to recall stories of evading cops, knowing the location of new underground cruising sites, or bearing witness to nice rides is an important part of their membership in this scene. Spending time with the boys at Freedom High School, I heard tale after tale of weekend cruising. The retelling of tales is as important as the experience itself, since it confirms having been there. I came to see this as an example of what Sarah Thornton termed subcultural capital—"a means by which youth imagine their own and other social groups, assert their distinctive character and affirm that they are not anonymous members of an undifferentiated mass."[32]

In this sense, cruising is best described as an activity that enables young Chicanos to feel a sense of connection to an imagined community, a symbolic community through which they gain a sense of themselves as a collective based on their connection to particular practices (cruising) and particular places (Santa Clara Street), rather than to one another.[33] It is a community that exists in what the philosopher Charles Taylor has called the "social imaginary," a conceptual scheme by which "people imagine their social surroundings . . . that make possible common practices and a widely shared sense of legitimacy . . . [and] incorporates a sense of how we all fit together in carrying out common practices."[34] For these kids, the community they imagine and construct has deep national, cultural, and intergenerational ties, connecting them to a larger history of struggle over claims to space.

Many of these young Chicanos/as think about cruising in the abstract, as though it were a practice much larger than themselves. Tino, one of the young Chicano students from Freedom High School, who drives an old pickup truck with worn green paint and rust at its edges, tells me he doesn't cruise anymore. When I ask him to elaborate, he explains that he gets "followed by cops," and the kids who cruise don't even "know what it means." To many, he tells me, it is simply about "getting drunk." Tino expresses what is experienced as a loss of culture, a culture that at other moments had been held together through shared meanings of what cruising represented for the group. Seventeen-year-old Tino's nostalgia derives from the "stories, myth and legends" he has heard from older generations as much as it does from his own memories of cruising growing up.[35] Perhaps this explains why "tradition" is a term I hear over and over, as are phrases like "old school" and "back in the day," as I listen to the Chicano kids at Freedom High School imagine themselves a part of a larger intergenerational community in solidarity. The *New York Times* writer James Sterngold, reflecting on the evolution of lowriding, also recognized this practice among earlier lowriders: "Rather than use their cars as symbols of rejection of their elders" as youth from other ethnic groups had, "the lowriders were conspicuously reverent to their parents' generation. They embraced the zoot-suits and drooping mustaches of the so-called pachucos, hipsters of a previous generation, as well as Roman Catholic imagery in their search for an identity with roots in the past."[36] In their search for a concrete connection to the past, young Chicanos and Chicanas immersed in the culture of cruising spoke of fathers, uncles, grandfathers, and older cousins. Carla's narrative is particularly revealing in this regard.

> My dad, he loves cars, too, and him and my brother are talking, cause he has a Regal, a '86 Regal, and it's in the backyard and they're always talking about how they're going to fix it up and all these ideas and it's just kind of, they got me into that scene, you know. And they have posters on the walls and when I was back home I had posters of lowriders up on the wall and cause there's these beautiful cars.

Young Chicanos shared stories of working on cars together with older men from the neighborhood and their own memories of cruising as kids. "The past" was the most salient and consistent referent as they spoke about cruising today. David Madrid, a writer from San Jose, says, "When I talk to uncles and older cousins about the cruising scene back in the day, I hear stories of the El Camino, La Raza Park, and the Studio West. Some spots still remain even after decades, like First and Santa Clara Street and King Road. . . . Father and sons working together on their rides have deep roots in the lowrider culture. When I get together with my family I trip off the photo albums of old cars and the stories they tell." Older men are central figures in this cultural world, and there is a distinct reverence for them. "Old-timers" provide young Chicanas/os with details of the past through their storytelling and thus provide an opportunity for a younger generation to connect with something larger than themselves. Old-timers also embody the collective struggle of a community, since they were the first ones to be unfairly targeted and harassed as they struggled to stake a claim to public streets to cruise.[37] Like the Pachucos, the old-timers were unwilling to back down. This is evident from Carla's almost mythical construction of *veteranos*.

> *Veteranos*, they're like the old-time gangsters. Like the old school, that's what they call them, the old-school gangsters that kind of settled down, they have their families, they still have their car and they'll go out cruising with their family, you know with their wife and their kids and they just go out there, they're not really into causing trouble, everybody still respects them because they had a place in the *barrio* before, so they give them their respect.

For Carla and other young Chicanos/as like her, the shared history of which they become a part through lowriding is defined as a history of oppression and marginalization. Cruising is experienced through a lens of "us and them." Again, Carla elaborates:

> Chicanos have lowriding and they see it as art and they go out to show off their cars or whatever and like police, I don't know, they just don't like it or maybe they don't want to deal with, you know like, if gangs do show up they don't want to deal with it but they should give them a chance not just because they have a lowrider, because they're Chicano, Latino, like go and try to pull them over.

As young Mexican Americans are drawn into this world where lowriders rule, they are immersed in the interpretive contexts that help to define the symbolic boundaries of this world. They gain exposure to the interpretive frameworks that are central to maintaining a sense of solidarity among a very loosely organized group of people drawn together by a shared history of oppression and the increasingly abstract notion of La Raza.

Participating in the cruising scene itself serves to highlight these connections, making race political for these young adults, since it is often a site where they encounter what they define as an ugly racism displayed by police officers and other agents of the law. Carla recounts several run-ins with officers, aware of the injustice at work.

> *Carla*: Like my brother, I don't know if I mentioned to you, he got pulled over once cause he was driving his Regal, he had a rosary in the mirror.
>
> *AB*: I think you did tell me about it, but tell me again.
>
> *Carla*: And, well, he was cruising and like his car's lowered, he has the speakers, it doesn't have a paint job yet but it's still a lowrider, right? So and he was cruising, he was doing everything right, the police pulls him over and asks for his, you know, driver's license and registration and insurance whatever, and my brother gave it all to him and he's like, well, can I know the reason why you stopped me sir? And he's like, well, because there's something in the mirror and it's obstructing your view and it was a rosary and I mean how is a rosary, I mean it's not even on the mirror, it just hangs up. So my brother was just like, he didn't even want to argue cause he gets pulled over a lot because of that so the guys was just like, well, just be careful, and he didn't even give him a ticket or anything, just targeted him cause he had a lowrider.

Carla continues:

> Another time we were, it was, our whole family, we went out to go get, I think we went out for lunch, all of us went out and me and my brother were sitting in the front seat and my parents were in the back with my brother and the police, like he passed us up and then flipped it, you know, and just came right after us and turned on the light and pulled us over. So my brother pulls over and he was getting his stuff out again and then the police was like, so what are you doing, young man, and he's like, oh, I'm just going home, is there a problem? And he's like yeah, and he had his flashlight and he flashed it back and he sees my

parents in the back and he's all, what are you guys going? And then my brother's like we're just going home, we just came from dinner, he's like, Oh, are those your parents? And he's like, yeah, and he's like, Oh, hi, Sir. And my dad was mad, really mad, you know? And he's just like, I'm fine, and he's [the police officer] just like, well, I'm just making sure you guys have your seatbelts on, you guys don't have any grenades back there do you? And then my parents are like, No.

Many of these young adults see themselves as the objects of unnecessary roughness and ongoing verbal harassment. They recall suffering count-less indignities: being held at gunpoint, searched, or held on the ground for no apparent reason other than their having brown skin. With few exceptions, they narrate these encounters as racialized events, framed by and through the common expression "driving while brown." DWB as a racial discourse grew out of the lived experiences of black and brown men and women and has become shorthand for the widespread practice of racial profiling.[38] Importantly, DWB has emerged as a repository for the formation of a collective consciousness of racial injustice for Latino (and black) youth.[39] This discourse of racial injustice is easily harnessed because it is readily available and resonates with the lived experiences of kids of color, not just Chicanos. Both Jorge, seventeen, and Augusto, eighteen, provide accounts, compelling because of their seeming ordi-nariness.

> You get pulled over for no reason, I mean, DWB, driving while brown. I have a nice car, you know. If I have a beat to my car they're gonna be "He's a gansta'." So, um, I got pulled over one time downtown. Cop came over and he said, "Huh." I said, "What seems to be the problem, sir?" He says, "Aah, I thought you had a tail light out, but I guess not." And I said, "Okay, is there anything else?" And he said, "How are you doing?" "Fine." He says, "What are you doing tonight?" I said, "Just hanging out with some friends, going home. I go to school down the street here." He said, "I didn't ask where you went to school." "I go to Bernards College Prep." "Right," he said. "Oh, okay, can I see some ID?" So I had to have to show him my driver's license plus my student ID to prove that I go to Bernards. He goes, "Hum, so you go to Bernards, huh, interesting." I go whatever. I said "Well, is there any-thing else? What's the problem?" I was getting pissed off, and he says, "Are you taking a tone with me?" "No, sir, I don't know exactly why

you pulled me over." "Don't talk back to me, we can go downtown if you want to do this right now!" "Sir, I have no idea what you're talking about." I just kind of like shut up and looked forward.

Augusto describes a similar series of events.

Augusto: I've gotten pulled over in just about in every town from San Francisco to Gilroy. Uhhh . . . on the highway and on the town maybe . . . a lot of people stereotyping. Most of the time I would ask just to see why I got pulled over and the only answer I got was 'cause I look suspicious. Which kinda sucked.

Danette: How did that make you feel?

Augusto: Ugghh . . . angry . . . very upset. Many times I raised my voice at the officers 'cause I had did nothing. The same reason . . . last time I got pulled over I'm like, "why am I getting pulled over?" I'm like, "wait, hold on . . . because I'm suspicious?" And the officer said, "Yeah, pretty much . . . there was another car . . . same vehicle type, same everything," which is the same thing I get from each officer. And they were doing something they weren't supposed to.

Danette: How about umm . . . You said you felt that it was stereotypical, like all of those times. Can you tell me was it because of what you look like or the car type?

Augusto: I think both. They would see a young guy like me . . . you know, a young Hispanic guy in maybe a Mustang . . . back then it looked nice. And they're like, okay, what is this guy up to? I'm pretty sure they thought I was going to be some drugs or in possession of drugs or something like that. I couldn't walk away clean. So I think that's why they pulled me over.

Danette: Did they ever try to search you?

Augusto: Yeah! All the time. They searched us all the time. All my friends were . . . and one time all of us were in there [the car] and it was kinda weird 'cause we were . . . we were parked, but we were still inside and we were searching for quarters. We walked outside, two of us remained . . . two of them remained in the car looking for more quarters. And we were trying to put 'em in the meter, mind you, it's past meter hour . . . we don't know. Uhh, so a cop pulls over and turns on the lights, we're like, we can't see anything. Three or four more patrols pull up, and they totally just told us to get against the wall and don't move . . . at gunpoint. And I was . . . besides being scary I mean you get angry and all these emotions go through you and it's kinda sad in the end 'cause you realizes jeez just because I was looking for quarters and I'm getting gunpoint. The only reason they could come up with was . . . well, there's been people robbing the meters . . . and I'm like in a bright street people are robbing the meters, RIGHT! You could of come up with something better, but that's what I got.

As they cruise around town, young Chicanos come to see the shared sense of struggle between their generation and the generations of Chicanos/as before them. Out of these experiences that are at once shaped by and give expression to a discourse of racial injustice, these young Chicanas/os align themselves with lowriders of other generations, seeing little difference between the struggles of the Pachucos in 1940s Los Angeles and their own at the dawn of a new century in a very different world. They possess an unsettling awareness that, regardless of the cars they drive, they still carry the stigma of being brown.

Cinco de Mayo and Carnival Community

Youthful attempts to construct a sense of community belonging are perhaps most dramatic on the holiday Cinco de Mayo, when thousands gather to witness a parade and later to cruise down Santa Clara Street. Cinco de Mayo commemorates the hard-won victory of a Mexican peasant village against French imperialist soldiers at the Battle of Puebla on May 5, 1862, and is celebrated in San Jose by thousands of community members.[40] Cinco de Mayo, though not widely celebrated in Mexico, carries importance for Mexican Americans who draw parallels between the peasant struggle and their own. In this sense, Cinco de Mayo serves as an occasion to reaffirm one's membership in a community in struggle. In my field notes from one particular Cinco de Mayo celebration, I recorded the following:

I am near Santa Clara Street and see small groups walking. I approach the light to turn onto Santa Clara and sit as the car idles. The scene is almost entirely Chicano/a and Mexicano/a. The crowd is exuberant. I watch on as people dance in their cars and sometimes outside them. On the sidewalks, kids make their ways down street in swarms. There are tons of people on foot, young families with baby strollers and lots of young kids. With my windows down, I take in the sounds from outside. Music streams into the car, Mexican ballads mostly. The air is very warm and cars are at a literal standstill. The ubiquitous green, red, and white Mexican flag is flying everywhere. Three girls hold hands moving down the street, two wear halter tops designed as Mexican flags. Cars all around display the Mexican flag, many attached to the hood of the car. Large flags are flown outside car windows but most hang limp since few cars are actually moving. (May 2, 2004)

The cruising that customarily follows the Cinco de Mayo parade (which itself draws a more diverse crowd) is a ritual celebration enacted almost entirely by Chicanos and Chicanas.[41] The two times I participated in cruising on Cinco de Mayo, I appeared to be one of only a few Anglos.[42] This did not pass unnoticed. I vividly remember one police officer who was diverting traffic, ushering cruisers off of Santa Clara Street toward the end of the day, asking me if I wanted to drive through rather than be diverted with the group. He was confident that I, a light-skinned, red-headed woman driving a station wagon with an empty carseat in the back, couldn't possibly be there to cruise. While Friday and Saturday night cruising attracts a heterogeneous mix of youth, that can not said of Cinco de Mayo, and, in this sense, it is likely here that young Chicanos/as find the community they search for. I remember the excitement and intensity at Freedom High School the week of Cinco de Mayo as young Chicanos talked animatedly about the cruise, recalling farfetched and fanciful stories; four guys were shot by gang members, Tino tells me the day after Cinco de Mayo.[43] But Cinco de Mayo occurs once a year and in this way might be considered what the sociologist Zygmunt Bauman, in his book *Liquid Modernity*, refers to as a "carnival" community. Carnival communities need a spectacle to tie them together; they are principally events and thus not communities in a traditional sociological sense. Participants tend to dress according to particular dress codes, which provide uniformity among the group. Carnival communities have an explosive quality in that they are transient, with a single purpose, and they tend to be precarious and volatile. "Their lifetime is short but full of sound and fury."[44] For Bauman, the spectacle serves as a break from the mundane and "solitary struggles" of individuals, and in this sense they are born from the conditions of late-modern life where individuals are unencumbered by the constraints and controls of traditional communities but also lack the anchors they provide.[45] Thus, while Cinco de Mayo provides a sense of community for young Chicanos/as, it is, after all, a temporary one; Chicano/a youth must, in the end, return to their solitary struggles in school, at home, and elsewhere.

We Ain't Homeboys

As much as cruising is taken up by youth to create a sense of community belonging and to claim an ethnic identity, cruising also reveals the limits of these undertakings. Lowriding, if not the practice of cruising itself, emerges ironically as a symbol of intraethnic differences, etched within a context of changing economic realities for a number of Chicanos/as and the transformation of a group historically unified as much by class as by ethnicity. The comments of Cesar, a seventeen-year-old Mexican American senior from Freedom High School, are revealing in terms of the emerging divisions within the Chicano community.

> *Maria*: Do you guys go cruising?
> *Cesar*: No. We ain't homeboys.
> *Maria*: Huh?
> *Cesar*: (laughing) We ain't homeboys.
> *Maria*: (laughing) Ohhh.
> *Cesar*: Hell no we don't go cruising! Heeelllll no.
> *Maria*: Do you know anybody who goes cruising?
> *Cesar*: Homeboys, you know what I'm saying (laughing).
> *Maria*: What do you mean by homeboys?
> *Cesar*: Like the cholo crowd!

The divisions that exist within this Chicano community are also illustrated in a recent community struggle that revolved around the building of the downtown public library in San Jose.[46] A collection of artists had been commissioned to design a series of art installations that would speak to the diversity of San Jose. One artist (who was not Chicano) proposed an installation of lowrider tables and chairs, positioned low to the ground as lowrider cars themselves are typically. The proposal led to a series of public forums where the appropriateness of the installation was seriously debated. Many members of the Chicano and the broader Latino communities in the area were deeply troubled by this proposed installation, lamenting the lack of community involvement in the decision to commission this particular project. Many professionals in the community and students and professors at the state university felt that lowriders not only failed to represent the richness of the Chicano community but were ultimately a poor symbol. Given the representations of lowriders in popular media as criminals and gang members, it is easy to understand the concern articulated by this group. With the support of the National Association for Chicana and Chicano Studies, the group called for a public apology by the council and the artist for the "inappropriate image of the Chicana and the Chicano community and the negative depiction of lowriders in the mockup poster."[47] Defenders of the project, mostly local artists, rallied around the importance of freedom of expression. Ultimately, the lowrider table project was abandoned.

The struggle over lowrider art is a complicated one. At its center, it is a struggle for authentic representation of an ethnic community. But many differences exist within this community, and these make it very difficult to speak about a Chicano community rooted in shared experience. There are as many Chicano communities as there are situations that construct and sustain them. Constructing a cohesive Chicano community against a set of social conditions that has made the work of maintaining ethnic solidarity increasingly difficult remains a challenge for young Chicanos/as. Some, like Tino, become disillusioned, setting their sights on other sources of community belonging, in search of other anchors for identity construction. Other forces are at work, acting as obstacles to young Chicanos'/as' search for a coherent sense of community and ethnic identity. Santa Clara Street, a central place out of which young Chicanos/as formed their community and ethnic identities, is a site where different social terrains increasingly collide. This has far-reaching consequences for young Chicanos'/as' ability to maintain community ties as they come of age.

Keeping the Streets Clean

"Five or six years ago, when I worked normal patrol downtown, I would see a lot more lowriders and minitrucks and just more tricked-out old cars that had been souped up and they looked nice. Today I see a lot more kids driving their parents' vehicles, big SUVs, Mercedeses,

Lexuses, um, just nicer modern vehicles," says Steve, one of the handful of police officers I interviewed who works downtown on cruising nights. Steve is not alone in his observation of the changing cultural landscape downtown. By all accounts, the cruising scene in San Jose has changed significantly in the past decade. Once an activity largely dominated by Chicanos, cruising Santa Clara Street now consumes the evenings of many of San Jose's young.[48] A series of events conspired to alter the landscape of Santa Clara Street and thus young Chicanos'/as' ability to gain a sense of being Chicano/a through cruising. Today the downtown serves as a point of contact among individuals and groups that would otherwise have few opportunities for contact: youth from the surrounding suburbs, youth from the immediate city neighborhoods and from the *barrio* on the east side of San Jose, the homeless, state university students who frequent the happening and usually hopping clubs and bars that populate the downtown, and patrons of the theater and the growing number of high-end restaurants that have sprung up in recent years. There are also the police officers who work in the Cruise Management Division, a division of the San Jose Police Department that is responsible for patrolling Santa Clara Street and the surrounding area during peak cruise times.[49]

Cruising is officially illegal in San Jose and has been since a municipal anticruising ordinance was adopted in the early 1990s. Signs that read "No-Cruising Zone" (all in English) are posted on literally every other street corner along Santa Clara Street, and roaming police/peace officers can be spotted in the many parking lots that line the street. On a usual Saturday night, a group of up to ten police officers can also be seen standing in the middle of the road directing traffic, inspecting cars, and issuing tickets. Police officers like Steve have a solid and highly visible presence, as is clear from an observation I recorded in my field notes:

> It is almost ten o'clock and four cop cars are assembled in the middle lane of the street. Beside them stand six cops. I witness several cars as they are pulled over. The six cops stand in the middle of the road watching as the various cars pass, talking among themselves, having a laugh. They are highly visible, and I wonder about their safety standing in the middle of the street as hundred of cars pass. Suddenly, a cop's arm shoots up, and his finger directs a young driver into the center lane; moments later another cop does the same. (August 2001)

These officers are part of the Cruise Management Division of the San Jose Police Department. Their primary purpose is to manage and contain the car cruising scene, "to deter them from clogging up the streets," says Steve. They divert traffic, issue citations, and sweep the parking lots that line Santa Clara Street, "you know, so emergency vehicles, buses, and other public vehicles can use Santa Clara Street." On some occasions, an officer might issue "a cruise warning." Fines for an actual cruise violation can be hefty—"a $270 ticket, once they are given a cruise warning," I am told by Jeff, one of the officers. But tickets are rarely issued. Instead, officers issue countless "fix-it" tickets for minor infractions such as a missing front license plate. For the officers of the CMD, much of this is routine police work, done with the efficiency one would expect of a police department. Steve explains:

> They know that we're not out there to attack them or to pick on them. We do stop them. We'll educate them on the law. We'll violate 'em and that's for the citation, and move about your business. If you want to go talk to a girl down the street, go to the parking lot, out of my sight, and talk to the girl around the corner, don't do it here in front of me, cause I have a job to do. So they understand. I don't really have that many problems out here.

But these officers are also aware of the deeply political nature of their assignment, knowing as do I that their presence is about claims to turf and the protection of a sizable financial corporate investment in the redevelopment of the city's core. "I hate to say it, but I think deep down it's kind of a political thing," Steve explains, "keep the streets clean, clear as much as possible by issuing citations or diverting them away from the main corridor so that people who are coming downtown to spend money can do so." Jeff's statements echo Steve's: "We're there to keep the corridors open so that people that want to spend money can go down and spend money. Otherwise, why would it matter whether these kids drive around or not? They could drive around all day."[50] This was the case in the 1980s, when the downtown area drew little attention among developers or urban planners. Chicano kids more or less freely cruised the downtown area with little interference. Like other urban areas, the downtown was a forgotten space. But, in the 1980s, after a decade of economic decline and inactivity, the loss of city tax dollars, and the erosion of the city's residential and commercial base, the downtown eventually came to be defined as a problem area.[51] "There was a big problem there, ah, and not only was there cruising but other major crimes associated with it, stabbings, shootings," Chris, one of the officers, explains. "It's not a serious problem like it was, I mean, definitely it's not where like it was ten, fifteen years ago. I mean it's mellow compared to that. And that has to do with all them, you know, the whole crime statistics," Jeff, another officer, offers. But this was soon to change.[52]

In the early 1990s, as San Jose emerged from the economic slump of the 1980s, the downtown area was officially designated as "blighted." The group responsible was the San Jose Redevelopment Agency, whose role was to "stimulate private investment in hotels, office towers and retail destination, especially in the Downtown core."[53] This designation catalyzed a sea of changes in the downtown both in the built environment and in social relations, as San Jose was refashioned as a "new space for urban consumption."[54] Important among these changes was an anticruising ordinance and the formation of the Cruise Management Division. Many community activists who observed the key changes in the downtown argued that the economic interests of corporate developers is ultimately what led to the adoption of the anticruising ordinance and the formation the Cruise Management Division. This is likely, since the Cruise Management Division (originally and transparently called the Youth Service Detail) first emerged during the massive program of urban revitalization and the funneling of millions in public funds and private investments into the downtown.[55] Explaining the emergence of the CMD, Ron, another officer, offered this: "I think it mostly started because people that want to go downtown that used to go to restaurants or whatever couldn't move because of so many cars coming and it gets gridlock really quickly."

From a government perspective, the San Jose Redevelopment Agency is widely known as a benchmark of "smart" redevelopment of America's urban core. Responsible for various initiatives involving city beautification, revitalization of public parks, restoration of historic sites, and neighborhood crime reduction programs, the Redevelopment Agency has played a powerful role in improving the quality of life in the downtown area. Santa Clara Street has become a thriving commercial district and an upscale residential zone, though it is still peppered with abandoned store fronts.

But gentrification and urban revitalization have fundamentally changed the actors and activities that occupy this cityscape. Many local groups, such as the Coalition for Redevelopment Reform, an organization against redevelopment abuse, regard the downtown as a virtual "nonplace." Traci Hukill, a writer for *Metro*, a local publication, wrote, "The Redevelopment Agency has played a critical role in the downtown crackdown on kids both directly and indirectly . . . [with] the enactment of teen curfews in 1994." Many long time community members have been dislocated. Mexicano, Filipino, and Vietnamese small-business owners who were central players in keeping this city afloat during the 1980s have been displaced by the ever-escalating rents and by the San Jose Redevelopment Agency's right to assert eminent domain in "blighted areas." Longtime cruisers have also been displaced, though cruising itself remains a widely popular activity. "It's no secret that anti-cruising ordinances target minority youngsters. For kids who have no place to go and can't afford the twenty dollars it costs to take a date to a movies or out to dinner, cruising is a natural option. It's also a generations-old Latino institution," Hukill, writes.[56]

In terms of cruising, "there is a different economic group here now," Officer Steve explains. "You're not looking at these kids who have built these cars up from nothing, and they are living in the ghetto. I mean, yeah, some of those kids are still out there, but most of these kids, they're driving better cars than I can afford to drive." "It's not the same kids seven or eight years ago," Steve continues. "I mean these kids, there's a lot more put-on status, the clothes they wear, they're all wearing these designer clothes, everybody wants to look cool, fit in, and now they're driving nicer cars, and I don't think people are so much looking at the, uh, the old cars that have been remodeled and souped up, they're driving, asking their parents if they can take out these really nice cars and it's more of a status thing." I, too, notice this upscaling of cars as I take note of the many expensive cars that cruise the strip: BMWs, Mercedes-Benzes, Cadillac Escalades, Lincoln Navigators, Yukons. In many ways, this reflects broader trends toward the upscaling of "life-style" norms and the competitive consumerism that I discuss in chapter 5. The revitalization of downtown has also drawn many youth from the suburbs. Earlier, in the 1970s and 1980s, affluent suburban kids primarily cruised down El Camino Real, a long strip of road flanked by strip malls in one of the more suburban areas just outside the city limits. But an anticruising ordinance adopted there combined with the urban revitalization efforts already discussed shifted these kids downtown, as it came to be seen as a more desirable social space.

Young Chicanos/as continue to make up a significant and visible slice of the downtown cruising scene. But this activity is no longer exclusively Chicano. It is taken up by young folks from all over the county and beyond. The changes in the downtown—a change in actors, greater police presence, more visible signs of wealth, and the greater financial investment—have transformed the experience of cruising and thus the meaning this activity carries for young Chicanos. One of the most significant changes has been more intensive policing of the downtown. The increased policing and surveillance of the area have meant that the young Chicanos, those most likely to be regarded with suspicion in this community and who had once claimed this space for themselves, have been subject to organized efforts of displacement. Many have simply left on their own accord; like Tino, they grew tired of being followed by cops. But there is also a sense that these brown kids were pushed out and unfairly targeted as gang members. A number of the kids who cruise believe that Chicanos and other young men of color were unjustly harassed. One writer, David Madrid, recollects:

> Now with San Jose trying to maintain its image of an orderly city, it's just a matter of time for cops to come flashing their lights, making threats and herding cars into the street like cattle. Cops have turned the cruising scene into a game of cat and mouse. Take the checkpoint at First and Santa Clara for instance, which is essentially a bunch of cops standing in the middle of the street profiling the cars stopped at the red light. If you're a carload of homeboys or flossin' too hard, you're most likely to get pulled.[57]

Keisha's depiction of the scene downtown is not too far from David's depiction.

> *Keisha*: When I go downtown, you know whole bunch of cops are in the middle of the street.
> *AB*: Oh, on Santa Clara Street?
> *Keisha*: Yeah, yeah, and pulling, pulling, you know, I've seen them pulling like if there's a bunch of Mexican men, young men, Mexican men, black men, pulled over. I've seen them looking to see if you have your

seatbelt on, checking your tags, with the, you know, the light in the car to see, to see, that's if they don't have an excuse. But sometimes, they don't need an excuse to pull you over anyway, so. And like all my male friends say the same thing, they all, all of them that are black have experienced.

Even the officers, who have been the subject of increasingly organized and sophisticated criticism for racial profiling, indirectly recognize that the displacement of young Chicanos has been a central part of their work managing the downtown. "It's difficult for people that want to come down here and enjoy themselves have to come down and listen to people blaring their music, you know maybe some of the people riding, lowriders doing their lowrider thing in their car," Chris, one of the officers, explains. "You know and to some people it's intimidating and that's why we're out there." Clearly the people to whom he refers are people not "of" the city but from outside it, residing in the various suburban settlements that border the downtown. For Chris, this explains why he and his fellow officers have been called upon to keep the cruising under control. "It [the CMD] initialized when downtown was kind of recreated, you know, so families and people could go down there and feel comfortable." Mike Davis, in *City of Quartz*, details the urban reforms focused on Los Angeles's public space, calling these efforts "a cold war on the streets of downtown," a storm of repressive security efforts that created a new kind of urban apartheid as they also eroded once-shared pedestrian spaces in order to secure the high-stakes financial interests of what sociologists call "capitalists of place."[58] Certain parallels might be drawn here, since much of what motivates these shifts are both present and future financial investments in the downtown.

The fights over space both fuel and reflect ongoing debates around issues of race and claims to public space for the community at large.[59] In a few instances, the increased policing in the area led to violence. This was the case during a Cinco de Mayo celebration in 1997, when exchanges of words quickly escalated as bottles were thrown at storefronts and the police made mass arrests.[60] Though newspapers reported that the conflict originated between rival gangs, it was also clear that the violence had escalated as officers intervened. Cinco de Mayo celebrations have been under close watch since then, with police officers out in full force.[61]

When young adults attempt to carve out public space, their efforts rarely go unchallenged. The controlling of space, concerted efforts to bar access from particular public places, and attempts to overcome this exclusion from public life are fundamental to the story of youth.[62] But this struggle often occurs in the context of race. Young Anglo men and women who come to participate in the cruise seem to escape the high levels of surveillance these young Chicanos/as confront as they claim space for themselves on this street and others. Young Anglos are free to wear red and blue in this space without drawing the attention that young Chicanos draw, whether they are "flying" these colors as a sign of gang membership or simply wearing them. In the end, these dynamics stand behind young Chicanos' desire to claim a coherent ethnic identity. At the same time, they pose a significant challenge to Chicanos'/as' attempts to do so, since the imagined community these young Chicanos/as create is disrupted by dramatic changes in the life of the downtown area and by the organized and repeated efforts to remove Chicano/a kids from this space.

Claiming Cars

As much as the emergence of cruising as a popular social activity for postwar youth reflected a set of changes in modern social life—suburbanization, the expansion of the leisure industries, and the emergence of a commodity culture, a changing reality of adolescence defined by greater freedom and autonomy—the same might also be said of today. The present cruising scene can be understood in terms of a new set of changes in social life: the reworking of America's urban core, the dissolving boundaries between suburban and city life, and the growing diversity in suburbs and city that are a consequence of an emerging global culture and the trend toward transnationalism. In many ways, the changing streetscape discussed in this chapter reveals the locality of relations and the economic processes that have shaped them. Large-scale efforts at urban renewal have developed alongside Silicon Valley's emerging role in a postindustrial economy as the center of high tech, expressing the city's desire to draw business and people to the downtown.

This has meaningful consequences in terms of how young Chicanos/as construct community belonging and ethnic identities. Participating in the cruise is central to "claiming" an ethnic identity for young Chicanos in San Jose and beyond. But shifts in the social organization of the downtown have made the work of constructing ethnic identity more tenuous. In this sense, car cruising in the downtown reflects changing racial maps that structure U.S. communities and youths' relationships to places within them. These racial maps frame the cultural identities youth are given and those they claim as they travel in and around "old places" that have become "new social terrains." These spatial relations, grafted onto the racial landscape of the downtown (and other ethnically segmented areas of San Jose), give rise to the formation of a collective race consciousness. This can be seen as young folks invest in their cars and in the practices of cruising as an expression of ethnic identity and their ongoing struggle against racial oppression.

Cars and the social relations that surround them reflect what Arthur Schlesinger has called the "cult of ethnicity."[63] Cars are a means to both solidify and protect racial and ethnic identity and, in some instances, to counter the stigmatization of those identities for youth. Kids increasingly use cars as a means to identify ethnically, to "claim" membership in an ethnic group. In the increasingly diverse communities of northern California, where ethnicity plays a heavy role in deciding where you live, where you work, where you go to school, and the group you hang with, identifying ethnically through one's car is a way to belong. Youth attach ethnic meaning to cars by the rosary beads and bucco shells they hang from rearview mirrors, the symbols and icons they attach to the cars, and the customized license plates that affirm their racial and ethnic identity.

Many scholars have observed that the turn toward ethnic identification occurs at a time when the traditional anchors through which our collective and individual identities were formed have eroded. Likewise seeing the focus on community occurring at a time when its absence is glaring.[64] As people respond to and make sense of the world around them, a world that lacks the coherence and stability provided by the grand narratives of what Zygmunt Bauman calls "solid modernity," they struggle to belong to something in an increasingly mobile world that lacks any sense of permanence. In this context, identities are fashioned through ethnic symbols and histories are arranged and reinterpreted in ways that allow for the formation of fluid collectives to which individuals can claim membership. It is in this context that we must understand Chicanos'/as' heightened awareness of ethnicity and their attempt to construct a coherent narrative of identity and community through cruising.

The increasing importance of ethnic identification and ethnic attachment among youth also reflects meaningful demographic shifts. While San Jose itself is a "minority majority" city with established middle-class and lower-income ethnic enclaves, it is the young, not the adults, who are the most ethically diverse. In terms of total numbers, the young are more racially diverse than the overall U.S. population with the percentage of Latino, African American, and Asian American youth all above the overall national average. The young have the most contact with ethnic groups other than their own, are the most likely to participate in interracial relationships, and are most likely to have a close friend who is from a racial or ethnic group different from their own. Young people increasingly live their lives differently as Chicana, queer, urban working class, suburban upper-middle class, or immigrant. "This fragmentation," the historians Joe Austin and Michael Willard argue, "facilitates both a multiplicity of youth culture and a wide range of hybrid identities."[65] Youth themselves play an active role in shaping and reshaping, inventing and reinventing ethnic formations. This can be seen in the racial repertoires these Chicano/a youth use to narrate their experience of cruising. Through cruising, they come to see themselves as belonging to a larger intergenerational community born out of cultural struggle. In this sense, these young Chicanos and Chicanas belong to the same interpretive community, even if they live miles apart.[66] Yet other Chicanos, like Cesar, distance themselves from cruising, seeing it as representative of a particular kind of Chicano. Perhaps, some young Chicanos distance themselves from this activity because it carries the weight of the stigma assigned to it by those in power.[67]

Lowriders and cruising carry a "spirit of liberation for those embedded in the social reality of subordination and domination."[68] Importantly, it is through cars and their engagement in car spaces that youth sometimes come to think more critically about the world and their place in it. This can be seen in how young Chicanos/as come to define their encounters with police officers as symptoms of widespread racial injustice. They understand the political implications of these encounters, seeing them as central to the racial persecution of generations of Chicanos/as. In this limited sense, cars carry a transformative potential that can inspire an emerging youth activism. This was the case in Oakland, California, where young African Americans fought against what was commonly seen as "racially unfair cruising ordinances at Oakland's Lake Merritt."[69]

Yet, as much as San Jose's downtown cruising scene carries a spirit of community for young Chicanos, it is also steeped in other social histories. What of the girls, for example, who cruise? Some are Chicanas, but many are not. How do they travel within this space? In the following chapter, I return to the downtown scene, seeing it as these girls might.

2

Sex-in' the Car
Girls and Car Cruising

On a warm night only weeks after the summer has begun, I drive downtown to Santa Clara Street to cruise. I arrive to a scene bursting at its seams. Not unlike the other nights I have come to cruise, a chain of cars stretch far beyond what the eye can see. Moving at the characteristic nearly-nothing pace, I pass a grocery store parking lot on my left. The lot is empty except for four cars, parked in a row. The sound of muffled music emanates from one of the four cars. For each car, there are three to four young men, standing around as car after car rolls by. All the men appear to be in their early twenties. A number wear baseball caps atop cleanly cut hair, a noticeable number wear football jerseys, oversized of course, many bearing the Oakland Raiders' black and silver. One group of boys huddles around a blue Chevelle, marking the car as the lot's centerpiece, that is, until a motorcycle drives by with a young woman wearing denim short shorts known colloquially as "Daisy Dukes," sitting on the back, her arms tightly clasped around the waist of the male driver. One of the young men steps onto the sidewalk; leaning forward he roars, "Booootie!" and then casually returns to what moments before had occupied his attention. A few parked cars down, I spot two guys sitting in the front seats of a silver Mustang. They sit silently, face forward, music booming out of the car as they look out on to the street. Farther down the street, three cars sit in the Chevron station; four young men are gathered under the hood of another Mustang, this time bright yellow. A few feet from where they stand, I spot two girls walking down the drag. They are perhaps eighteen or nineteen, have long hair; each is wearing a miniskirt, a colored halter top, and high-heeled sandals. I wonder if they are walking to someplace or if the walking itself is the event. The lively chatter of a group of three girls drifts from the Honda Accord beside me as I pull up behind two cars, one a convertible; both are full of young men. I see out of the corner of my eye the driver, a slim guy no more than twenty, with a baseball cap and flannel shirt, smoking. I fix my attention on the convertible in front of me, as I watch the two boys in the back moving easily around as they chatter; "No seatbelts," I think. I can sense their excitement, and perhaps I even catch a little of it. In my rearview mirror, I see a young man who has just stepped out from the back seat of a 1980s BMW. Appearing drunk, he stumbles over to a bright green VW Bug, which holds three young women engrossed in conversation. Perhaps that's why they don't realize the young man has now opened the door of their car, attempting to get inside. One yells, "Get out!" as the driver pulls up a few feet, causing the young man to lose his balance. Catching himself, he turns and slinks back to the BMW, where three other young men who have already begun a diatribe of heavy ribbing and howls wait.

I pass a group of four young men on foot as they disappear into a darkened parking lot, each separately emerging moments later readjusting the zippers on their pants. Inching down the street, I can see off in the distance a group of young men, eight or so, hanging out on the sidewalk. Several hold soda bottles in their hands, and I wonder if there is liquor in there, too. One car stops before them, a black Cadillac Escalade, and one of the guys ambles over. He leans over the window, half of his body almost inside the car. I watch as the others point out different cars, perhaps evaluating. They hoot and holler, dancing to music as different cars pass. A car peels out, and I hear the group cheer with excitement. This cheering is momentarily interrupted as two women pass dressed for a "night out." They cheer for the women, actually at them, as the women rush on, revealing only the slightest of smiles, as if to suggest this is all a matter of course. I move on, happy to be in my car and not on foot like these two girls.

Santa Clara Street has long been a space where groups of young men and women come together on summer nights in the late hours, lingering after the clubs and bars that line this downtown street have closed usually until the cops usher them elsewhere.[1] Car after car, mostly full of young men, they congregate on Santa Clara Street on these hot summer nights, accompanied by a cacophony of hoots and hollers directed at young women as they travel in small armies in cars and on foot, up and down the street. That young men dominate this car scene, though an unremarkable fact, does not pass unnoticed by me or by the hundreds of young women who move in and out of this space regularly. Car cruisin' has long been understood as a masculine activity taken up by men, not women. The historians Michael Witzel and Kent Bash write, in *Cruisin': Car Culture in America,* a historical account of the youth car culture of the 1950s and 1960s in Southern California, "Without a doubt, a cool car was a prerequisite to get girls and get laid. If the car was a racy, sexy hot rod one had a good shot. So car owners became aware of the numero uno reason for cruising: driving an awesome automobile was the most effective way to attract females and keep their interest." Witzel and Bash, two self-proclaimed insiders, suggest a troubling geography of gender for this cruising world, complicated further by the seemingly inescapable logic of heterosexuality. The link between cars and masculinity is probably as old as cars themselves.[2] But this fact should not eclipse another one—young women play important supporting roles in American car cultures. A quick flip through the many car magazines available today shows endless images of women as objects of display.[3] In *Lowrider* and *Street Truck,* two notable car rags, women are rarely featured behind the wheel but can be regularly found draped across the hood of car after car, usually wearing very little. In the April 2001 edition of *Lowrider* magazine, I counted thirty-one pictures of women wearing bikinis and high heels either atop a car, bending over, or straddling the hood of a car (this excludes the magazine cover, which always features a bathing suit–clad woman and a car).[4] In the same monthly edition, I found only one picture of a woman seated in the driver's seat.[5] While the types of cars featured regularly change, the images of hypersexualized young women rarely do.[6]

Hardly invisible as they often are in other male-dominated cultural scenes, young women exist under a spotlight of peering eyes, cast as objects whose bodies are inspected much as the body of a car would be. American car cultures' very organization depends on young women's presence as sexual objects in that they affirm a heterosexual world of masculine competition and bravado; their existence helps to define their opposite, the subjects of this world, young men, *as* men.[7] As feminist scholars argued long ago, it is through girls' bodies that masculine power effectively works.[8] In this sense, this (mis)use of girls' bodies is a familiar tale.

But what does this mean for the young women who bravely traverse this gendered world?[9] Why do young women participate in a cultural scene where they appear to gain so little? To answer these questions and others, this chapter focuses in on young women's participation in the local world of car cruising, an activity that occurs regularly on late weekend summer nights on public streets, spaces historically off limits to "good" women.[10] Cruising, while an activity that ostensibly brings young men and women into the same physical space, largely remains a sex-segregated activity. Young men and women regularly talk across cars, but rarely does one see a car transporting a young man and young woman. Most cars contain two to five people, almost always all of the same sex. This gender scheme reflects (and reproduces) a rigid set of rules of sexual conduct for young women, requiring them (and young men) to actively manage their identities as young women as they and the boys move in and out of this shared public space.

Hanging with the Girls

I arrive to the sorority house on a Wednesday evening around six o'clock for an interview with a group of college-age Chicanas to talk about cruising. It is still light out, and will be for the next several hours since it is the height of summer. My knock brings Marisol, a slender young woman of twenty in shorts and a tank top, her dark hair wrapped in a sleek bun, to the door. Marisol is a member a multicultural sorority at the state university, blocks from Santa Clara Street.[11]

I walk into the living room, a small dark room that opens to an equally dark kitchen. Carla, who is now six months pregnant, is sitting at the kitchen table with three of her sorority sisters, Lydia, Lupe, and Teresa, talking about baby strollers and her upcoming baby shower. Carla, whom I interviewed last month, coordinated this evening. She tells me we are expecting a large group (eleven in total) and that we should wait for a few minutes before we get started. I take this time to scope out the scene. Theirs is like no other sorority house I have seen. No clean white walls, plush pastel-colored carpeting, or floral chintz drapes; instead, vinyl flooring that extends from the kitchen into the living room, dark wood paneling on the walls, and a single window in the living room which is without coverings. In the small living room, there are two old, unmatching couches, a wooden chair, and a small television sitting on a dented metal TV stand. I sit down on the dark green vinyl couch next to Carla, and we chat as Vanessa, Maria, and Felicia trickle in. Three more girls, Yesina, Deisy, and Claudia, will arrive later in the evening.

The young women are seated on the floor or the stairs leading to the second floor, and the small room almost feels overcrowded (and quite warm, since there is no air conditioning). I set the recorder on a chair in the middle of the room, and the evening is under way. I ask them to tell me about cruising, an activity that has consumed many of their weekend nights since high school. For these girls, Santa Clara Street is a well-traveled road. Felicia is the first to speak, taking obvious pleasure in her description.

> We just like roll down the windows and we get all dressed up, even though we're not going to meet [anyone] you know, out there, we're not going to be walking. We just get dressed up, turn up, turn on the music really loud and just sit there and look at the cars you know and if there's like cute guys passing by or standing whatever, we'll wave to them and stuff like.

With years of practice, much of this is routine. They enjoy the activities of getting ready; often the partying begins with drinks as they collectively prepare for an evening out. The girls clearly enjoy the hours they spend sitting in their cars, a meaningful social space, traveling up and down the drag, seeing and being seen. They are at once participants in and observers of this cultural scene: agents and objects. They objectify as easily as they are objectified. "It's crowded and you're dead stuck in the middle of traffic," Lupe explains, "then the little breezies will go out there and flaunt their little bodies around. There's fat girls out there, and there's everything. Big, little, small, black, white, you name it."

Though time spent inside the car with girlfriends watching others carries significance for these women, ultimately the night is about boys, meeting them and being noticed by them. Talk of boys occupies much of our evening together as they collectively and individually describe their various encounters with young men. Carla offers,

> Yeah, well last year I went with my friends, my sorority sisters, it was really fun and um, it's funny because all the guys jump out at all the girls; like they practically try to go into the car windows and when we were stopped at a red light this guy came over and asked my friend for her number. So she got it and he ended up calling the next day and him and a couple of friends came over and that's where I met my fiancé.

That Carla met her fiancé through cruising is novel for these girls. Few have expectations that any long-term relationship will develop from cruising. Instead, the night is about fleeting interludes, a succession of momentary connections, a game—young men and women coming into contact with the objective to "get holla'd at" and to be recognized by as many as possible. Ariana explains,

> You go out there and you're driving up and down Santa Domingo Street and a bunch of cars, and all these guys, and some of them come down and try to holla at you in your window, and then you try to give them your number. In all reality, what the hell you giving them? Seven little numbers he ain't ever gonna use, they never call you. Nobody ever really calls back. And if they do, maybe sometimes they do, like it could be a way to meet new people, but more than 90 percent of the time, every time I've given out my number or taken a number, I've never called it back.

Undeniably, impressions are important. In my observations, I witnessed a carefully crafted performance by both boys and girls, each playing different parts but for same audience, that is, the boys who reign over this space, who claim streets like Santa Clara as their own. The metaphors of performance and the stage, first used by the sociologist Erving Goffman to describe the ritual enactment of the everyday world, are rich in meaning and useful in understanding this cultural space where the boundaries between pleasure and desire, power and exploitation explode.[12] Hundreds of young men and women crowd into this space to put on a good show as much as they come to watch one. The street is their stage, the cars their props, and young women's bodies the key resources in the decadent play of identities and the transgression of moral boundaries. Jorge's words are revealing in this regard.

> *Jorge*: Me and my boys grab our cameras and go strippin' the streets on the convertible. Flashing. I mean random. ooooh man.
> *Maria*: Wait a minute, who's flashing? (laughing)
> *Jorge*: Random . . . oooh. Man. Just random . . . oooh. And you pull over post up and you park your car and it's so packed that you can actually walk up to a car and talk to a girl for a good five, ten minutes before they have to move.

Maria: Oh yeah.

Jorge: So you hit on them, get some numbers. You might even make out with little random.

Maria: You've made out with some girls?

Jorge: Just random girls that pull out their titties and let people suck on them.

Maria: Seriously?

Jorge: We have it on tape. Oh my God!

Maria: So these girls that are doing the flashing are they younger girls?

Jorge: Eighteen or something to their early twenties. Yeah, yeah. It's off the hook. We had, dude had a camera and we just had girls "Hey, hey, what up, come pull over." Dude, girls will do anything in front of a camera, they'll bend over let us pull out their thong, just take off stuff.

Like Jorge, I observed countless young men with handheld camcorders, repeatedly zeroing in on young women's bodies, their breasts and backsides.[13] Perhaps their intention is to leave with lasting records of having witnessed "the little breezies" out there to "flaunt their little bodies."

The elements of fanciful play, licentiousness, and playful deviance captured in Jorge's depiction of Santa Clara Street are central to understanding how Santa Clara Street comes to life on these weekend nights. The fluidity of interactional rituals, the pleasures of the body, the parade and performance of utter excess contribute to the sense that, on Santa Clara Street, "anything goes."[14] Indeed, there were times when I felt this to be the case. But what I came to realize is that Santa Clara Street is a space governed by a distinct set of interactional rules that function more than anything else to give the appearance of the absence of rules. These hidden rules of conduct, which govern how men and women come together and move apart, are carefully veiled by a parade of recklessly extravagant performances as conventional gender scripts are activated for the explicit purpose of disrupting them. Young men initiate much of the action, but the social encounters themselves revolve around women's bodies. And thus it is women's identities as much as the men's that are at stake. Much relies on young women's willingness to play their part.

While a large number of girls display a willingness to be seen on the one hand, they also work to express a cool disinterest on the other, as if to say, "I don't mind your looking, but don't expect anything else unless I am willing to give it." Young men are repeatedly "dissed" in this scene. But that is all a part of the exchange. Boys hoot and holler across cars to gain the passing attention of girls. Boys' efforts to command the attentions of a car full of young women ultimately are what enable them to be recognized as "players" and "pimps" by their peers—other young men.

Girls can decide how to respond—to engage fully by talking or giving out their telephone number, to acknowledge the boys but not respond, gesturing with a slight smile or flip of the hair, or to ignore them completely. If the guy is ignored, he will often move on, laughing it off with his buddies. If the young man is unable to recover from this "diss," thereby losing face, the young woman who was the object of his attention can suddenly become the object of his wrath. Not surprisingly, girls are regularly charged with being "bitches," or worse.

Having a cool car is the key to gaining visibility for boys in this cultural scene. "You have to have a nice car. You don't want to go out there with a Pinto 'cause then you're really not gonna get holla'd at," Vanessa explains, her comments followed by this from Teresa: "If the guy rolls up in a beat-up old car and tries to pick up on you, they're [the girls are] gonna walk away, they're not gonna be talking to a guy in a beat-up car, it just doesn't happen." But, this is not the case for young women. "I mean, guys don't care, I was in a junked-up car, and they were like, Hey baby what's up, if you're cute they don't care," Deisy offers. Few women have the sort of cars that draw any sustained attention (those outfitted with after-market parts), in large part because few are willing or able to make such a sizable investment; such a car costs dearly. But what women do have time and money to invest in is their appearance. They are well aware that how they look serves as the basis of whether a boy will look *at* or *through* them. Thus, visibility is gained primarily through how they display their bodies. "Like, these guys get to see your face so if you don't have like a nice face, you're not gonna get hollered at." To be seen, a girl must convey a willingness to be looked at. After all, to be invisible in this scene is the worst kind of slight, essentially defeating the purpose of being there in the first place.

Cautionary Tales and Boys' Outrageous Acts

These girls clearly delight in talking about the scene, recounting to me, an obvious outsider, with noticeable excitement stories from the field.

They seem to enjoy shocking me with the outrageous tales of boys jumping in girls' cars. The wild excitement and the heightened emotional experience they feel as they play with and push the moral boundaries that in other settings fence them in help to explain their willingness to return to Santa Clara Street in the first place. But their excitement is tempered as their talk turns to the unfair and quite often downright bad behavior of boys. In describing this scene, the girls identify a pervasive double standard: one set of rules for the boys, another for the girls.[15] This double standard helps explains why the girls, even those who have boyfriends, never cruise with them. Talking about her old boyfriend, Marisol explains:

> He'll sit there and stare at girls, or he'll like look, I'm like, Oh my God. And then like one time this guy waved to me and I was like, huh? and he's like, cusses, mother fucker, I didn't want to look at him. He was like, you know that guy waved to you, I'm like, he did? [laughter from the group] It's like break your neck just to look at a girl, he can't wait to meet them, I was like, oh my god. We left the strip because he was an asshole.

But it is not the apparent double standard that bothers these girls. This they accept as a matter of course. What bothers them is the fact that the boys' behavior encroaches on the girls' freedom to move in and around this space with ease. "Guys are really aggressive during that time . . . [it's like] cruising gives them the right to act that way or, I don't know, it's just, they're more aggressive toward females," Vanessa explains, adding, "All these guys jumping at you, and getting in your car, and doing this and that and camcorders and this and that and the other thing." Hardly worth their weight in salt, guys are not to be trusted, Teresa advises:

> All the guys want to do is see, you know, girls. They just want sex. Lots of times guys are drunk so they approach you like you know, right away they'll just come up to you and like try to touch you and all that. They'll go to the windows of girls' [cars] and stick their head in there.

Though they are reluctant to admit it, on some level it is clear these girls at times feel threatened by boys, as Marisol's statement reveals: "They come in big groups, you don't want them to do anything to your car, you know."

Though rare, anger and a sense of injustice at times inflect their voices as the girls talk about the transgressions of boys. What bothers them is not simply that they become the objects of boys' transgressions but that their ability to then transgress their own boundaries as subjects in their own right is eclipsed by the actions of boys. Lupe speaks animatedly: "Along the strip, there are guys who will just get out of their cars, hang out on the wall, drink and stuff and they'll do the cat calls as you're driving by . . . we would get mad but it really gets me mad." Yesina interrupts, "You know what's the worst part? When they hang something onto your car." The excitement of the group seems to reach a crescendo as each of the girls jumps in with a tale more outrageous than the last. "They try to jump in the car they try to open ya, they try to get, 'can I have your number?' and you know to roll up the windows cause, shoot, you think they're gonna go in there and something like freaking attack you."

Accounts by police officers resemble those of the women. Jay, one officer who works in the cruise management division, offers, "This last 'Cinco' . . . there are so many girls downtown, these guys are cruising jumping out of their cars and grabbing their breasts, or their buttocks." Steve, another cop who works in the Cruise Management Division, says, "They're [women] walking through the cruising areas, and they're on foot in groups, groups of boys, and they'll . . . kind of surround these women and they start getting aggressive, almost, I don't want to make a bad analogy, but like a pack of wolves, and they're surrounding and then they start acting, ah, more and more aggressive with these women." I witnessed several attempts by boys to get into cars driven by young women, recalling the scene described earlier in the chapter. And I watched as boys moved their hands over and across girls' bodies as they passed each other on the street.

As our night together unfolds, the stories the girls share move beyond a realm of questionable conduct to one where young women's safety is compromised as the aggressiveness of the boys sometimes escalates.

I remember one time these guys drove up and were like, Hey girls, where's the party at? What's your number? What's your name? You guys want a ride? What are you guys doing out so late? you know, Do you guys need a guy to walk you somewhere? and we were just like, No thanks. We were being nice about it, we were like no thanks and we smiled and we kept walking. It was like three of us and it was probably five guys in the car and they kept following us so we started to get scared and one of my friends she was like, Don't you get it, we don't want to talk to you, and then they were just like, God, you know. They got kind of mad but they kept on persisting and then one of my friends, she was joking around but she said, "Oh, well, if your car was a little better maybe we would think about it." You know, and then all of a sudden laughing because she was just joking around but the guys got really mad and they were like, Oh you stuck-up bitches, you're not all that anyways, you're ugly, and they just started telling all these things and then my friend, she got mad and she started you know telling them off too and she went off on them and we were just like calm down because there's five guys and only three of us. Finally we got into the car and we were going to get in and the guys threw a bottle at us and then sped off, so, yeah, the guys do get you know aggressive if the girls turn them down or whatever. So, it was kind of scary but I didn't think much of it until later, you know I was like, okay we were stupid, we shouldn't have got them mad but you didn't think about it, at the time it was funny.

The girls' emerging concern for their safety seems justified as things quickly spiral out of control. When the girls attempt to "tell it straight" (after several attempts at polite refusals), the boys' anger ignites, eroding any opportunity for the boys to "save face." In the end, these girls hold themselves largely responsible, seeing their own actions as "stupid."

Allowing the boys to save face is a theme that regularly emerges in the accounts young women provide about their encounters with young men.

Like, if they start smiling at me or whatever, I'll just kind of smile but not really or if they're like hey girl, what's your number, I'll just be like, I'll roll my eyes or look away and then they'll kind of get the hint but yeah. But they're just like really, some of them think that you're playing hard to get and so they'll just keep trying to talk to you and sometimes they'll follow you.

Their comments highlight the work involved in the performance that is expected of girls as they interact with boys within this sexually charged space and others like it. While they are willing to tolerate many of the actions of boys, the efforts involved in managing these emotional terrains are considerable. They must carefully deflect unwanted attention without creating a scene and ensure their own safety without letting on that this is what they are doing. Lots of girls give out their telephone numbers (or fake ones), even though they do not want to, because it is easier than having to say no to those boys who are unrelenting. "I really didn't want to give him my number, ya know, they weren't that cute."

Boys' expectations of girls' "ritual deference," to borrow again from Erving Goffman, curtail the chance for them to get in on the fun, to feel the excitement gained by being a participant in the playful, wicked, and decadent performance of excess, to soak up and soak in the cultural scene. The boys' expectations of ritual deference by girls also shows an important component of this cultural scene, which is that it is the boys who hold the cards. They govern the fields of meaning, the "ritual codes" and the "expressive fabric" that order and define this space and the encounters therein.[16] Also revealing is that the boys depend on the girls' honoring this expressive order to support an image of themselves for the audience that matters most, that is, other boys—their homies. The girls' unwillingness to participate in what Goffman called "status rituals" where their appreciation and submission are symbolically conveyed serves to disrupt the image of the masculine self these young men work to maintain through their encounters with young women.[17] It is especially meaningful that the girls in the first scenario mocked the boys because of their car, an important marker of their being legitimate men, thereby not only failing to support an image of the boys' masculine selves but calling it into question.

The girls' stories also reveal the limits they place on themselves as they attempt to circumvent situations that at times leave them feeling threatened. "You don't want to be a single soldier out there, no, don't ever. Two people I don't know, three's a crowd, so you're better with three you know," Ariana shares. These eleven young women rarely venture beyond the group or move outside the cars. But others girls do, Carla is quick to share with me: "Some people don't have cars they'll just go out there and stand on the street and look at cars. But when I go, I don't like to be out there because I'm kind of scared." Lydia says, "I just stay in the car and even then, you know, they try and jump into cars and it's just, they can get out of hand." The girls share a number of cautionary tales of girls venturing beyond the car, perhaps told as much for me as for each other. "You don't wanna be the only girl in the car with like six guys," one of the young women warns. "If they have a nice car, they'll be like, Oh, do you want to go cruising with me? and probably the girl's going to be like, Okay, and bring like a friend along or whatever. Usually they won't go by themselves cause they don't know the guy. They'll just go in maybe for a block, just be in the car for like a block and then get off and then [he] tells his friends all these lies." This explains why Lydia thinks it better to just stick to yourself. "I don't' really talk to no one out of their car."

These cautionary tales told by and among these young women, all friends and insiders to this cultural scene, operate on many different levels of meaning. At one level, these tales seem to be exchanged in a genuine attempt to protect themselves and others from what are perceived as legitimate dangers. On another level, these cautionary tales form the basis of the girls' shared experience, of "having been there," and in this sense serve to solidify their identity as a collective. But there is also more to these tales. For the teller, the detailing of what many would consider alarming encounters is also part and parcel of the performance of femininity, testimony of their successfully embodying the desired (though perhaps not desiring) heterosexual girl. Just as recounting stories of battle for soldiers serve as testimonies of masculinity, the sharing of these types of stories serve as a kind of feminine claims-making in that they reveal one's feminine visibility.[18] It is in this sense that young women are active in the social reproduction of gender.

Context matters here, since this performance of femininity takes shape in a space where young women come together in and against the sweeping tides of the collective power of boys. They accept boys' power in this space, and the double standard through which this power is upheld even as they sometimes express a sense of anger about it. But these women refuse to see themselves as victims, preferring instead to recall the close calls where they outwitted the boys and perhaps by sheer luck alone emerged all right.

In some ways, their testimonies are examples of the "risk narratives" that the adolescent psychologist Cynthia Lightfoot argues is central to the culture of risk-taking among youth.[19] Risky activity, according to Lightfoot, is conceptualized among youth as a transforming experience, providing opportunity to push one's personal limits and test one's inner strength, learn about one's self and others, and exercise control over one's self and surroundings. The sharing of these narratives is important in groups. The fact that their stories focus on risk of sexual violence reveals the role gender plays in organizing risk narratives and the gendered pathways through which young women and men differently move through cultures of risk.[20] Sexual violence is a primary risk for young women. That these narratives all recall "close calls" where sexual violence was successfully avoided positions the women as in control both of the event and of the retelling of it, even while the control they did have seems jarringly fragile to me as I listen.

Notably, rather than generating any sustainable critique of how boys control social spaces through intimidation and threats of violence and exercise an unreasonable sense of entitlement to young women's bodies, the girls offer testimonies of their ability to cleverly maneuver in a world where boys seem to be holding all the cards. Their insistence seems to parallel the new kind of girlhood Lyn Mikel Brown identified in her book, *Girlfighting*. Brown argues that "new versions of girlhood have emerged: girls as smart, strong, athletic, brave and resistant. Out of these versions a new popular ideal, some might say a counterideal, has developed: girl as fighter. In response to girl as victim, which fed off stereotypes of femininity as passive and vulnerable, girl as fighter is assertive, usually smart, psychologically tough and physically strong."[21] This emergent girlhood celebrates girl power, perhaps to the point of ignoring the obvious absence of it.

The Dangers of Being a Girl

Rarely do the girls confront the arrangements in this scene, believing that its form was cemented long before their arrival. In a space where boys not only outnumber them but also appear to control the fields of meaning, these girls impose a feminine code of conduct as they rein themselves and other girls in through their disapproving talk. Girls who express too much interest in cars or the public space where car cultures take shape risk the label of "hood rat," "hoochie," or "slut," labels not surprisingly assigned by both young men and women. Those deserving of such labels are women who give into a man too quickly, eagerly jumping into a strange boy's car, for example. To do so essentially means "they don't care enough about themselves." The girl who escapes a suspect sexual label is one who gives primacy to her girlfriends over a boy (unless he is a serious boyfriend) in this cultural scene.[22] She never leaves her friends or ventures outside her friend's car to cruise with a boy she doesn't know. "When I am cruising alone with the sisters I won't get out of the car. . . . In your car, you're in this little confined bubble, and you feel safe."

Dress and deportment are key markers in this scene. "I did wear a short dress one time. It wasn't really revealing, but it was short or whatever, and I got a lot of unwanted attention. Like all the guys immediately assume that you're easy, that they can grab you, you know." At the same time, they symbolically, if not physically, distance themselves from girls who are seen as sexually suspect: "a lot of girls start flashing guys and wearing skimpy little clothes," Marisol explains, but she and her friends don't. Carla offers, "Guys, they're just, 'Hey girl, let's hook up and I'll show you something in my car,' and like other girls would just laugh, but I kind of felt uncomfortable." These girls invoke a typology of girls that is ever shifting, depending on its creator. Vanessa chimes in at a particularly raucous point in the evening, "We don't go flashing people or grabbing guys or whatever, you know, we don't do that but you know we still talk to the guys and joke with them or whatever, but when there's like a girl and she's doing all that, letting herself be grabbed or showing her, whatever, we'll be like, uh, that hood rat."

For this group of college women, the division between the good girl and the bad girl is reframed in terms of high school girls and college girls. High school girls are cast as insipid and trifling girls, willing to flash their breasts in exchange for attention. Carla explains,

> College girls, they're, I don't know, they're more restricted to the way they act like what they're wearing, they, while they might be wearing something revealing, but they won't do the things that other girls don't do, and you can usually tell right away and like, us we're, like when I go with my friends we don't, we don't go flashing people or grabbing guys or whatever, you know, we don't do that, but, you know, we still talk to the guys and joke with them or whatever, but when there's like a girl and she's doing all that, letting herself be grabbed or showing her, whatever, we'll be like, uh, that hood rat, you know, uh, that hoochie.

Ultimately, the younger girls are seen by these college women as unable to distinguish between those boys out for a good time at their expense and the few boys who are to be trusted. These young women pride themselves on being able to recognize a "player" or a "pimp."[23] One can't help sensing that these young women are responding not only to younger women of the here and now but perhaps to the actions of their younger selves. Yet I find myself returning to Carla's words, troubled most by her statement about college girls: "they're more restricted to the way they act." The college girls, these girls, are the ones she sees as in control, yet they also appear to be subject to more restrictions in terms of dress and deportment as they reel themselves in. What becomes clear is that these young women are active creators of the gendered realities that often bind and limit them.

Getting One Over: Girls Resist

These girls demand that I see this scene for what it is, a complex space where the power of boys is both illusory and real. As I step from this late-night scene, taking it in, I am gripped by a naggingly persistent sense that reality is not as it seems, that these young women's claims to this space are held together by thin threads. Like birds on a wire, however, a thin thread is apparently enough for them to etch out their collective path through the cat calls—to be "holla'd" at in the right way, to gain the right kinds of attention from boys, and to successfully deflect the wrong sort.

All girls must manage this sexual terrain, yet many playfully negotiate its perimeters. Girls often travel across this space in large numbers, which at times enables them to engage the game on terms slightly different from those set by the boys. These women engage in what the sociologist Mimi Schippers calls "gender maneuvering," an interactive process central to identity formation that involves reworking the interactional patterns that preserve hierarchical relations between and among masculinities and femininities. Schippers investigates an alternative hard rock scene, zeroing in on the everyday strategies young men and women use to "push, pull, challenge and fortify the rules of gender and sexuality,"[24] arguing that, as they gender maneuver, they carefully, though not always consciously, craft an alternative order. One way through which young women negotiate the sexual field of cruising is by trying "to get over on a guy." A young woman I interviewed, delighted in being able to outsmart a guy, said, "We used to be like we're all sisters and we'd have names that rhymed. . . . We'd be like Mina, Tina, and Nina. . . . They'd catch on, but we'd get a good laugh out of it." Other girls, like

Lupe, told tales of giving out fraudulent pager or telephone numbers in an attempt to have a laugh.

> Well when I go with my girlfriends, we just roll down the windows and we get dressed up, even though we're not going to meet you know out there, we're not going to be walking . . . we turn up the music really loud and just sit there and look at the cars you know and if there's like cute guys passing by or standing we'll wave to them but if we're not attracted to them we'll give them fake names and numbers most of the time. Everybody does that. . . . Like I have so many fake names and them like you'll see this guy walking down the street and he'll be calling you by your fake name and you're like you know I totally forgot. It's so funny.

Carla adds,

> Um, I've given Regina, cause that's my like, my like first communion name, and then I'll give fake numbers, but if the guy's really annoying I'll be like, okay, my number's 123-4567 and they'll know right away, okay she does not want to give me her number cause it's obvious it's a fake number.

With hundreds of young women and men participating in this space, girls have some degree of anonymity that allows them opportunity to invent themselves, testing out different ways of being a girl. They can be "Mina" or "Tina" or anyone else momentarily, and their girlfriends are almost always willing conspirators.

Many of these young women also relish the opportunity to make fun of young men. Beating them at their own game, they enjoy those moments when young men reveal themselves as fakes and posers. Consider the story Marisol and Maria convey:

> *Maria:* I knew a guy on Santa Clara, he actually rented a car. Me and my friends ended up going on a ride on an Expedition, and he's was like, oh you know. I wanted cigarettes, and I pulled open the compartment and I saw like it was from Enterprise.
> *Marisol:* It's so sad.
> *AB:* Did you get out?

Maria: Yeah, we got out.
Maria: He was like, I just bought it, I just, I . . .

When asked how she knows a player when she sees one, Marisol explains that it's really the whole package, "the car, their mannerisms, if you see they've filmed us and then . . . start filming another group of girls. Gettin' their numbers and comin' back and gettin' mine. You can watch them down the strip." To make sure I don't misunderstand and think that girls are terribly bothered by these players, Vanessa quickly adds, "They roll up just a little bit so you can see them up ahead or right behind you, and then you just make fun of them, mess with them." Here they have power, not the boys, because they refuse to be taken in by the sham.

AB: Do they know that you are making fun of them?
Maria: Sometimes.
AB: Do you make fun of them in front of them?
Marisol: Yeah.
Vanessa: If you think you're all that and you're not, you know.

Their laughter explodes as Vanessa offers, "They are getting smarter, dude, now they want to dial [the number] right then and there."

When I ask if the guys keep track of how many numbers they can get, they are quick to remind me that girls play that game, too. "Girls, too," several say in unison. Vanessa elaborates, "You wanna see how many people you can talk to, but, when I used to go to high school, we used to be like, we used to have contests to see who could get the most numbers." Rarely do these result in lengthy telephone conversations the next day. These girls disrupts what Lyn Mikel Brown calls the "good girl code" as they play with and stretch the boundaries of being bad girls in these moments: they hang out of the window of their cars, screaming and yelling as boys pass, getting one over, having a laugh.[25]

In these ways, the girls resist the ways boys monopolize this space and the ways boys define them in this space as objects and not subjects in their own right. For these girls, it seems that they can be both: objects of attention and visible subjects. They also seem to resist the encroaching tides of conventional femininity that overwhelm them in their family and school lives, their romantic relationships with boys, and even in spaces such as this. They enjoy being able to disrupt how they appear as if to say, "Things are not entirely as they seem because I am not entirely the girl you think I am."[26]

Girls struggle to lay claim to this cultural space and the possibilities it offers: fun, freedom visibility, and adventure, all things the boys at least appear to already have.[27] Girls carve a space for themselves, however small, in order to feel the freedom boys feel, to live a life that wasn't given to them. But part of doing so for many of these girls means accepting a set of terms set by boys and not by them. These girls find ways to ignore what many would consider to be intolerable, perhaps because not to do so, in the end, would mean to pass on the freedom that defines the basis of being young in American culture.

Of course, few young men and women are free in any true sense. Girls grow accustomed to the absence of freedom as they venture to social spaces like bars and clubs and public streets where cruising occurs, even as they attempt to claim it. Adopting various strategies to insulate themselves from the possibility that a line will be crossed, they stay in their cars and enjoy a set of private activities in a public space. They distance themselves from the girl whose identity is sexually precarious, while also attempting to walk around the boundaries that contain her.

Being and Living Chicana

Why would young women participate in a cultural scene where they appear to lose as much as they gain? For Carla, cruising was first an activity she shared with her family. After church, her father, mother, and brothers would crowd into the family car to cruise the strip in Salinas, a central California town, home to both migrant farm workers and settled working-class Chicanos.

> Well I would cruise with my older brother and like, everybody in my town knew that we were brother and sister, and a lot of people who didn't always thought that he was my boyfriend or whatever 'cause we would always cruise, and it was, I don't know, it was like a time to relax I'd listen to oldies and just cruise you know? It's just, you're just cruising and it's nice. Sometimes I would go with my dad and he doesn't have a lowrider, but if he would drive my brother's car he would like

remember when he was younger 'cause he owned an Impala when he was younger, and he said that was like his pride and joy, you know. So he understands kind of where we're coming from and like kind of grateful that he does know that because I know that a lot of parents are like, why are you wasting your gas cruising, you know, it's just a waste of money and my dad, he's kind of like, kick back about it and he likes it, he enjoys it, and sometimes he'll take my mom cruising, and it's cute to see them out there and know that they're not trying to pick up on guys and girls you know, it's cute. . . . I think my parents were more lenient with me cruising because they had another picture of what cruising was 'cause of when they would cruise, it was kind of like kick back and cruise, right, you drive, you take in the scenes, listen to music to show off your car, and they would do it as a couple, so, you know, my dad never had a problem with me cruising or cruising with my brother or whatever, and that's what I always thought cruising was, like you know.

And while Carla concedes that the scene has changed some since her parents cruised, she awaits the day when her daughter will cruise.

When my child, he, he or she wants to cruise, I will want them to cruise in that way, but I mean I don't know that cruising is still allowed, you can still see it at the car show and things like that and I mean that's the cruising I like 'cause it's to show off your car and see other people's cars, take in the scene, like, you know, that time on a Sunday afternoon and it's kick back, it's mellow and I would let my child cruise that type of cruise.

After all, Carla met her fiancé through cruising. She explains,

This guy came over and asked my friend for her number. So he got it, and he ended up calling the next day and him and a couple of friends came over and that's where I met my fiancé. He just started calling me every day after that and like, probably three months later we got together and we've been together since and now we're having a baby so.[28]

Cruising remains a popular community activity for Chicanos/as, as I discussed in chapter 1. The Mariachi festival, Cinco de Mayo, and Mexican Independence Day draw large crowds, mostly from the Latino communities of San Jose. Participation in the local car cruising culture fosters a sense of being, living, and staying "Chicana" for this group of young women. This group of young women is made up of first-generation college students living on or near campus, many within the sorority house. Their everyday lives are tied to school. As first-generation college students, their lives are less connected to their communities. Education promises a more secure future for them,[29] but education also distances them from the largely working-class ethnic communities from which they came.[30] In particular, they have gained distance from their brothers, male cousins, and the other men in their lives.

Perhaps this explains why these young women largely align themselves with the boys who cruise. And while these girls may be critical of some of these young men for their outrageous acts, any sustained critiques of injustice are usually directed toward police officers, who also play an important role in this space, as I discussed in chapter 1. Consider Maria's statement:

> If you're cruising, you know, cops are like just waiting for the moment to fuck you like they are ready to attack, you know, they are expecting the worst, it's just the fact that like they know it's young people . . . I think it has a lot to do with minorities. It's a minority culture to go cruising, it is mainly Latinos, it is mainly African Americans, that are out there. I think it's, um, Latinos, like a lot on the strip that are like me.

Maria's story is echoed by others. Teresa adds,

> Yeah, we were walking down Santa Clara and, um, this guy I guess he wanted to talk to us, I don't know, we were trying like, he just, he made a U-turn, and I guess the cop, like, was in back and like and then he parked in a red zone, and I don't remember he was like slowing down. . . .

As Teresa's voice trails off, Yesina literally finishes her sentence: "Yeah, and he was just like, pulled over, took out his license, and gave him a ticket. They've just treated the guys like dogs, Especially during cruising hours." Here the hint of anger that emerged earlier at the boys is rechanneled, directed at the police officers for what is defined as unreasonable and unjust attention toward "our guys." The loyalty these young women demonstrate toward the young men with whom they share this space emerges from the repeated racial profiling they have witnessed by the police officers. The racism they see targeting their fathers, their brothers, their cousins, and the men they hope to marry helps to explain their tolerance of the behaviors discussed earlier. Under other circumstances, these young women might define some of the acts and actions discussed here as unacceptable. But one can't help being concerned that the loyalty that ignites their anger against the treatment of "minority" men seems to censor the possibility of articulating their collective anger toward these young men. The social scientists Michelle Fine and Lois Weis identify the in-group solidarity among Latinas as a "tunnel of cultural loyalty" that ultimately prevents them from fully confronting the mistreatment of women by men within working-class Latino communities.

One also wonders about the other girls who cruise but have no ties to the Chicano community. As I discussed in chapter 1, Santa Clara Street is a changed scene tied less to the Chicano community than it was in earlier decades. Renewal of San Jose's downtown has drawn young men and women from various ethnic groups to Santa Clara Street to cruise. There is a clear sense that this scene's appeal has much to do with the parade of excess, the pleasure of transgressing boundaries of social life, the chance to play with identities in a setting where the possibilities to craft alternative selves seem endless. In those moments when the excitement intensifies, threatening to explode, and one feels the emotional rush of an experience that lies just beyond the moral boundaries of the everyday world of work and school, life must seem limitless.

Beyond Hoodrats: The Struggle for Self Determination in a Boy's World

Young women's relationships to the cruising scene is tenuous, having much to do with the troubling gendered divisions between public and private spaces feminists scholars documented long ago. As I think about this point, my thoughts drift to the spate of anticruising ordinances invoked in California in the 1960s, their emergence tied to a growing concern with female respectability, the rise of juvenile delinquency among females, and what was understood as the decline of the "adolescent girl."[31] That the image of the wayward adolescent girl helped catalyze campaigns to prohibit car cruising, a popular evening activity for many suburban teens in the 1950s and 1960s, both expressed and affirmed the prevailing sexual order rooted in conventional gender scripts that then and now limited young women in profound ways as they struggled to make claims to public space and to solidify their identities in public ways.

As girls gain visibility in this scene where cars rule, they both gain and lose power over self, body, and situation. Girls in this cultural scene move under the specter of a crude masculine power that is ritually expressed and enacted through the physical and symbolic forms that define this scene's very essence. Though it is unclear whether the girls see the world as I see it, what is clear is their own unwillingness to see this scene in one-dimensional terms. They stubbornly refuse any sort of easy explanation of what it means for them to participate in a set of activities where it often seems like they lose as much as they gain.

These girls travel to boys' worlds at some risk to themselves in the hope of being noticed in a crowd of other girls by those who really matter—young men. Yet, as much as girls' desire for recognition by boys continues to direct their action, these girls see themselves as independent and as wise to the ways of boys. They reject any suggestion that they are also victims of a culture that continues to denigrate femininity and girls as it excuses a range of bad behaviors by boys. They refuse to see themselves as victims of boys' antics. Instead these girls see themselves as part of a new generation of girls. They are aware of the fact that the new girl is in control of herself. She is empowered. This is because emancipation is conceptualized in popular thought today as something a girl can achieve through a transformation in self, if she is willing to undertake the project of self-change.[32] If a girl *feels* oppressed, then she has only herself to blame, because she is the one who must take charge of her emancipation. In this changing cultural context, it makes sense for girls to distance themselves from any sense of feeling victimized, which is central to the formation of a collective critique and the demand for social change.

These girls act out a new kind of girl, influenced by the popular rhetoric of a postfeminism that repudiates any organized social movement for gender justice and celebrates the power over others that individuals may gain, instead of the shared power that comes from collective action.[33] Their tales reveal meaningful contradictions that arise as they struggle to narrate their role in this space as self-determining in and against an obdurate reality that suggests otherwise. In many ways, their narrative attempts to present themselves as in control hides the indignities and injustices that they encounter in this space and beyond.

Their words depict a cultural scene made all the more complex by their participation in it. Their stories about their adventures cruising reflect their much larger struggles for visibility. Such struggles are central to this cruising scene's enduring significance and cultural importance and are also meaningful (as I explained in chapter 1) to our understanding of why boys, many of whom are low income and of color, return to Santa Clara Street every weekend of the summer. "Everybody's out there, everybody's trying to get their face seen, and they're trying to get holla'd at," as one of the young women explained. But girls' struggles for visibility and recognition here and elsewhere differ from boys' in several ways. Their struggles to gain visibility occur within a intricate web of cultural relations where femininity is at once idealized and devalued, where girls are objectified and dismissed more often than not, where gaining visibility centers on the body, and where recognition by boys is ultimately what matters most. In this sense, girls' struggle for visibility carries the contradictions of the larger culture in which these struggles occur. Ours is a culture that values the power of self-determination, yet denies it to girls.

As I think about this, I am reminded of another interview conducted with a young woman, also a regular weekend cruiser, whose boyfriend was seriously "into" cars, as was she by extension. She spoke at length about cars and clearly was very knowledgeable. I was impressed by her ability to engage in car talk and also by her obvious delight in her ability to do so with me during the interview. The source of her delight seemed to stem from the fact that she was able enjoy the power associated with the terrain of boys by engaging in a sort of talk that is largely dominated by male voices. The appeal of cars and spaces where cars rule, like Santa Clara Street, for young women seems to have much to do with the power boys express and the freedom they enjoy, which remain so very elusive for girls.

3

Race-ing Men
Boys, Risk, and the Politics of Race

On a warm Tuesday morning at Freedom High School, I find myself at "auto shop" class. The room is cavernous and full of the sort of clutter one would expect to find at an actual mechanic's garage: soiled rags blackened by oil and grease strewn throughout the room, a small mountain of safety glasses in one corner, a dust-covered windshield in another, rows of tires stacked like doughnuts, metal cabinets spilling over with an assortment of tools. I spend much of my morning moving between the groups of boys who are scattered throughout the room before making my way over to a small huddle of boys working on a Honda CRX, a beat-up car that officially belongs to the auto shop. Right now they are working on recharging the car's battery, since it won't start. Moments before, two of the boys, Justin and David, had pushed the CRX over beside a much newer Honda Civic parked in the car lot a few feet from the car bays. The Civic is painted a purplish-blue and is equipped with a sleek body kit and shiny chrome rims. Its frame rests much lower to the ground than any stock Honda, but just enough above the shiny rims to still be "street legal." I ask the group whose car it is and a tall South Asian boy whom I come to know as Shrini offers up, "Mine." Don, who is sitting in the driver's seat of the CRX, his hands firmly placed on the steering wheel, sticks his head out the car's window to ask if I like it, which causes the group to erupt into laughter. "You can buy it if you want," Shrini tells me with a more serious tone. I ask him why he's selling it. He explains he wants to get a Subaru STi, which is much faster. Tim, a classmate, has a Subaru, the very one Shrini hopes to get after he unloads this car. Nearly all agree Tim's is the fastest car in school. And they should know. These boys and a string of others are "racers," a tag they use to distinguish themselves from the "cruisers," "lowriders," "gang-bangers,"[1] and the endless variety of other "subcultural" groups of boys at their school.[2]

Shrini's car is an automatic, a point he reluctantly offers only after I ask. Though his car has undergone some changes to the body, there have been no performance upgrades. Right now, the car doesn't run fast enough, and since it is automatic, it is unlikely it ever will. A slow car confers little status to its owner among the street racers, especially if its exterior has been customized to look fast. Such a look eventually discredits racers, attaching to them what is arguably the worst sort of shame. Speed, driver skill, and a willingness to take risks behind the wheel are what matter most in the world of street and organized racing. A slow car, no matter its appearance, provides little opportunity to demonstrate any of these virtues.

This band of boys race imports: Honda Civics and Accords, Nissans and Acura Integras, all cars imported from Japan, where a vibrant and parallel racing scene has also emerged.[3] They are part of what has been called "the Import Car Scene," which originated in southern California in the early 1990s but has spread north to San Jose and San Francisco and east beyond California. The import scene in southern California and in San Jose is dominated by Asian and Asian American young men in their teens and twenties.[4]

These young men are all Asian, first- and second-generation Chinese, Indian, and Vietnamese mostly, with exceptions like Daniel, who is Méxican. And they are students at Freedom High School, one of a handful of "low-income schools" in San Jose that has an overrepresentation of immigrants and kids of color and is also underserved in terms of both academic resources and avenues of upward mobility. The kids make up a loosely organized group of small crews that know each other mostly by the cars they drive.

Most in this group at Freedom High School own used cars, almost all purchased for less than $5,000 and almost all having anywhere between 100,000 and 150,000 miles already logged before the new owners get behind the wheel. Justin, who drives an emerald green Acura, bought his car for a clean $3,500 almost four months ago and currently has 127,000 miles logged on the odometer. For most in the group, these low-priced cars serve as templates for a series of costly modifications that in the end can more than double the initial cost of the car. Body kits, lowered suspensions, engine upgrades, multimedia systems, and altered exhaust systems make up a multibillion-dollar industry of aftermarket car parts, an industry largely supported by these young men and others like them who on weekend nights gather in the early hours of the morning in abandoned industrial zones and business parks to see whose car will outdrive all the others.

How do they afford these expensive car modifications? For a small number of young men tied to the import car scene, parents finance these indulgences, but not for these boys. Long hours stocking shelves, slinging burgers, punching cash register keys, and mopping floors provide just enough disposable income for them to gain access to this dizzying world of pulleys and bbk's, h-pipes, adjustable struts, sway bars, intercooler kits, and injectors called alternately "moding" or "tuning." They spend hours surfing the Web in search of a deal, special struts for $100 each on eBay, for example, and are proud of their ability to know a good deal when they see one. Few in the group drive new cars because they can not afford them, but others in the import car scene do. The middle- and upper-middle-class Asian American young men from Orange County, California in Victoria Namkung's 2004 study of Asian American youth culture and the import car scene all appeared to drive new cars, spending upwards of $25,000 when including the initial cost of the car and the upgrades. Many of the young men in Namkung's study came from far more affluent families than the boys at Freedom High School and were already in college, with a lot more of their own disposable income than these high schoolers. Within the broader import scene in San Jose, this is also the case.

For this group of high school boys, life revolves around their cars and racing. Economic constraint keeps them from funneling the same kind of cash into their cars that upper-income and older kids do, but it doesn't prevent them from putting whatever money they do have into "tuning" their cars. Thuy Vo, who drives a customized Honda Civic hatchback, works at Great America, a local theme park where many youth work the rides in exchange for baseline wages.[5] *All* his money, he tells me, goes to transforming his car's engine and exterior. So far he has installed a sway bar, which enables him to better handle turns at high speeds, and a new exhaust. He has shaved his door handles and removed the windshield wipers. In their place he has sprayed "Rain Off" on the windshield, a commercial product which is supposed to repel the rain. The car has been lowered several inches, the "H" that normally resides on the car's hood has been removed, and the back lights have been replaced. These exterior changes enable Thuy Vo to achieve what he considers "a cleaner look." I heard many of these import racers describe a "clean look" as a car's ideal. In many ways, this clean look achieves "an aesthetic of speed." With its sleek streamlining, its center of gravity hugging the road, the car visually appears to look fast and not "frumpy" and "rumpled" like the standard stock Civic hatchback or, worse, a lumbering American giant like a Dodge or Chevy. Beyond these changes, his car has been painted "egg-shell white," a custom color, and he has installed red car seats, new "racing" seat belts, a new steering wheel, a red racing stripe, and red and gold rims, which he painted himself to resemble from a distance a very expensive set of rims he admits he can not afford. Thuy Vo, like a number of these boys, uses auto shop to make as many of these modifications to his car as is possible given the limited resources of the school (sometimes at the expense of completing the official class projects assigned by Mr. O'Malley, the auto shop teacher). On the weekends, Thuy Vo, along with the others in his crew, travels to meeting spots to race against other imports. During the week, he spends his time outside work and school driving around malls, local streets in the neighborhood and sometimes Santa Clara Street in the hope that his car will be recognized, especially now that he has all but finished customizing it.[6] Thuy Vo's car, which was always parked just outside the car bays despite a school policy that restricts students from parking in that specific school lot, was the subject of much discussion among the students, racers and nonracers alike, in the three other classes I observed. On one occasion, two boys came by to take digital pictures of the car. When I asked Don, one of the students, about the picture taking, he explained, "See, we see cars as artistic, like artwork. . . . Taking pictures is a way to show appreciation for the car and the work that has gone into it." On another occasion, I overheard one of the boys from a class remark to another, "Daammmn, I see that car everywhere." Thuy Vo has gained what he had hoped to achieve, a much-sought-after visibility for his individual style and a collectively recognized one through his car.

Imports versus American Muscle

Thuy Vo, Don, Shrini, Vicrum, and Justin, along with other boys who participate in the import car scene, distinguish themselves from another groups of racers, those who have declared a devout allegiance to American Muscle, Ford and Chevy drivers who at Freedom High School represent at best a handful of boys. (Among the four auto shop classes I observed only one boy, Jeff, identified himself with American Muscle. He drove a 1966 Chevelle that he was restoring with his father).[7] Since the 1950s, American Muscle has stood at the center of the "illegal" street and "legal" organized car racing and hot-rodding scenes. However, in the past decade, the flourishing import scene has given hot rodders a run for their money. Writing on the cultural relevance of the import car scene in southern California, Victoria Namkung has argued that "the growing import racing scene has unquestionably changed the automotive industry and altered the dynamics of the vibrant car culture. . . . Import racing has propelled a historically invisible ethnic group onto center stage of the previously Anglo-dominated consumer market and culture."[8] Many would agree that the ascendance of import racing and import racers in the commercial world and the world of car enthusiasts has subverted the longstanding rivalry between Chevy and Ford, replacing it with a new one—a rivalry between domestics and imports. Two different value systems organize the domestic and import scenes. Within the world of American Muscle, having a car that is either "fast," "loud," or "big," a car with "hog power," that is, translates into what the late French scholar Pierre Bourdieu, writing on the social practices that produce social distinctions and symbolic boundaries, called "symbolic capital."[9]

A car's muscle is not celebrated among participants in the import scene, where far less emphasis is placed on horsepower or having a large engine. Quick, lightweight cars reign over the import scene. Acuras and Hondas are regarded as superior to Mustangs, the reigning modern American muscle car. They are low cost and lightweight, and their more powerful Honda engines (like the Prelude's) can be dropped easily into the car. The more powerful engine in a lightweight car can make the car very fast, particularly if it also has a nitrous oxide boost (usually called NOS by insiders to this world). The boys from Freedom High School swear to me that such a Honda could outrun a 4.6- or 5.0-liter Mustang in a second. This claim, of course, is met by howling protestations by those who align themselves with American Muscle, like Kenny and Tom, who both currently drive modified Mustangs and are part of the same crew. When I ask if they ever race against the imports, they are sure to let me know theirs is the superior car, working hard to convince me that it could barely be considered a "fair" race. "It's not worth it," Tom says with a firm shake of his head. "If you call it racing," Kenny, smirking, adds. "Their car's really slow; my car's really fast."

By all accounts, the car racing scene, made up of these so-called street racers, is "big" in San Jose. This despite increasing efforts by Bay Area police to dampen these underground activities. In June 2001, fifty officers from a South Bay task force discovered 247 cars at one of the business parks during a bust of an illegal street race, which led to nineteen cars being seized and fourteen arrests, according to the *San Francisco Chronicle*.[10] San Jose is not distinct in this regard. Street racing is popular in a lot of places where the boundaries between urban and suburban life are blurry, where cars can traverse long stretches of empty (and not-so-empty) road. Imports and American muscle serve as the two pivotal points around which this scene, fluid in its form, membership, rituals and rules, codes and conduct coalesces. These two groups regularly gather in the same meeting places, but import racers and domestics race primarily against cars of the same kind; every once in a while, they go head to head. The groups are largely ethnically split. "You got your Asian rice rockets. Honda Civics that are souped up, got their Na's, their flo masters and stuff. So, you have that and Latinos, Mexicans, with their old-school muscle cars," JP, an Anglo kid and self-described racer who drives a Chevy, explains. Melissa, who as a young woman resides at the periphery of these overlapping scenes, echoes JP's remarks: "Trust me, if you go out there and look, you'll see a complete difference between a Vietnamese car and a white person's car. I feel like I'm being racist, but I'm not. . . . Asian cars, they'll always do a body kit. And that's why they call them Rice Rockets. Because their cars sound a lot different than . . . they do something different with their mufflers and their intakes." These groups have become increasingly antagonistic as loyalists to American Muscle have attempted to reassert their dominance over the car-racing scene.

Formally and informally, the racing scene operates as a space of competition and antagonism, where racers regularly challenge other racers. Respect and recognition are extended to those who can "step up" and "hold their own" against those already recognized as the most skilled drivers with the fastest cars. Impromptu street racing is also common among those whose cars can compete, and a shared code of communication, the revving of an engine at a stop light or a quick nod to the rival driver, signals a willingness to race. Suffice it say, not to engage is to lose face. "You'll be at a stop light and guys pull up and you know they antagonize, you race. If a guy comes up and challenges you, then you race him," explains Trevor, who also drives a modified Mustang.

"Even if I don't race him, you have to respond in some type of way. If you're not going to race, then you bark at him and how you bark at him is by revving your engine, just to let him know, you know, I'm not scared but at a different time."

Street racing and car customizing are activities shared among men—a set of social practices and relations from which young men work to construct and articulate coherent narratives that solidify a sense of being men. It is this heightened sense of competition that fortifies the enduring link between cars and masculinity. Perhaps this helps to explain why high-level risk-taking assumes such significance for these young men; the level of risk one is willing to take becomes the means to set oneself apart from other men.

Risky Business: Boys Who Race

AB: Um, what's the fastest you've ever driven?

Kenny: One hundred forty-two miles an hour.

AB: Really, on a highway?

Kenny: Uh-huh, on the freeway.

AB: Um, what, was it, like late at night, or?

Kenny: Yeah, it was coming home from those races you were talking about.

AB: Oh, my gosh. Did you have people in the car?

Kenny: Four people.

AB: Were you scared?

Kenny: Yeah.

AB: Well, describe what it's like. I mean, I've never driven that fast.

Kenny: It's a rush, it's like crazy, like.

AB: Well, how do you feel?

Kenny: Calm, I feel really calm when I do it, like I don't know, it just feels like you're flying or something. Yeah, it feels like you're floating across the road.

Daring, danger, and peril reside at the center of this competitive world of racing.[11] These boys travel to forbidden territories, abandoned industrial zones, in search of a profound "experience" that will enable them to transcend the shackles of time and place, to step outside the self as they step into the flow, to engage risk and defeat it. They race to *feel* the intense sensation, difficult to describe in words, that provides the means to anchor themselves within a physical world where one's existence is known because it is felt.[12] Their desire to do so at times almost overwhelms them. These boys talk incessantly about the rush they gain from racing, of being in the flow, the "high" they get from being at the edge, almost losing control and somehow finding their way back. "It is all about the rush," I hear over and over from this group of boys and others who race. The source of the rush? Testing themselves against themselves and against others, since displays of danger and daring are the principal means to gain respect and recognition. Perhaps that is why, when not racing, they spend hours with others in their crew reliving stories of near-peril, sharing what the adolescent psychologist Cynthia Lightfoot regards as "risk narratives."[13] These narratives make up these boys' "storyworlds," where their reality is constructed as much as it is expressed, through which they gain recognition and visibility. The auto shop is a particularly strategic space in this regard, since it provides opportunity to talk about cars, risk, danger, and peril of all sorts, and talk they do. The boys spend much of their time rehashing details of past races, whose car outdrove whose. Talk about speed, how fast they drive, and the fastest they have ever driven is regularly interjected into conversation as they debate what counts as "sick" driving, celebrating those who are willing to do "crazy shit." Their stories serve to signify a life lived at the edge. I hear countless stories of driving that seem to provide opportunity for these young men to flaunt, above all else, their own driving skill, since they did, after all, live to tell the tale. "I used to race people on the freeway 'cause this car it always attracts people that want to race me so I always end up racing," Olie, a young man, explains. "Sundays are really good days for when guys are out like older, like little thirty-years-olds in their Corvettes or whatever who want to race. I'm down, I'm okay. 'Cause I'm really good at maneuvering through traffic, and I make really crazy moves and stuff." On another morning, boys trickle into class, settling into their seats as they talk about the events of the past weekend. I overhear two of the boys rehash the race that occurred between two other boys in the class. This is interrupted by John, another student, also a racer, who begins to recount to Mr. O'Malley his race at Sacramento raceway over the weekend with a friend. He flips through an auto parts magazines, describing how the rear axle and the drive shaft broke on his friend's Camaro SS as a large number of the students now listen in. I am suddenly reminded of Daniel telling me last week how he had blown up the engine of his Civic in a race the weekend before. Beyond this, I hear countless stories of driving on bald tires, stripped struts, and ever-thinning break pads that seemed to be a way to affirm their participation in a world of risk.[14]

I hear several stories of tickets, like the story George, who drives a Jetta, told me one morning during class, as the two of us watched Rich sand down one of the side panels on his white pickup truck. Last month, George was racing down the road neck and neck with Rich. As the two lanes of the road merged into one, George pulled ahead of Rich. Neither noticed the cop car parked in the side street. The race resulted in a $400 fine for George, since his car was in the lead; Rich barely escaped. Speeding tickets, especially tickets issued for "exhibition speed" and "reckless driving," which carry hefty fines, are badges of courage and bravery, since such violations provide evidence of a life lived on the edge. I talk to David as he measures the tire pressure of one the cars as several hover around passing the time. "I have a Civic at home," he tells me, but he is not allowed to drive it since he has a suspended license, he says as he chuckles to himself. When I ask why, he responds, "Reckless driving." He and another guy were "just fooling around" in a parking lot. He says earnestly, "We weren't even racing," but the cops stopped them and checked their car "because they think we do drugs." This resulted in a $1,500 ticket and a suspended license, which won't be returned until some ten months hence. Strangely, he seems only slightly upset by this turn of events. Perhaps it is because he has simply resigned himself to the fact. Or perhaps it is because this has become a good story to tell, a story that secures his rightful place as a man among men.

Cops are important to the storyworlds these boys construct, since their presence helps to define racing as a risk activity that involves more than just the obvious physical risks taken for driving at breakneck speeds. Cops serve as reminders of the boys' willingness to put their life at risk in other ways. These young men risk arrest, tickets, fines, possible jail time, and the disruption of their futures. In short, they are willing to risk it all. I can't help wondering if taking such significant risks is a way to remain in control of their lives. This is a group whose lives are largely defined by a set of circumstances that are beyond their control. As low-income kids with few secure or promising avenues available to them, their futures beyond high school remain largely uncertain.[15] These risk narratives, which construct their reality as much as express it, seem to be a way to manage, if not control, the uncertainty of their future. Within their storyworlds, what lies ahead rests squarely within their own hands. They are the narrators of their own lives, and if they mess up they have only themselves to hold responsible. This is after all the model of the autonomous, self-determining individual to which many Americans aspire and upon which masculine status rests.

The Need for Speed: Masculinity and Performance Vehicles

Cars have long served as objects for men to position themselves in terms of masculinity, enabling an elaborated performance of the masculine. But the relationship these young men forge between cars and being masculine is far from uncomplicated; rather, it is fraught with messy contradictions and struggle. To understand the nature of this struggle, which is the subject of the rest of this chapter, requires an understanding of the world in which boys are becoming men. The sociologist Michael Kimmel, among other scholars, has argued that modern masculinity is in crisis, its foundation rapidly crumbling as the traditional anchors of manhood recede in importance or become all but impossible to obtain.[16] Financial independence is increasingly an empty pursuit, since most young men will be unable to provide for themselves, let alone for others, if they are to continue to reside in communities like San Jose. Outside the realm of sports, physical competence, a traditional marker of masculinity, carries little occupational prestige in a world organized around the exchange of information, not displays of muscle.[17] In an increasingly posttraditional world, where social roles (e.g., being the breadwinner) are less likely to serve as guides for action and identity formation, young men inevitably will face an existential crisis.[18] Their participation in the world of cars and car racing provides a space to manage the existential dilemmas of masculinity, where these young men work to construct and sometimes repair a set of boundaries through which masculine power is reasserted.

These boys invest in fast cars and this fast scene as they traverse a changing world in search of recognition, visibility, and respect when the traditional ways to gain respect as men is unavailable. They also confront other problems because their struggle to become men occurs in a context where masculinity is increasingly transparent as a social construct. (Consider, for example, the ways masculinity is increasingly parodied and satirized in the popular media.) In a so-called postmodern world of hyperreality, where there is no original, no "real," behind the imitation but only other imitations, as Baudrillard has argued, the struggle to gain recognition as masculine requires a far more nuanced and subtle performance to be believable.[19] Against a masculinity that reveals itself to others as a fake, as a performance, these boys struggle to be "authentically men."

Perhaps this explains why boys are increasingly called upon to monitor their own masculinity, to demonstrate a self-awareness that the performance of the masculine self is after all a performance. "I think, um, there's always some internalized pressures to drive a certain way in terms of my gender. There seems to be some expectation to drive fast and live and do everything fast," Richard, one particularly insightful twenty-year-old, remarked. "Like every time I see my little rearview mirror and I see people trailing behind me and I think oh maybe I should go faster . . . I feel those pressures."

These young men must be convincing as men not only for an ever-increasing group of skeptics and ironists but also to themselves.[20] Identity formation today occurs in a context where "the self is seen as a reflexive project for which the individual is responsible."[21] In a media-saturated culture where images and parodies of men are profuse, men are increasingly expected to be reflective about their manhood. Hypermasculine men are ones who are "unreflective about manhood." They are seen as not self-actualized and thus not in control of themselves.[22]

The shifting ground on which these "reflective masculinities" are mapped has consequences for understanding the struggle for masculinity of these young men who participate in the car-racing scene. Racers walk a thin line because the car-racing scene is often regarded as a hypermasculine space to outsiders (this given its ties to white working-class masculine culture).[23] This point is clearly illustrated in the following conversation with two young men who stand outside the car-racing scene. Here they link cars and "macho" as they attempt to present themselves as authentically masculine against macho men, men who are largely regarded as imposters.

> *Robert*: I think it's kind of a macho thing to like, I don't know, I've heard people like, I can drive when I'm drunk and like, oh you can't do it? So it's just . . .
>
> *AB*: What do you think about that, the whole macho thing?

Robert: Stupid.

Mitch: I don't know, I'm not a macho person, so I'm not going to try and play it off.

AB: So what defines like a macho person?

Mitch: Someone with flows and big subwoofers in the cars and—

Robert: Yeah.

AB: Well, I was going to ask actually because you had said earlier that you were not the type to do all that stuff to your car and um, and . . .

Robert: A sound system might be different because I really like music, but I'm not going to, like, put a lift on my car, get big twenty-inch wheels or whatever. What some people do to their car, like what they put into it, is so amazing.

Mitch: That's what the parking lot's [at school] like. It's like a battle between who has the loudest bass on their car or . . .

AB: Really?

Mitch: Yeah.

Robert: Or, who . . .

Mitch: The loudest engine.

AB: What do you think about that?

Robert: I think it's silly, yeah. I like to watch people, like while you're spinning out your tires, so you'll have to be like, you know, spending three hundred dollars on new tires like, you know, five months earlier than I am.

Young men today parody others and themselves for performances of masculinity that are too obviously fakes. This is perhaps especially apparent around cars because they have long been associated with masculinity and also provide ground for competition. A number of these boys sought to expose the ways some men use their cars as a status means to "get" women, lest they be accused of doing precisely that themselves. Trying to explain why he has such disdain for car cruising, Aldo offers, "I don't know, like, guys being dogged, you know trying to say, 'What's up baby?' you know, 'What's your number?'" Scott explains why he was not into "one of those big macho cars." "Why bother? I have nothing to show off." This young man saw having a "big macho car" as a feeble attempt "to get into somebody's pants." For Olie, talk about cars becomes a space to parody himself, perhaps before someone else does. "I was just pulling into the movie theater like I thought I was really cool 'cause I was with a girl and stuff. Yeah, you know what I'm saying and I didn't see one of those cement blocks and I was like, oh shit."[24]

Many young men today, whether racers or not, distance themselves from "macho"—the hypermasculine "straw man" as they solidify their own identities as authentic men. But their reflections and parodies fall short of actually subverting the privilege accorded to them by the mere fact that they are men. To the contrary, this kind of talk is central to reaffirming the power of masculinity that ultimately establishes, regulates, and sometimes rewards these young men.

Trevor, an African American young man who did not get his license until he was twenty-one, reveals, "I was ashamed of it [not having a license]. Ah man, you know, my girl drives me around. My friends kind of let me hear about it a lot. It's something you have to swallow and get on with life." Trevor now has a black Ford Mustang GT, a car with considerable power, especially following various engine modifications. Explaining why he chose to modify the engine, he remarked with a surprising frankness, "It makes it louder, meaner and tougher. . . . Like I said, some guys they pull up and they want to show off and they rev their cars, you know, and if you can't, you know, you feel embarrassed, stupid, so you got to get that." This sense of struggle to achieve masculinity by debasing and discrediting other men is well illustrated in the following example drawn from one of the countless electronic bulletin boards organized around street racing. The following posts represent an ongoing conversation, occurring over several days, about the meaning of a "real" racer.[25]

Malachi #1:

I've been in the game since '94. Not that duration is important, but for the last 9 years I've eaten, slept, dreamed and worked for going faster. My driving is always being examined, and my mechanical skills are always improving. The name racer always sounded stupid to me, but it's what I am. Who here is a real racer? Post up and tell me why. *Do not post if your just gonna list the parts you bought, and why your euro style tailights were a performance upgrade.*[26]

Green Goblin #2 is the first to respond, offering the following:

A racer is a one who races. I drive a Ford Explorer, but I've raced other SUVs. I know it isn't the fastest vehicle on the road, and I don't act like it is, but it IS at least faster than a lot of other SUVs. I don't go around places saying "I am a racer" but I have raced others in the past and I still do, so therefore, I am a racer.

This is followed by a series of messages. The conversation rapidly becomes hostile, with repeated attempts by these men to distance themselves from and to debase other young men as they talk about their own relationship to cars.[27] They position themselves against a particular group of racers who are recognized as "all show and no go," the aforementioned "ricers."

Abcd123 #3:

> I see what you're getting at. I have a few friends like that. Some keep at it for more power, some keep at it, but for more speed. I don't consider myself a real racer. Maybe back in the day, I would drag anything that moved. Cars weren't as powerful, and the police was not an issue. There was more emphasis on being able to cut through traffic than actual horsepower, since mods were unheard off.

SL porn series #4:

> I've been racing since 94 also back in high school. I guess I caught the bug from when pops was a kid. He raced anything from lola's old chevy station wagon, his triple deuce, GTO, Sting ray, Vet, his Suburban. We always BS about comparing apples vs oranges as no replacement to displacement. etc. . . . He's a strong vette follower and a supervisor mechanic for PG&E. He's a real racer from drag to autoX, to go carts, to road courses. He's pretty impressed with imports and he also likes driving my turbo hatch I do it for fun and not to be trendy. I've dragged charged buicks, Pop's C5, and a lot of Hondas. I respect anybody that races and works on their cars. I do it for sport. *Unlike most ricers these days who drive to be trendy and be "noticed". Peace!*

Sleeper #5:

> *Street . . . well that's just full of posers . . . it would be so easy for me to claim something that my car obviously does do . . . but it happens at the scene all the time (we usually call them ricers or idiots). I do push my car to the limits on the way back roads . . . if I have to drive 2 hours*

to find a remote spot, I will . . . with minimal risk to me, my car and more importantly others who wish not to be involved. I also, usually don't take anyone with me . . . the main reason is that most of the people in my town are all talk and I don't trust the abilities of other drivers. I do accept the risks and have no problem taking tickets if I'm doing something wrong . . . cops usually respect that too. I accept responsibility for my mistakes.

Lt. What? #6:

Fake racer. I pretend to drive my cars. They really drive themselves, they're the real racer.

Another thing, you ignorant prick, if you're going to talk shit in your sig, you might want to spell check. I'm sure you'll respond saying I don't know anything about the english language, much the same as engines, and 'your are' is proper english.

Lastly, did you really need to include a setup for your little rib at Nick? I'm sure only one with your intellect could put together that the comment in YOUR sig was FROM you. Thank you for labeling it for us mere mortals. *Eat a dick, bitch.*

333racer #7:

however i need to bring up another point, for all those people who proclaim they are "real" street racers. i find that term to be absolute BS. true you may be racing on the streets, but i noticed that all those who were from back in the day they don't admit to racing on the streets and many more are actually ashamed to say they do. i think that the term street racer has turned into a trendy little label to make people feel like they are important. real racers know the importance of keeping the racing secret.

Runner #8:

Let's not get into what is racing and what is not. I really don't like to drag now. I road race exclusively. I will drag once in a while though, I haven't for few years though.

I wrench, I don't really like to. But when it's my ass on the line, I gotta know my car will be there for me. I don't trust anyone. I've been screwed. No one will care like I do. I've only bought one aftermarket body panel in my life, a Spoon CF lip for my old EG. I drive a WRX now. It's ugly and fast as fock. Not done yet, it's being built as a well rounded car. Suspension/Brakes/Power-Driving skill. That's all that matters to me. No euro tails, no Z3 gills, no supra headlights, no lighted washer nozels and no 15 year old on my hood! But the WRX will have some nicer panels in the end.

I remember when the scene was pure. When all we wanted to do was go faster. I sold my civic because I was tired of being associated with scum. Too harsh? Stop doing ghetto shit to the car, get rid of the euro tail lights.

These young men draw on the language of purity and pollution, what the anthropologist Mary Douglas regards as central to the hierarchical distinctions groups invoke as they draw distinct moral boundaries between us and them. In the words of Runner #8, "I remember when the scene was pure."[28] These writers/racers define the boundaries clearly: "real" racers modify the performance of their cars, and "fakers" make modifications for aesthetic appeal.[29] In this sense, gender tropes are clearly in play as examples of display are linked to feminine activity. In their struggle to be recognized as real racers, these young men distance themselves from feminine practices of paying too much attention to the body (car body or otherwise), since the car body can be seen as a metaphor for the physical body. Spending too much time "primping" is decidedly unmasculine; recall from chapter 2 the time girls spent getting ready for their night out cruising. This can be seen primarily in the recurring challenge to needless and gratuitous display that emerges beginning in the first instance with Malachi: "*Do not post if your just gonna list the parts you bought, and why your euro style tailights were a performance upgrade.*" At several points, driving skill is privileged over aesthetic changes as they draw lines between those who are rightful insiders and those who are outsiders—those who are men and those who are not.

I also witnessed attempts to draw distinctions between real racers and fakers in the auto shop class. On one occasion, a group of import racers, Ping, Brad, and Vicrum, are at work on Ping's Civic hatchback. They are planning to attach a black lip to the bottom. Other kids hover around watching them as they work to figure how precisely they are to attach this lip. As I look on, I ask why they want to attach the lip to the car, and one of the guys, the only nonimport racer in the group, responds with noted sarcasm, "To make it *look* lower," as he chuckles to himself before walking off. A few moments later, another nonimport racer approaches, asking the group at work sarcastically, "Does it make it faster?" Interestingly, though these young men are questioned about the types of modifications they are doing, because they are doing the work themselves, they are not discredited as "half men." As SL porn series #4 remarked in his post, "I respect anybody that races and works on their cars."

In this competitive context, having knowledge about car parts and how cars work serves as a key cultural resource affirming one's status within the group, solidifying a hierarchy of respect, and serving as a basis of exclusivity.[30] Boys who pay someone else to customize or modify their cars accrue less status than those boys who are able to work on their cars themselves, because they are seen as imposters.[31] This explains why a car that is fast but has only limited visual appeal is often regarded as a "work in progress," which enables its owner to claim respect. A primed hood, for example, becomes a way to announce that this car is being worked on by oneself. As a useful point of comparison, consider my earlier comments about Shrini's car, which had significant visual appeal but no speed. Shrini was actively trying to sell this car, lest he be discredited as "all show and no go."[32] Having to pay someone to fix and modify one's car can also serve to discredit a racer. It is in this sense that knowledge of car parts and cars themselves communicates what Sarah Thornton has termed "subcultural capital," a type of capital that structures an alternative hierarchy by which people vie for status—a social good that can be bestowed only by others and not awarded by oneself.[33]

American Muscle and Talking Trash

The comments posted on the bulletin boards that defined racers who focus on exterior changes rather than performance upgrades as "ricers" is quite telling.[34] As SL porn series #4 remarked in his post, "most ricers these days who drive to be trendy and be noticed." Runner #8 comments, "I remember when the scene was pure. When all we wanted to do was go faster. I sold my Civic because I was tired of being associated with scum. Too harsh? Stop doing ghetto shit to the car, get rid of the euro tail lights." Sleep #5 writes, "Street . . . well that's just full of posers . . . it would be so easy for me to claim something that my car obviously does do . . . but it happens at the scene all the time (we usually call them ricers or idiots)." Within the world of car racing, the term *ricer* or *rice rocket* is used interchangeably with the term "import." Ricers and rice rockets are Hondas, Nissan, and Acuras. Fords and Chevys are never called rice rockets.

The condemnation of "ricers" was widespread on these message boards and elsewhere. The following rap, entitled "The Ricer Anthem," appeared on one of the message boards where import and domestic racers routinely post messages, debate the merits of different cars, and constitute the moral and cultural perimeters of the racing world.

The Ricer Anthem

Hi! My name is (who?) . . . my name is (what) . . . my name is (scratches)
. . . Rice Burner!
Hi Kids, do you like 5 inch tips?
Wanna see me stick chrome fender flares over each of my Konigs?
Wanna follow me and do exactly as I did?
Try NAWS and get your motor fucked up worse than my life is?
My brains' dead weight, I'm trying to get my head on straight
But I can't figure out which sticker to put on my license plate.
And the mechanic says "Rice burner you's a crack head "Nu-uh" "Then
    why's your car dead man its wasted"
Well since age 9 I've wanted an SI so I could put chrome 18s on it and
    make it run 16.9's.
Got pissed off and ripped all my Honda emblems off,
And replaced them with "R" badges so people know I'm not soft.
I smoke a big bowl of chronic, and lay in my lawn,
For longer then it took me to put my altezzas on.
"Come here bastard" "Dude, wait a minute that a viper dawg!!"
I don't give a fuck, I'll just fly by and put my hazards on!!!

After this anthem was posted on the message board, a number of writers posted replies, including jdanger, who wrote, "This rice burner anthem, it says exactly what needs to be said. Ricer burners want to look performance but can't perform. I would rather have performance than looks." Another wrote, "all show and no go, that's rice."

The distinction between an authentic racer, somebody who is focused on power, speed, and skill, and a "poser" is presented through racialized metaphors that align cars and aesthetics with particular ethnic or racial groups. This rivalry might be explained by the fact that these car scenes are ethnically organized. American Muscle continues to be dominated largely by Anglos, while the import scene is predominantly Asian. Recall also my earlier comments that American Muscle's hegemony in the racing world has been challenged in recent years as imports have posed a legitimate threat that must be taken seriously. American Muscle racers have managed this threat through attempts to discredit imports and import racers and by physically and discursively distancing themselves from this group. I repeatedly listened to young Anglo, Mexican, and African American men aligned with domestics denounce any association with the import car scene, the cars, rice rockets, and the drivers, known as "ricers." "Yeah, I'm not into the car scene where they all like rice rockets," seventeen-year-old Cesar explains. Jorge echoes Cesar: "Rice rockets the small, you know, Hondas, I don't like 'em. Honda Civics souped up, stereotypically Asian. . . . I have no respect for imports . . . they give them too much credit . . . for what they've done and if it wasn't for I guess the American cars you've got bigger muscle cars . . . they wouldn't be around. And they still have to give respect to those cars 'cause you know who you're messing with and who you're not messing with [laughing]." Even within the group of import racers, the distinction between ricer and racer was clearly drawn. Brad tells me, "To hot rodders and cruisers we're all ricers in the [import] racer community." But to Brad and his friends, there is a difference between an import racer and a ricer. In the words of the sociologist Erving Goffman, they "stratify their own," a common enough strategy among those who must routinely manage a stigmatized identity.[35] Brad and his friends distance themselves from those racers who make "excessive" exterior changes (pointing out some of the cars in the lot that are "ricers" or "border-on-ricers") as they struggle to maintain legitimacy within this world of risk and competition.

This condemning talk directed at import racers and the racial logic upon which it rests is also visible in a conversation that occurred during one of the focus group interviews at Weston High School. While this was a racially mixed group of kids, importantly, no Asian kids were present in this group. As was the case in other focus groups, the young men dominated the conversation. In this particular focus group, one of the boys, JP, an Anglo kid and the oldest in the group, initiated much of the dialogue.

> *JP*: I don't like imports.
> *AB*: You don't like imports, how come?
> *JP*: I just don't
> *AB*: So what do you like then, like what's kind of . . .
> *JP*: Oh no, I have, I respect them, I don't say anything about them at all, I just . . .
> *AB*: It's just not your style?
> *JP*: Like them, they don't like muscle cars, and then they actually do go and talk crap about muscle cars.
> *AB*: Who's they?
> *Adam*: I know.
> *JP*: Imports.
> *Adam*: Asian people.
> *JP*: If you think about it, you go buy a $20,000 car okay, it might have some advantages like air conditioning, CD player, and all that, but then you get a car for half the price, an American one, and it ends up out running all those cars, for half that price, and you put, you work that other half of the money into your car, and then you have a machine . . . it's crazy.
> *Adam*: What you call them is you call them imports and domestics, me and him both drive domestics, so that's Chevy, Ford, all those, those are domestics.
> *JP*: And then you got your imports, which is like Honda, your Integra.
> *Adam*: Your Acuras.
> *Tom*: Integra.
> *JP*: All that crap is imports and that's the ones you hear nnneeeennneeee goin' down the street, and stuff like . . . See, I just like domestic cars a lot better, and like lowriders, they're cool, but I hate, why are you going to do that to an American car? I hate that, because when you see all them lowriders doing all their hydraulics.

JP starts out talking about cars but ends up talking about the drivers, too. Ricers are no longer cars but people, Asians, as he attempts to denounce imports and import racers. Racial tropes are mobilized as JP defines the values of this cultural scene. Asians are constructed as the outsiders—the others against which he and other hot rodders solidify their identities as men. This is further illustrated by additional comments he makes in the course of the focus group. He draws specifically on the emergent stereotype of Asians as "bad drivers" as he again attempts to discredit not simply the import scene but an entire racial group.

> *JP*: I think Chinese shouldn't really drive because they don't even really know how to drive.
> *Cynthia*: Oh my God.
> *AB*: Who?
> *Adam*: Asian people.
> *JP*: No actually a lot of Asians.
> *AB*: So why do you think that?
> *JP*: [imitating a Chinese accent] Ohhhh, oh, you son of bitch, you wreck my car.
> [laughter from the group]
> *AB*: Well, what about American-born Asians?
> *JP*: Then they get out and they start yelling at you for parking your car.
> *AB*: What do other folks think? So, is this like all Asian folks, like Asian born folks or . . .
> *JP*: They can't see.
> [Laughter again from the group]
> *AB*: [referring to a comment by AS] Well, okay, well, he just said that your comment was racist.
> *Tom*: No, actually Asian people are very good at racing, like I know lots of guys . . .
> *AB*: [referring to DH] You just said it's because they are rich?
> *DH*: 'Cause they always have nice cars.
> *AB*: So are there any Asian kids that go to this school?
> *TH*: A lot.
> *AB*: So, well, what do you think about that? So what if there was an Asian person sitting here right now, would you be saying the same thing, or . . .
> *CJ*: Maybe.
> AM: I don't think so.
> *AB*: You don't think so.
> CC: I don't think so.
> *CJ*: But, I mean they can't drive, seriously, they can't drive, they drive piece of shit cars, sounds like a goddamn mouse running through

your house. It's like come on now, get a real car. I don't like the ones
that make so damn, so much noise, like the, the ones they call "rice
rockets."

The idea that Asians can't drive also emerged in auto shop class. On
one occasion, a group of us are gathered around Brad's red Civic hatchback. He is balancing what are horribly bald tires. The group of young
Asian men around the car is talking about another car on the lot whose
fender has a deep and sizable scratch, and Sean, one of the Asian boys,
remarks, as he explains the scrape, "He can't drive. He's Asian." Incred-
ulous, Daniel, the only Mexican boy who hangs around with the import
racers, responds, "Daaaammmnnn, and you're Asian." To this Sean
retorts, "Yeah, I can't drive, I can admit it," as the groups collapses in
laughter.

Interpreted one way, this comment reflects the psychosocial dynamics of racial dominance, revealing a pattern of internalized oppression,
what Paulo Friere has called "horizontal violence." After all, this statement is articulated by a young Asian man and is met with laughter by
other young Asian men and in this sense reflects what Goffman called
"identity ambivalence." But, interpreted another way, this comment
about Asian drivers in the context of this largely Asian, all-male group
is a way to manage the enduring stereotypes, what Patricia Hill Collins
refers to as "controlling images," used to discredit them as less than
men and thus to justify their subordination. These boys know that JP is
not alone in his condemnation of the import car scene or of Asians. By
preemptively making the charge, they can control the joke themselves.
In various ways, these young men are engaged in what Goffman regarded as interactional strategies to manage the stigma of race as they
attempt to preserve a sense of being men in a context of an intense competition over the symbolic resources that define masculinity.

This point is also illustrated in another instance. One early evening I
am driving across town to a restaurant for dinner, and I pull up behind
a Honda Civic at a stop light; it is an older model of the very car I have,
but, unlike mine, its suspension has been lowered, and while my muffler
is barely audible, its exhaust buzzes each time the driver, a young Asian
guy with short black hair shaped into small spikes, taps his foot on the
accelerator. As I sit waiting for the light to turn green, I inspect this car,
curious about its driver, who he is and where he's going. I notice that
just above the car's back bumper is written in white script "*Got Rice?*"

Within moments the light turns green, and the small vehicle idling in front of me is gone; its rear lights fade as the distance between us grows. I am left in its wake. I imagine a scenario where this car is racing against another on a highway or empty street; it pulls ahead, leaving its rival behind, with a derisive *Got Rice? Got Rice?,* all the more powerful as the last word, is loaded with intention and mocking, a means to invert and convert the pejorative meaning of *ricer.*[36] It is a call to war, an attempt to inflame the animosity that inspired the term in the first place and to subvert the hegemony of American Muscle.

The sociologist Paul Connolly argues that young men express deep racial animus in situations of tense competition, though they might not in other situations. Certainly car racing is a space of hypercompetition, since the activity is not only organized around winners and losers but emerges as a terrain of claims to dominance and superiority. Imports and domestics are locked in a battle over not simply whose cars are faster but also what constitutes the basis of legitimate masculinity for these young men coming of age in a posttraditional society. Because many import drivers are Asian, this struggle over dominance is largely directed toward Asian men and reflects the historical legacy of anti-Asian, nativist rhetoric.

Racial constructions are routinely used to work out deep anxieties about masculinity, to define who is authentically masculine and who is not. The sociologist R. W. Connell's understanding of race and what he calls "hegemonic masculinity," defined in part by invisible whiteness and reliance on the hypermasculinization of black men and the hyper-feminization of Asian men, is useful for making sense of these exchanges among young men who participate in the car-racing scene.[37] Asian import racers as a group, who have historically been feminized, get discredited in this car world as others actively (re)feminize them. The sociologist Yen Le Espirtu has argued, "Asian American men have been excluded from white-based cultural notions of the masculine," noting that Asian American men are regularly depicted in the media as "impotent eunuchs" and emasculated "model minorities."[38]

The feminization of Asian men is achieved in two specific ways. First, by arguing Asians can't drive, detractors position Asian men outside a masculine world of skill, risk, and competence. Similar arguments made about women drivers also once served as justification to keep women off the road.[39] Second, the cars of Asian import drivers are feminized as "rice rockets," cars with gratuitous display. Consider the comments of jdanger: "I hope you guys see where I am coming from. These little jap cars are nothing but the nastiest, dumbest girl in school with plastic surgery."

One might also consider the possibility that attempts to discredit import racers as ricers through a critique of gratuitous display is also part of an intense backlash against Asians and Asian immigrants in post-1965 America. Changes in immigrant policy in the mid-1960s led to an influx of immigrant groups in the 1980s and 1990s, a time of eroding economic opportunity as hundreds of thousands of manufacturing jobs were lost in the United States. A number of scholars and activists have identified a heightened anti-Asian, anti-immigrant sentiment in California and nationally in the context of economic uncertainty.[40] The charge of gratuitous display against "ricers" appears to be tied to nativist critiques of conspicuous consumption directed at Asians and Asian Americans that grows from the perception that they are claiming too large of a piece of the proverbial pie, thereby displacing other groups competing for employment and housing opportunities.[41] A deep racial animus against upwardly mobile Asians is present in JP's focus group where all Asians are defined as "being rich." Indeed, this has served as the very basis of the model-minority myth that continues to target Asians as interlopers.[42]

A larger narrative is at work here that reflects deepening inequalities and conflict in an increasingly global world marked by ever-growing economic and social polarization. The rise of distinct ethnically based car scenes and the emerging rivalry between domestics and (Asian) imports are consequences of a changing, competitive global world order where the perception that "Americans" must continually reassert their supremacy in the face of unwarranted attacks by outsiders and foreigners is intense and pervasive. Consider these comments, posted on another message board by jdanger:

You guys that LOVE imports can say all you want about how they're cool and stuff, but they still will be little jap cars. You can say NOS this and turbo that, but nothing is gonna beat American Muscle. I know maybe some American companies are manufacturing in other countries but they still make better cars than Honda, acura and all the other jap brands. I do want to ask you one question . . . why fix up little crappy 4 bangers, when you can fix up a muscle car and get at least twice the power?

Posted comments of this kind often become the source of disagreement but seem to reflect longstanding anti-Asian ideas that led to a century of reactionary policies, panics, and sentiments against Asians and Asian countries, from the Immigration Exclusion Acts of the 1800s and 1900s, directed at Chinese immigrants and others, to the Japanese internment camps during World War II, to the "Buy American" movements that emerged in the 1970s and 1980s as U.S. multinationals halted production in the United States and relocated to other countries with cheaper labor and fewer environmental restrictions while U.S. laborers (many of whom were white union men) lost their jobs. Even some of the racers, though failing to see the broader historical context that has given rise to the anti-Asian sentiments that lurk beneath the anti-import rhetoric, recognize the narrow Americanism that is operating. Consider the following post, written by "Nissan Fan":

> If you were a true car fan you would see past all the "American Pride in Our Cars" shit who the fuck cares what country it came from look at the car not at the country . . . just because you hopped on the bandwagon of biased Yankee car lovers does not mean that Japanese cars suck . . . P.S. jdanger what your saying is very stereotypical.

LancasterWannaBE wrote, "I don't understand why there's always so much fuss about tuning Japanese cars. Last time I looked there were also many Jettas on the road—and guess what, they're imports too. I never hear anyone complaining about someone else tuning an Audi." The sociologist Lillian Rubin (2004) has argued that anti-immigrant sentiments are often articulated by white working-class men because they are the ones who have lost the most and who are increasingly vulnerable in a postindustrial America.[43]

Brave Men in a Brave New World: Global Masculinities

At the center of this competitive and antagonist world, where what you know serves to define where you are and where the level of risk you're willing to take is the measure of a man, is an ongoing and often heated rivalry between domestics and imports: Hondas against Mustangs, "Ricers" against "American Muscle." A quick car versus a powerful one. Asian versus Anglo. Who are the better drivers? Who has the fastest cars? Who can beat whom? Young men who participate in this world spend hours debating these points as clear and distinct lines are firmly etched. I have argued that this struggle, because it is organized to position Anglos and Asian at odds, is racialized. By this I mean that racist ideologies that have long suppressed and oppressed Asian men are used as a way to reaffirm white masculinities.

Phrases like *rice rockets, ricers,* and *riced out* operate as code words, allowing kids to talk about race, to participate in racial discourses, to express a deep racial animus, and to uphold a veiled racism that is taken as something else. All the kids I interviewed were familiar with these phrases and could use them easily. What stands behind these racial repertoires are young men's struggle for masculinity in a context where the traditional measures of being a man are increasingly out of their reach. For young men of color perhaps this has always been so. But for young white men who align themselves with American Muscle, many of whom are working class and have experienced a loss of status as they confront eroding job opportunities and as those jobs that remain open to them in the service economy are defined as women's work, they struggle to reassert their dominance in other ways. In this instance, it is through the symbolic work of distinction. As Sarah Thornton has argued in her writing about the social logic of subcultural capital, "Distinctions are never just assertions of equal distance; they usually entail some claim to authority and presume the inferiority of others."[44] Masculine identity construction for these young men occurs within a play of global and racial forces. Cars reveal some of the complexities that surround the process of becoming men and the role of symbolic boundaries.

An interesting parallel can be drawn between the work young men do on their cars and the work young women do on their bodies as both prepare to participate in spaces where the car rules. Boys work on their cars as a way to work on their masculinity, just as girls work on their bodies as a way to work on their femininity. Both converge in these car spaces, where boys' cars are presented for display much in the same way as girls' bodies are, that is, for boys to see. One might conclude that in these spaces, boys rule as much as cars do. Yet, one also wonders whether girls realize the time and energy boys direct towards fashioning their cars. Certainly, there are times when it exceeds the work young women do in fashioning their bodies.

In these spaces where boys and girls cruise "together but apart"[45] and where boys race against themselves and each other, young people search for recognition and visibility, for connection and belonging. They travel into these spaces where cars rule, where pleasure, desire, power, and struggle converge, to experience an intensity of emotion as they construct, play with, puzzle over, and defend who they are.

PART II

Fast Times

4

Car Privileges
Family Rules and Permission to Drive

Jorge, a bright seventeen-year-old Latino, is a senior at Bernards, a prestigious private boys' school in San Jose.[1] Jorge is a lot like the other young men who attend Bernards: his priorities are academic, he is actively involved in a host of extracurricular activities intended to bolster his college applications, and he feels assured that his dreams of a bright future will be realized. On every day of his first two years of high school, after finishing football practice or one of the many other school-based extracurricular activities he pursues, Jorge boarded two buses for the two-hour ride that would bring him across town to the East Side, where he lives with his mother and father. To outsiders, the East Side of San Jose is viewed as a hotbed of gang activity. But the East Side is also home to among the largest Vietnamese and Latino communities in the county. And while it has more than its share of rundown houses, overcrowded apartments, and families living on the edge, the East Side is also home to many middle-class families. Jorge comes from one such family. To guarantee they stay that way, his mother and father travel forty-plus miles each morning to their jobs. From their combined income, his parents pay a mortgage on a modest home, his mother drives an Infiniti, a mid-priced luxury sedan, and for their only child they are able to finance the cost of a private school education. Last Christmas, they surprised Jorge with a 1998 Ford Explorer. The impetus: "They don't have time to drive me, so they got me my own car," Jorge explains. Like most kids at this prestigious all-boys school, Jorge doesn't work. "School is my job," he offers, though he adds, "I want to get a job and try to lift that burden off my parents." But Jorge is simply too busy with extracurricular activities to find the time. For now, he is just happy he no longer has to ride the two buses each afternoon to get home.

When asked if he has ever lost his car privileges, he answers in a matter-of-fact tone, "It's not worth taking away the keys. I do a lot of stuff.

They feel bad taking away my extracurriculars." He adds a few moments later, "My curriculars are more than just hanging out with friends. I do a lot of stuff at school." Besides, to take Jorge's car privileges would impose greater time demands on his parents, on top of those already placed on them by their busy work schedules.

By just about anybody's standards, Jorge is a good kid: earning high marks in school, getting along with fellow classmates, being involved in school athletics and several academic clubs.[2] For many middle-class parents like Jorge's, it is a matter of good practical sense to get their child a car once he or she can legally drive. Driving even one child, much less more than one, to and from the seemingly endless stream of organized activities, in addition to managing two busy professional schedules of their own, is almost impossible.[3] This is the "time bind" Arlie Hochschild so cogently described in her book by the same name. For middle- and upper-middle-class children struggling to gain an edge in what can only be described as the increasingly competitive marketplace of high-stakes education, all of this is a matter of course.[4] As Latinos, Jorge's parents also struggle to carve out a better life for themselves and their son against the legacy of racism that has consequences for where they live and where they work and to realize that elusive American dream that brought their family to California in the first place. A lot is riding on Jorge's success in school that is not simply about his future but also about the future of his family and the Latino community from which he comes.

Jorge's story about how he came to have his own car is an interesting one, because it provides important clues about not only the decisions parents and their young adult children make regarding teens' changing roles and responsibilities inside and outside the family as they move into adulthood but also how these decisions are made and the social forces that influence them. While Jorge's story seems to reveal something about the increasing independence of children of working parents and the intense academic demands for college-bound kids, it also points to the central role of class and the demands of work in structuring these family decisions. Jorge's car ownership is important to his family's ability to manage the fraying ties that hold them together. Especially at a time when most parents must work but have less control over their work lives; when the demands placed on parents to care for young and old family members are greater, but their financial resources fewer;

where children and their parents live out their lives in increasingly separate spheres.

Against this backdrop, parental anxieties and fears about their loosening grip over the fate of their children intensify.[5] Concern about their children's safety, about their children's futures, about risk and danger and success and failure have deepened as parents are challenged by what are often regarded as the growing risks in modern life. As Ulrich Beck, author of *Risk Society,* has argued, we are a society that has come up against its own limitations: "Modernity creates the very risk it attempts to control."[6] The sense that there is much to fear reflects a shift in our cultural thinking, defined by the emergence of "a risk consciousness," Frank Furedi, author of *Culture of Fear* argues, in which a "precautionary principle" and a "doctrine of limits" prevail, where caution is institutionalized, and where safety experts weigh in on everything as they attempt to predict and prevent what Furedi calls the big "A"—accidents.[7] In a discourse of fear, children are powerful symbols.[8] Parents tend to worry most about the supposedly boundless risks children face at school, at home, and on the road.[9] This parental anxiety is exploited by media "fear mongering," used to boost both television ratings and levels of parental worry, often unjustified, as well as create financial gain for media corporations.[10] For example, over and over, the media reports that traffic accidents are the leading cause of death among teens, while failing to mention that teens today die from few other causes,[11] and that rates of traffic accidents and traffic fatalities among teens have declined steadily over the past twenty-five years, as have rates of drinking and driving.[12] Nevertheless, parents are often left with the impression that the risks their children face today are countless and far more serious than those that existed in generations past.

Given this, it is hardly surprising that cars and driving are the subject of lengthy conversations and sometimes heated debate between parents and their kids as parents are forced to manage the tensions arising from competing frames: fear for the child on the road, respect for their child's desire for greater independence, a wish to not spoil their child, and their recognition of the freedoms they as parents gain once their child is able to drive. Parents and teen children negotiate these cultural contradictions as they make decisions, often informed by class realities and gender stereotypes, about when a teenager should get a driver's license and have his or her own car. Parents and kids struggle together and apart to make sense of changing family responsibilities and roles in contemporary American life arising from the changing demands of work, growing economic pressures on American families, the dwindling of free time, and more varied family formations.[13] Negotiations around the car provide meaningful clues about the nature of this struggle. In this chapter, as in the others, it is young people's accounts that direct the discussion, which would surely sound different if told by parents.

Slow Starts: Gaining Access to the Road

Gripped by concern for their children's safety, parents often award rights to the road reluctantly.[14] For better or for worse, parents exercise considerable control over their young adult children, placing limits on how they may drive and when and where and with whom they may drive.[15] Mena, for example, was required to wait until she turned seventeen (one year older than is required by California law) before getting her license. She was then allowed to drive only under the direct supervision of her mother for an additional year. "I was just like, basically that one year, it's just like I was driving with my mom like to errands and stuff." Olie was expected to wait an additional two years beyond the legal age requirement before getting his license. That Mena's and Olie's parents were recent immigrants to the United States may help to explain this, since most kids were allowed to seek a driver's license by parents if legally permitted by the state. The imposition of age restrictions beyond those imposed by the state is a strategy these immigrant parents used to monitor and possibly curtail their children's participation in American youth culture.[16] Immigrant kids' participation in the culture of MTV and Britney Spears is often a source of great anxiety for many immigrant parents, not only because they fear for their safety in a world they know little about, but also because of their concern for the loss of the home culture.[17] Postponing the license essentially works to limit teens' access to public spaces, keeping kids close to family and home. Without the means to get somewhere, wherever that where may be, teens usually spend their free time at home. But the consequence is that many young people feel stranded. This was the case for Allison, a young woman of twenty-two who recalls her life before a driver's license, before a car. "If I was lucky, my sister would take me out. She had a car and she was more of a homebody, so she just used her car for the basic necessities, if

I need to go to the library or deliver something or do a task for my parents. But I always wanted to go somewhere and so I had to beg her, please, please, you know. If I was nice or she was like, Okay, make me a sandwich, you know, then I could go and she would be my ride. My folks worked a lot."

Much changes when a teen gets a driver's license; a world of endless possibility beyond the home opens up. But most young adults must manage their parents' concern for them and their rules, no matter how unreasonable they may seem. When asking to borrow her mother's car, Lucena explains that sometimes, "they would be like, No, you can't take the car, but it wouldn't be like for punishment, it's just that they didn't want me to. They didn't feel like it [laughs]." Hortencia, a high school student, explains:

> My parents I don't think they were strict, but then again they weren't maybe because I challenged them on it, I mean, it wasn't, when they would say no to something I would say, but why?, here are my reasons why I can do this, what are your reasons? So I kind of engaged them in a conversation and because like I was always totally involved in school when I was, it was just like by chance if I went somewhere, like I didn't, I didn't, for me like, I was never into drinking, I was never into, so I knew what I was doing was fine. After I talked to them they would let me go.

Christina's situation was especially difficult. Her mother prohibited her from using the bus and wouldn't allow her to ride with her friends in their cars or to drive herself, seeing all these options as unsafe. Christina sees her mother as shamelessly holding things over her head, insensitively stalling her and ultimately preventing her from getting a license.

> I got my permit when I was fifteen and I had kept wanting to go get my license. I took all the driving lessons and everything. My mom finally decided you know 'we'll just put this off, put this off.' So when I was eighteen I got my license on my own. Since [parents] don't have to sign anything. [My mom] used it as a punishment because I wanted to drive myself to school and work and everything else . . . umm . . . she would say "No, no, no, you have to do things my way," and if they weren't done the right way, "You can't get your license."

Christina had to rely on her mother to drive her, lest she be left at home. Other parents were unwilling to allow their kids to use public transit, one of the only viable alternatives for getting around for those without a car. Many of the middle-class and upper-middle-class kids remarked that their parents perceived public transit to be unsafe (mistakenly, since the city's public transportation was well known for its impressive safety record). This was the case for Lenny, who in the end was able to use this as a means to negotiate for his own car. "My parents didn't want me to use the bus, it's not safe, but they didn't always want to give me a ride so 'well if you don't want to give me a ride I'm just gonna use the bus and . . . give me a ride if you don't want me to use the bus."[18]

The Double Standard: Boys, Girls, and Driving

Keeping kids safe was paramount for parents but played out in often dramatically different ways for sons and daughters.[19] Amanda and Mena, two young women, elucidate the situation:

> *Amanda*: My parents had like rules.
>
> *AB*: What were the rules?
>
> *Amanda*: The rules were that I couldn't have very many people in the car or the music, always music. Yeah, because there's so much distraction going on, but I did it anyway. It's just one of those things . . . they didn't want me driving, like my sister's friends, they didn't want me driving my sister's friends home because they didn't have an okay from their parents in case anything happens and they're in the car then I'm responsible.

> *Mena*: I never got to drive it to school; my dad would not let me drive it to school.
>
> *AB*: How come?
>
> *Mena*: Just because he's like, no, it's too risky and then your friends probably want, you have to probably pick up your friends cause that was a big deal, like, oh pick me up I don't have to go take the bus or something. And he's like, I don't want, you just started driving and then they get in the car it's, you know, it could be dangerous and all that. And I remember one time, I almost got my mom to let me take the car

and not tell him, but she got kind of nervous too, she's like, no, 'cause what if somebody, something happens and then I'm going to be the one to blame, so I could never take the car to school as much as I wanted to.

What is most striking here is not the rules themselves but their arbitrary assignment. Brothers and sisters were often subject to a different set of restrictions in terms of driving curfews and even punishments for traffic violations. While second-generation South Asian and Latino teens cited a gender double standard more often than Anglo and African American teens, this was apparent in nearly all of the interviews. For Mena, a South Asian young woman, gender is especially relevant insofar as she and her sister experienced a different set of restrictions from her brother.

> *Mena:* My dad didn't want to give us the responsibility of driving . . . I got it [the driver's license] at seventeen because he knew I would be going to college, I would have to commute so I would be better if I got it then and be able to, you know, drive and practice before I started going to college by myself. So, he gave me my license.
>
> *AB:* So, how did you learn how to drive?
>
> *Mena:* My dad had, he, 'cause I think at, oh maybe that's after a certain age, cause you're suppose to take twelve hours or six hours of driving lessons? There's a certain number that has to be, but then I went through a school and he had us take at least twenty-four hours of driving school. 'Cause he's so paranoid and so he's just like put us through that . . . me and my sister went through it kind of similarly . . . But my brother was like, not so much of a training.

For Sarah, a middle-class girl of sixteen, the gender subtext is particularly evident in her words.

> *AB:* Do you have a car?
>
> *Sarah:* I'm gonna get a car when I have money. Yeah my parents don't like me and they don't like the fact that I would ever get a car because I'm a B-I, B with an itch, and I would probably run people off the road, trust me PMS straight out . . . I'll get my driver's license but no car.
>
> *AB:* Will your parents let you drive their car?
>
> *Sarah:* I don't think they trust me.

Nearly all the young women identified rules their parents had invoked around driving, while only a few men identified having to obey parental driving rules or getting in trouble when such rules were violated. Jorge is the exception to the rule.

> Yeah, I stayed out too late one night. I was out with a girl, stayed out too late, and they took my keys away for about a week. I was supposed to be home at midnight. I walked in the door very scared, scared shit-less at about 2:30. So, my pops came out and ooooh, Bronx Puerto Rican at his best, cursing me out in Spanish and English. Took my keys.

It is likely that some boys, mindful of how they appeared in the in-terviews, withheld information about their parents' rules. Yet boys, in general, seemed to enjoy far greater freedom and fewer restrictions. This may be explained by the continued pressures to maintain a young woman's virtue; young women continue to be seen as needing watching over by parents, cousins, and older siblings.[20] This has significant conse-quences for how girls then move around (or don't) in public settings such as school, social events, shopping malls, and public streets.

Feminist scholars have shown how our understanding of adolescence is primarily a masculine one. Restlessness and risk and testing of one's power are themes that define the period of adolescence, yet these themes tend to be associated largely with boys.[21] Girls' participation in the activities that conventionally define adolescence, "risky" driving, for ex-ample, may be more closely monitored and ultimately curtailed in part because these activities are at odds with prevailing codes of feminine conduct.[22] On the surface, this may mean that girls remain safer than boys; indeed, statistics on seatbelt use, traffic accidents, traffic fatalities, and speeding indicate that high-risk driving is far more common among boys.[23] But this also suggests that, in relation to cars, some forms of boundary pushing, which have been long recognized as central to healthy development, is suppressed for girls. For a large number of boys who participate in risk activities that would cause their parents to wince, they face the contradictions inherent in becoming masculine; they face legal sanctions for risk-taking behaviors, even while, by partic-ipating in these risk activities, they receive the rewards of masculinity not only from girls and other boys but from a culture that celebrates the James Deans and other tragic masculine figures, even as it shakes its collective head for knowing the perils that lie further down such a dangerous road. Chapters 2 and 3 detailed many of these gender dynamics and the ways they played out differently in the car-cruising and car-racing scenes for young men and women. But it is important to note that, for young men and women, ideas about gender also play out at home.

Hiding, Lying, and Other Tall Tales

Though many young adults saw their parents' rules as reasonable and as motivated by love and concern for the teens' well-being, as one might expect, these rules were not always honored.[24] Like Justin, who remarked, "What he doesn't know won't hurt him," a number of young adults follow their parents' rules selectively. As one young woman said, "They told me not to take my friends around, but I did. I was the first one to have a car so I took everyone around and it was about fun and enjoyment." Natalie offered this:

> *Natalie*: There was like written-out rules, my Dad had typed out these rules, it must be cleaned once a week. . . . He writes them down and he thinks that you know, it's going to work, and it never works.
> *AB*: So he like wrote it out as kind of a contract and did you sign it?
> *Natalie*: Yeah, we both signed it.

For some young adults, managing parental anxiety and control involves telling tall tales to avoid the truth. Marisol explains, "I wouldn't sneak out. My parents are way too strict. I was just like, you know, tell them I was like going to her [pointing to Adrianna] house and we would cruise, I would never sneak out of the house." Recounting the time when she crashed her father's car to the focus group, Sandy explains,

> *Sandy*: I wrapped my dad's Toyota around a light post.
> *Jamie*: There's something to brag about.
> *AB*: Did you get in trouble?
> *Sandy*: Well, yeah but no. I blamed it on my cousin 'cause she was in the car with me and she kind a took the blame 'cause she is older than me, and so she knew that she wouldn't get in that much trouble anyways.

Sometimes the lengths gone to hide the truth are considerable. Here is Mena, who, you'll recall was prohibited from driving on her own the first year she had her license:

> I had one accident which my dad knew about and the second accident . . . I rear-ended somebody while going to school and it was because I was putting on makeup so that was my mistake and I totally had to lie and change the story. . . . Then I got in an accident in my new car, it was two days after I had gotten it, and I, what happened was I thought this guy was going to go, he was yielding and there was enough space and I thought he left but he didn't so I sped up and I rear-ended him. And I was so nervous like oh, my God, what am I going to do, what am I going to do, so luckily he was just like, don't worry, he didn't say anything, he just came out of his car and looked to see if anything was wrong and he just like left, he didn't even speak to me and I remember I was just like crying and I was like, oh my God, oh my God you know. . . . And after the accident I had pulled into a gas station and I thought everything was fine but afterwards I noticed there was a dent in my bumper and so what I went home and told my dad was that somebody hit me in the parking lot. . . . I still remember when I came home I was bawling my eyes out trying to make it seem like oh my new car got hit and stuff . . . maybe, you know, a few years down the line it'll be something to laugh at with my dad . . . I don't really mind because it's not very visible you know so at least I got away with it you know, so I was happy about that.

When later asked if she had ever been pulled over, Mena elaborates on another incident:

> Yeah, we did get pulled over one time for not wearing our seat belts. Yeah, and my dad doesn't know about that 'cause we sent the ticket 'cause it doesn't go on your record, it's not a moving violation. So we just, I had it sent to like my friend's work and then I just paid it off.

Lying to parents or withholding the truth until a later date are strategies many teens use to manage the often opposing pressures of parental expectation and American youth culture and that, for better or worse, enables them to keep conflicts to a minimum.[25] But, again, what is most striking is the obvious gender double standard. It is largely young women who admit to telling these tales, and not young men. Young men's voices are remarkably silent in this regard. Possibly the boys didn't reveal their tall tales so as to appear in control in the interviews, but I suspect that also at work here is the gendered double standard. Boys are encouraged to take risks, and girls are not. Given this apparent difference, it seems likely that these tall tales arise when parents attempt to restrict girls' access to spaces beyond the home, while rarely reeling their boys in. Like parental rules themselves, these tall tales reveal the role gender continues to play in family life. Boy and girl teens seem to live in separate and, in some respects, unequal family worlds, subject to different rules and saddled with different expectations for behavior. Girls often must craft elaborate strategies to enjoy the freedom that boys enjoy simply because they are boys.

Wheels of One's Own

Despite their anxieties about allowing their children on the road, parents are far more likely to provide or help finance a car for their child today than at any other time in U.S. history. As Jorge's story at the beginning of the chapter demonstrates, the demands of work, urban sprawl, growing commuting distances, a general distrust of public transit, and the absence of government dollars for funding accessible public transportation create a situation where kids increasingly need cars. Kids spoke at length about the hassles of dealing with parents' busy work schedules and the difficulty of trying to resolve scheduling conflicts as key reasons why they wanted their own car. Marisol explains, "I started driving because I needed a ride to go to school and [my parents] can't take me to school, so that's why I started driving. [But], um, I can only go to school and back home and they, if they wanted me to do some like, run some errands or something they will give me the car." Today, the time parents and their children spend apart from one another, at work, school, or extracurricular and leisure activities, is considerable.[26] Jorge explains, "All of us are so busy. Since I got my own car, we're like three units. 'Cause we have our own work. My mom works in Oakland now. I do all my stuff at school like I said, so I don't get home until five or six. My dad doesn't get home until six or seven. We all arrive home at different times we do our own things on the weekend."[27] Mena's comments are also revealing in this regard. "I needed the car and my mom needed a car for work and it was kind of getting difficult where you know if she needed the car on her days off and I would have to revolve my schedule around her and stuff. . . . I was sharing it. It was like between me, my mom, and my sister and like, the way it was set up was my sister would carpool with her friend to school and that would be the days that my mom would take it to work and then a couple of days it would be home because my mom needed to run errands or whatnot." Eventually these scheduling problems became too great. Mena was given a new Honda Civic during her junior year in college. "I remember I started telling my parents I want a new car, I want a new car, I totally initiated it. So now all of us, all my friends, I can remember we all had an old car and now all of us, you know, have gotten new cars within like a year, a year and a half." Mena and Jorge are certainly not alone. Lots of young adults have their own cars. Recall that 40 percent of students in college have their own cars, and a growing number of the cars are new, since car dealerships are far more likely to finance young car buyers than they were a few decades ago.[28] The percentage of thirteen- to seventeen-year-olds who could say that a car was "the newest thing bought" grew from 4 percent to 10 percent between 1998 and 2002.[29] In 2004, buyers under twenty accounted for almost 600,000 new car sales nationally.[30]

Cars in a Class by Themselves

Parents often decide to give a car to their child to celebrate a milestone, usually educational, in their kids' lives. Graduation from high school, graduation from college, and the start of college, while socially defined as special occasions in their own right, are elevated in importance, as is the parent's role in these events, when such an expensive gift is given. As one might expect, the ability to bestow such an expensive gift is far more common in middle- and upper-middle-class households, since these parents are far more likely to have the necessary economic resources. Amanda, who was given a brand-new red Pontiac Firebird for her sixteenth birthday, explained:

> They paid [for the car and related expenses] because I was in high school and I didn't have a job, you know, my parents wanted me to focus on school and sports and I didn't have time to do a job after that.

So that was my job, basically . . . my parents just never like, you know, said don't worry about it.

Because of her family's affluence, this young woman got a car and didn't have to compromise her free time.[31]

These negotiations make clear, perhaps painfully so, the economic reality of their family lives. Decisions over whether to buy a car and the kind of car bought reveal to kids (though likely not for the first time) how their parents think about spending money, what sort of disposable income they have, and, sometimes, their willingness to assume additional debt. Cars serve as meaningful symbols of class membership and belonging. Through these decisions, young adults reaffirm their own and their families' place in the class structure and whether they have particular kinds of symbolic capital that determine their rank in the class hierarchy.[32] That young adults are now more likely to be given *new* cars as gifts reveal the logic of competitive spending and the upscaling of lifestyle norms that Juliet Schor and other scholars recognize as increasingly a part of American family and community life.[33]

These negotiations are also occasion for young adults to formulate their own ideas about financial spending and conspicuous displays. This seemed evident when I talked with a number of kids, all squarely middle class, about having an expensive car. They all knew kids who had been given what were seen as unreasonably expensive cars as gifts by parents; a number of them were critical of this decision and objected on moral grounds. Invoking the importance of cultivating a "work ethic," one middle-class seventeen-year-old young man who drove a used Ford Taurus wagon, which he had financed almost entirely himself from money his parents had put aside from his modeling as a child, remarked, "They're not going to appreciate their car because they didn't work for it, they just kind of got it." Banji, also middle class, who drove her father's four-year-old Camry at twenty, offered a similar story:

One of my dad's friends, he's a doctor and he got his daughter a Mercedes convertible and so I was like, I was a little bit jealous, I was like jeez . . . but then again I don't know, that sounds like you're spoiling your kids a little bit.

Almost everyone seemed to have a story to tell about an overindulged child.

I have a neighbor and she just got her license and she's a junior and her dad bought her a BMW. And I was like, whaaaaat, and I wasn't hating on her like hey, if that's what you're going to get for your first car, go for it. But I don't know, knowing that it's your first car most likely, hopefully not, but most likely if you're not an experienced driver you know what I mean. Something can happen.

Robert, an upper-middle-class high schooler from exclusive Woodside, a pricey area outside San Jose, who was given his grandfather's relatively new Grand Jeep Cherokee, offered:

I find it kind of funny when you know someone who like got a brand-new car and totaled it. Then, like, her mom gets her a brand-new car, I mean, you know, it's fine because, that's what her mom chose to do and everything, but I, I don't, maybe she'll get the impression that cars can be, you know, just tossed away and you'll get a new one for free.

Different ideological threads get knotted as Robert struggles to resolve the contradictions inherent in buying a teenage child a high-priced luxury car. The debate between freedom of (parental) choice, a premium value in American culture, and the shameless indulgence of a child's every want reveals the conflicting American ideals of deferred gratification and conspicuous consumption. Their reflections also reveal taken-for-granted ideas about who in American culture deserves to consume expensive objects. Since teens are generally regarded as economically inactive (even though nearly 70 percent of teenagers work full- or part-time), they are often seen as undeserving.[34]

While some parents are willing and able to buy a car for their child, others expect their kids to also contribute. "They were paying the payments under their name and I was paying them cash every month for my car. I would pay like $200, and it was like $350 so they would like pay [the remaining amount], you know what I mean," Natalie, the daughter of two professional parents, who was given a new Volkswagen Jetta (a coveted car among youth), explains.

Many parents are without the financial resources to hand over a large sum of money to finance such a significant purchase. In these instances, parents use other means to help their children gain autonomy and independence. This was the case for Trevor, a lower-middle-class college kid. His parents did not have the money to buy him a car, but his mother was able to help him find the sort of work that would enable him to pull together a solid down payment.

> I was working, um, I had got this job through my mother's, one of my mother's coworkers. It was a bad job, that's why I'm always thankful that I have a good job now. It was like janitorial work and yeah, so I had to commute all the way from the south side of San Jose all the way to like Fair Oaks, which is in Sunnyvale, and it was, it was a horrible job, but I did that for three months and I just saved and saved and saved and saved until I had like $3,000 and I went put a, got my Probe.

This was also the case for Lucena, whose father, a laborer, helped her to save enough to buy a car.

> My dad took me to the bank my freshman year, he took me to the bank and he said, "Okay Mija, we're going to open you a student account and a savings account." And I said, "Okay." You know, and little by little my dad would put money in the bank and stuff for me, and then I started to work and then little by little I would start putting money in the bank myself. Because he felt it was unfair because my two older sisters like, my dad bought them their first cars like full, you know what I mean. And with me, I had to do it by myself, you know what I mean, and so my dad said this is only fair. He'd put like $50 sometimes, like little, but over four years it counts you know what I mean, And then when it came time, I never . . . I just totally forgot about the money and when it came senior year, I was just like, how much do I have in the bank, and my dad was like, Well, you have almost ten thousand in the bank. I was like, whaaaaaaat? Swear to God. I was ecstatic, you know what I mean. I can buy whatever car I want. I could put a down payment on any car I want.

In several instances, parents were not alone in these decisions or financial contributions. Extended kin, aunts, uncles, and cousins, were often central to the ability to purchase a car. A number of kids turned to their relatives for financial help. Banji, the daughter of Indian immigrants, and Richard, an immigrant himself, relied on the networks of extended kin that is characteristic of many immigrant families. As Richard explains,

[The] aunt I lived with for seven years, she helped me with a lot, she gave me $5,000 that I didn't have to return and then an additional $3,000 loan and um, a relative in Taiwan, my uncle, these are all my mom's side, contributed $2,000 that I didn't have to return, so that helped a lot.

Banji offers this:

My dad wanted a dependable car and to him a dependable car is another Camry, so I got, he got me a, they went to the dealership just my dad and my mom and they found a pretty good deal on the Camry, it was between the Camry and this old Accord. It wasn't that old, it was only like three years old, but you know there's there is a money difference, and so I'm like okay, I'll go with the old, you know, Accord, it doesn't matter to me, but my mom and dad were like, if we're going to buy you a car, we might as well buy you a new one. And my grandma wanted to buy me a car, too, so my grandma chipped in and my mom chipped in and they bought me my car. And then what happened was my brother had gone with my mom and dad and then mom and my brother went again and then they took me along to look at it and I'm just like, it's a nice car, I liked it.

Teens' ability to financially contribute was often critical to the move toward purchasing a car and was generally seen by young adults as a sign of their growing maturity and movement into adulthood. For Mena, her ability to cover monthly payments was key, enabling her to persuade her father to agree to the car.

I was like, I think I have enough money where if you guys put the down payment maybe I could make the monthly payments, you know. And then they were just like, hmmm, we'll see, we'll see, don't worry about it . . . coming around. So I used that as an excuse. I was like, come on you know and then I think either my brother got a raise or something, something happened where he, I asked him to help me out. So then we came up with a plan, okay, if my dad put the down payment then we would both pay half of the monthly. And so but they were still kind of like, yeah we'll see, we'll see, and then my dad got a new car, so I kind of laid a guilt trip on him. I was like, well, you got a car and my sister

got a car when she went to State, so did my brother, and now I'm starting and my birthday's coming up, you know that kind of a thing, and
so they ended up getting me a car, and now I have to pay half the
monthly installments.

While some parents partly or fully finance the cost of buying a new or
used car for their child, it is often with the expectation that the child
will contribute to other car-related expenses, such as fines for traffic violations, repairs after car accidents, insurance payments, and gas and
upkeep. Amanda was given a gas allowance with the understanding that
if she exceeded the allowance, she had to pay the overage. While no
doubt these are lessons in financial responsibility for young adults, they
are also examples of parental control and monitoring. Parents indirectly, though perhaps not always effectively, exercise control over their
kids, regulating and monitoring their whereabouts and how they spend
their own money. Middle- and lower-income kids must often find part-
time employment to cover these expenses, which consumes much of
their free time outside school; the money they generate from these jobs
often goes directly to cover car costs, rather than being spent on other
items or activities. As parents' and teenagers' daily lives are increasingly
spent apart, this becomes one way for parents to maintain their hold
over their children.

Grades and Gas Money: Cars as Control

The loss of car privileges is common among teen drivers, often resulting
from activities and behaviors entirely unrelated to driving.[35] "My dad's
actually gonna give me a car this summer, but I can't drive it until next
year 'cause I kind of got in trouble," one young woman explained in a
focus group interview. Referring to the car, upper-middle-class Andrea
offers this:

Andrea: It was basically kind of like held over my head a lot, you clean
your room or you don't get the car this weekend. Always, you know,
the car was always taken away if I didn't do what they wanted.
AB: Did you lose your car a lot?
Andrea: Yeah. I was pretty good, but my dad was big on keeping the car

clean, keeping your room clean, it was mostly household chores, it was a way to get me to do things, and I didn't do them all the time so I would get my car taken away a lot.

Importantly, it was only parents who had helped finance their child's car who were able to revoke car privileges. Those kids whose parents did not buy them a car rarely mentioned the use of the car as a source of parental control. When asked if his mother helped finance his car, eighteen-year-old Kenny, who drives a fully loaded Mustang GT, offered this:

> *Kenny*: No. She didn't know about it, she almost disowned me for it, actually.
>
> *AB*: Tell me about that, what happened?
>
> *Kenny*: She just didn't think I needed it and I didn't need it, but I wanted it and I normally do whatever I want. It sounds weird, but I normally don't listen to my mother very much, so. She didn't have any say in what I did, really. She just didn't talk to me for a week, and then she got over it.

Kenny's unwillingness to defer to his mother might also be explained by the fact that, as a single parent, she seemed to possess little authority in negotiations with Kenny. This point is meaningful in relation to the fact that when young adults talked of their parents revoking car privileges, they most often talked about their fathers, not their mothers. Car privileges seemed to be awarded and revoked by fathers or by mothers and fathers *together* but rarely by mothers alone, again demonstrating that, when it comes to cars, there is often a gender-based double standard.

While some parents take their teen's car away as a punishment, parents also use the promise of a car as an incentive to elicit a desired behavior. The stakes are high, since cars (especially new ones) are highly desired objects but beyond most young adults' means. "I want to get a sports utility . . . my parents said they would help me buy a new car if I move back in, so that's another reason I want to move back into my parents' house," Aldo explained. Lots of parents use the car as leverage in arguments over performance in school and decisions over future career and educational plans. This was the case for Augusto, a middle-income eighteen-year-old: "Okay, my first car I uhhh . . . I got uhhh . . .

it was a present to me. If I graduated high school with good credits and high grades . . . so I did. High grades uhhh . . . got a couple of awards and stuff and I got the car." Natalie's words are revealing:

AB: Oh, so you didn't get it [your license] when you were sixteen?

Natalie: No.

AB: How come?

Natalie: I didn't get it because I was very lazy and the classes that you had to take for that were tedious to me and I was not into that. I was very, I was the type of high school student that enjoyed the weather a little too much. Didn't really enjoy going to ten-hour classes on a Saturday to learn driving skills, so my parents offered to buy me a car and that's when I was getting the motivation to be like, okay I'll do it, if I pay for the insurance and the gas and the tune up.

AB: So you get a car for your seventeenth birthday, was that?

Natalie: Not for my birthday, but after I graduated and I graduated high school when I was seventeen, so, 'cause I was a younger one.

Some kids even identified their parents' attempts as bribes. Mike, a wealthy kid who had attended a prestigious private school all his life, spoke repeatedly about the control his parents exerted over him. "Yeah, they're strict. They're still trying to be strict, but I'm kind of like hard to control." In the course of the interview, I learned that his relationship with his folks had been turbulent. Mike had been kicked out of his parents' house a few times, on one occasion being left with little choice but to live in his car temporarily. According to Mike, direct attempts to punish him rarely worked. In a desperate attempt to bring Mike under control, his parents, both professionals in San Jose's high-tech corridor, had offered to buy him a very expensive car if he agreed to commit himself to his college studies.

They'll probably buy the next car, half of it or most of it. They're talking about getting me a new car, and getting me the one I want if I do well in college. There's the ultimatum. But I'm totally ready for that and I hella want to. Six years of suffering for an Audi S4. It's like a $41,000 car, that's really nice.

This particular strategy is tied to the middle-class value placed on education as the primary means by which the middle class reproduces itself.

In the context of high-stakes education, where wealthy parents clamor to enroll even the youngest of their brood in premier preschools, it is not much of a stretch that middle- and upper-middle-class parents might also feel the pressure for their kids to do well in school in order to do well in life.[36]

In many ways, this reflects the class-specific parenting practices that the sociologist Annette Lareau in, her book *Unequal Childhoods,* came to see as she observed the daily rituals and routines of working-class and professional parents. Lareau argues that middle- and upper-middle-class mothers and fathers parent according to the logic of what she calls "concerted cultivation," which she defines as a commitment to "developing" the child through involvement in an array of educational and extracurricular activities intended to provide enrichment and an expanded cultural repertoire. Attempts to instill desired behavior through offerings such as a car can be seen as expressions of the interventionist role middle and upper-middle-class parents play as they direct and narrow the courses of action their children may follow, with the goal of instilling in them the cultural capital that will serve as the basis for entry into the upper and upper-middle classes.[37]

Having a Car Is Work

In exchange for car privileges, many kids find themselves suddenly saddled with greater responsibility to the family. These responsibilities include driving other family members around—younger brothers and sisters to school, grandparents to the doctor—and running errands for the family, such as picking up groceries. "I have to go to the laundry and pick up groceries and stuff." Crystal, a young woman from a middle-income family, offered during an interview. Eve, a young woman whose immigrant parents spent much of their life working in factory and field, explains her situation.

> *Eve:* My dad wanted me to take my mom out shopping and take the responsibilities that he didn't want to do anymore.
> *AB:* Did your mom not drive?
> *Eve:* She never learned.
> *AB:* So when you had that responsibility, what were some of the things that you did?

Eve: Oh, just take her to the store, grocery shopping mostly, yeah, doctor's appointments and all that.

Amanda, the young woman given a brand new Pontiac Firebird upon turning sixteen, offered this:

AB: Your parents let you drive to school?
Amanda: Yeah. I dropped my sister, my sister didn't go to the same school as me at that time, she was in junior high, so I would drop her off.

Richard, whose mother resides in Taiwan but hopes to visit soon, encouraged him to get a car when he was twenty with the expectation that this would be beneficial for both of them: "I'll be able to drive her around and that seems like something that she really looks forward to." Hortencia, whose mother was collecting disability for a work-related injury and whose father was getting "too old" to drive, conceptualized these responsibilities in terms of her duties as a daughter. She offered this:

Well, the thing is in my situation I kinda had to learn how to drive. My parents are older, my mom is like fifty-something, fifty-five, and my dad's sixty-six, so they're older and my dad's sick, too, and huh, in case of an emergency, I need to know how to drive 'cause my sisters are way older than me. I'm like ten years younger than my younger sister. So, I'm like really young so I kinda had to learn just in case of an emergency if something happens, you need to learn to get yourself out of a situation or take somebody somewhere.

What is also meaningful to her story is that she had yet to get her license. The driving she did, mostly local driving, running errands and helping her parents out "in case of an emergency," was done at a considerable risk.

Like Hortencia, other young drivers explained that their parents let them drive locally, running family errands, without a driver's license. Brittany and Alexa, seventeen and sixteen, respectively, explained to Maria, one of the student researchers, the conditions under which their parents would allow them to drive even though neither has a license, despite their being old enough to get one.

Brittany: It is my mother's car.
Maria: And she knows, she lets you drive it.

Alexa: I share a car with my mom.

Maria: You do. So does she let you drive it occasionally? How often can you drive it?

Alexa: Only when they want stuff.

Brittany: Yeah.

Maria: Oh really?

Alexa: Occasionally I can drive by myself, but I drive all the time because I have to drive her around because she's sick.

Maria: Okay, you run errands for her, and you drive her around?

Brittany: Yeah, like to doctors and stuff. So all the time when I'm in the car with her and she has to go somewhere, I drive.

Maria: So, does she let you drive without, like if you want to go out or anything like that?

Alexa: No, not too much, maybe like once in a great while.

Brittany: [laughs]

Maria: And your parents let you drive it?

Brittany: No, they'll let me drive their truck for them.

Alexa: Errands.

Maria: For them.

Brittany: If they want to go to the store then.

Later in the interview Brittany explained that sometimes she is asked to drive when her father has had too much to drink. Moments later, Alexa reveals that she too has found herself in such a situation,

Brittany: My dad drinks a lot. And most of the time when he drinks, now that I'm older and I know how to drive. I drive when he's drinking, or when he drinks.

Maria: So you drive him, if you know he's been drinking?

Brittany: Yeah.

Alexa: My dad drinks and drives.

Augusto also found himself in situations where his father was easily willing to hand over the reins when having drunk too much. "I pretty much learned how to drive maybe at the age of thirteen. I was out driving with my father, uhh, he knew it was against the law but, uhh, you know, he still had us driving many times because he was under the influence or he just didn't feel like driving."

Curiously, these parents placed their families legally at risk by allowing an unlicensed driver behind the wheel. This might be explained by the fact that parents had come to see their adolescent children as more-or-less adults, having more-or-less adult responsibility and thus saw the matter of their not having a license as a minor oversight. This may be a consequence of the values arising from privatized childrearing; parents see themselves as the ones who govern their children's actions, rather than the state or any other institution. Notably, with the exception of Augusto, in these instances, it was girls who did the driving. Perhaps parents see their girl children as extensions of the family unit, whose first responsibility is to the family, or, given family gender roles, perhaps girls are just more likely to be seen as caretakers. Either way, the fact that on the one hand girls are likely to have greater parental restrictions placed on their freedom to drive and that on the other hand they are more likely to be responsible for driving the family places points to the double standards girls face in relation to gender and their cars.

Often parents are willing to cover car expenses in exchange for their children carrying some of the burden of family life. Mike explains, "They paid for everything. They still pay for my insurance. They're covering all that stuff. I just have to pick up my sister here and there. I really don't mind because my sister's like totally cool." Lenny, whose parents gave him a new Toyota 4Runner, explained, "All I had to do was drive my sister around, like from here to there. So like if she wants to go to dinner, I take her out to dinner and I like pay for it . . . or if she like wants to go to the mall, I'll drive her and her friends to the mall or to the movies." In exchange, his parents also pay his car insurance and other car-related expenses.

For many parents, a teen's license means greater freedom for them. As Matt explains, "My mom is glad that I have my license because then she doesn't have to come and pick me up at twelve o'clock and she's not too thrilled about doing that. So, she was counting the days of when I would get my license." The newfound freedom parents experience, combined with the need for kids to fulfill family responsibilities, often has consequences for the driving rules parents establish and enforce. Parents are often flexible on these matters because they gain as much freedom as their children. Mena elaborates:

> In high school, my parents were very strict so we [referring to her older sister] didn't really get to go out much. . . . I never had the car when I was in high school, so [her father] never restricted us. I don't think he

had much of a choice to restrict when we use to go to college together. We had to commute so if he took the car away from us then . . .

To impose restrictions would mean additional work for this parent. Mike further elaborates:

> They really couldn't take their car away from me for a while because of like the fact that my sister needed a ride to school and I was her ride to and from school. It was a necessity for me to be driving so I always pretty much have my car. Maybe if I were to do something really bad they'd take it away for like a week.

Both Mike and Mena demonstrate the importance of the car for modern families. The increasing workplace demands on parents in a postindustrial economy and at a time of eroding public services for families have created a situation where both parents must work to make ends meet.[38] This is increasingly the case particularly for families at the lower end of the wage continuum: immigrant laborers, single mothers, workers of color, and the downwardly mobile white working class.[39] It goes without saying that not working is rarely an option in single-parent households. These families, as they struggle to adapt to changing economic and social circumstances, *must* often rely on the family work (and sometimes paid work) their young adult children perform to survive as families. In these situations, it often makes economic sense to impose few driving restrictions and even to contribute a nominal sum toward the purchase of an inexpensive used car for their kids. This was the case with a number of kids I spoke to.

Middle-class and upper-middle-class parents, who have professional jobs with high salaries, also rely on their teen children to run errands and shuttle younger siblings around. But other forces are also at work. Recall for a moment Jorge's story, told in the beginning of this chapter, about managing the busy schedule required for a teen to succeed in high-stakes education and to meet the economic and time demands such a schedule requires of the parents of such children. For middle- and upper-middle-class kids in the suburbs where social life requires the ability to get around, cars are a necessity if they are to succeed in a hypercompetitive educational context. Gaining entry to prestigious colleges requires more effort than it did twenty years ago. In turn, where one attends college has some bearing on the type of job one will later hold. Parental anxieties about class reproduction bear on this process. Parents, overwhelmed and fearful about their young adult children "making it," encourage their children's participation in a range of extracurricular activities. But the demands of their work make it difficult for them to manage family life, parenting, and the educational needs of their young adult children. Buying their teen a car is an obvious and easy solution.

The difference, then, between upper-middle-class families like those of Amanda, Natalie, Mike, and Jorge and working-class families like those of Hortencia, Eve, Lucena, and Richard relates to economics. The work young adults perform in the family, for those at the lower end of the economic ladder, is usually not optional. This family work often frees up parents to create income. Lower-income families often live in communities with families in like economic situations, where all adult family members work, and thus they are unable to benefit from neighborhood carpools that usually require that one parent have free time away from work. For upper-middle-class families, buying a car for their teens makes good sense because it results in more free time for the parents.[40] Importantly, these dynamics reproduce as much as they express the current class order, making cars as transportation objects essential for kids and their families.

Drivers Needed

The economic context of families is meaningful for teens in countless ways.[41] My discussion here has focused on the ways changing economic realities and the increasing demands of work on parents shape how teens come to relate to and think about cars. The fact that working-class and lower-middle-class families depend on their teenage children to survive, while middle-class and upper-middle-class families rely on their teens for other reasons relating mostly to the reproduction of class across generations has consequences for teens' lives. Certainly, the car emerges as a meaningful resource here. The car serves to embed class in family life as a status-conferring symbol, while also embedding class concretely, since it operates as a material resource for families. In upper-middle-class families, the car is used as a bargaining chip to promote desired behavior and to gain teens' allegiance to parents' plans for their children's future. Cars and, perhaps more important, the decisions parents and teens make regarding them have significance for the reproduction of class divisions between families and teens.

Teens must manage a range of social forces as they come of age. In a cultural context where kids' lives play out in settings different from those their parents inhabit, parental anxieties and fears intensify, with consequences for young people's access to a public world beyond family. In these family negotiations, gender differences matter dearly as girls far more than boys are limited by the rules their parents impose. Girls more often than boys face familial expectations about their duties to family. Clearly, as families across class groups cope with the time constraints imposed by family demands and work, a large burden falls to girls to pick up the slack. Yet, class is hardly irrelevant. Amanda, Allison, and Natalie, all white and upper middle class, like their male counterparts, Lenny and Mike, were exempt from the bulk of these responsibilities. While Amanda was expected to drive her sister to school, she never spoke of any expectation that she sacrifice school, sports, or other activities to help her family out. Her burden was small in comparison to Hortencia's or Eve's, both daughters of immigrant laborers whose mothers are on disability. Hortencia didn't have a license, yet drove her mother places when she had to, placing herself and her family at risk. Her parents seemed to rely heavily on her, as Eve's did on her. This was also the case for other young working-class women, many of them the daughters of immigrants, with whom I spoke, revealing the importance of class, gender, and culture in shaping young women's and men's lives within families and beyond.

The theme of car privileges recurs in this chapter. It is a rich concept, since car privileges carry different meaning depending on the class and gender contexts in which they are invoked and revoked. I am reminded of the statement I've heard countless times in terms of youth and driving—"Driving is a privilege, not a right." True enough, but the class realities and gender stereotypes that are so powerfully important to who is able to access these car privileges are lost in such statements as the focus shifts to youth as a group, who are largely seen as undeserving of such privileges. In the next chapter, I again consider the importance of class to young adults' ability to move beyond the private world of family and to participate in American cultural and public life as they transition into adulthood, and the role cars play in this transition.

5

The Road to Nowhere
Consumer Culture and the Price of Freedom

Kenny has blonde hair and a slight frame and looks as though he has spent most of his life on the sunny beaches of California. He turned eighteen last April and in the two years since getting his driver's license has owned three cars, a 1990 Toyota 4Runner and a 1992 Toyota 4Runner. The first one, "My mom bought for me, I had it for about four months and I totaled it," Kenny explains. "Then a month and a half later I got my next one . . . the insurance bought me the second." But, in a replay of events, Kenny also totaled the second car. "Two months ago I hit a curb and rolled it all the way over." In both cases, he was "so innocent," he says pleadingly, "I was going under twenty miles an hour. Like, my 4Runner was jacked up pretty high and I had big tires and then I clipped the curb, couldn't steer, and it hit a lamp post and flipped over in the middle of traffic, didn't hit anyone else, no one was in my car, I didn't get hurt." His disappointment is evident as he describes what was clearly a cherished car. He had put a lot of money into the second car—new rims, a four-inch lift with new thirty-three-inch tires, "an expensive CD player," and "two subwoofers with a lot of bass." "You can feel your music," he tells me, not to mention "it's obnoxious," as he boasts about the fact that his bass can be felt by other cars around him on the road. Before totaling the second 4Runner, he had hoped to install a "VCR and DVD player with Nintendo hookup" like the one his friend had in his truck. Both cars behind him, now he drives a brand-new Mustang GT bought straight off the lot for a grand total of $30,000, with a large chunk in financing. Explaining why he bought a Mustang this time and not another truck, he offers, "My friend bought one. I fell in love with it, the way it looks, the way it drives, the way, *everything*, so I bought it." In the six months since getting the Mustang, he has already made several modifications, all paid out of pocket. "I got an exhaust on it, so it's louder, got a stereo system in it, got rims and tires." Between insurance and his car payment, Kenny pays more than $700 monthly and will do so for the next fifty-four months. In all, he considers the expense reasonable. His friend who leases a 2001 Chevy Silverado is "paying like $700 a month for three years or something and then at the end of that three years, he has to pay $21,000 just to have the truck." Just in case I may have missed the point, he adds, "He's paying $55,000 for this truck that's worth $30,000."

When asked how he covers the sizable expense, he replies simply, "Work. I make $14 an hour and work forty hours a week." After graduating from high school, Kenny found a job answering phones and delivering materials for a roofing company. On a national level, his is a pretty good wage, but sobering when taking into account the cost of living in the high-priced Silicon Valley, where rent is twice the national average. Luckily, Kenny lives with his mother's boyfriend and has to pay only $400 a month in rent.

"I work just for a car," he says with a matter-of-fact tone, as if to suggest this is not the least out of the ordinary. "I put almost half my income towards my car, more than half my income if you count insurance and gas and car payment and maintenance." Realizing this may sound like an awful lot of money to put toward a car, he is quick to let me know that he does draw the line somewhere. "I'd never put more than like three-quarters, no, like two-thirds of my income to . . . my car."

Kenny is not a rich kid, nor does he pretend to be one. He grew up in a quiet but changing town outside the city of San Jose with his mother, who has worked full-time since he can remember. He must work to cover the expense of his car but finds it worthwhile. "I love to drive fast, I love to have nice things, like a nice car, drive around everywhere." For Kenny, it is not just about having any car like all the other "old beatup cars" parked in his former high school parking lot. His car is his ticket to freedom, to mobility, his means to an end, his claim to visibility, to being a somebody and not a nobody invisible to the world around him. His car is his means to express his sense of self and at the same time to transcend it.

Tom, Kenny's best friend, has had a total of five cars in the two years since getting his license, awarded, he tells me, the very day he turned sixteen. The first car Tom bought was a 1972 Barracuda, but after a few months, "I bought my dad's car off of him, which was the Acura, early '90s Acura that we dropped an engine in right before I bought it. I sold that one for $3,500, and I bought a '72 El Camino." After six months he sold the El Camino, buying a '94 Camaro, this time with the help of his Mom, who was willing to cosign a loan from a bank. "That was the longest I've ever had a car, seven months I think, and then a month ago I sold that and I have the 2000 Mustang." The reason for the newest car Tom explains is the sixty miles he commutes each day to and from work, a distance that is more the rule than the exception in Silicon Valley. "The El Camino, the wheel fell off twice on the way to work." After providing a $3,000 down payment for his Mustang, Tom pays $365 each month for his car payment, in addition to the $300 he pays for car insurance.

Tom is not a rich kid, either, but squarely middle class. He attends a community college as a freshman, lives at home with his mother, who is a nurse, works full-time at a "good job distributing medical supplies at the hospital," and is thinking about one day becoming a cop.

Kenny and Tom are part of a teeming crop of young adults in their teens and early twenties whose sense of being is tied largely to their cars. For them, the car is a central means by which they participate in cultural and economic life, navigating their ways around today's consumer society. Amid a rapidly changing world where traditional anchors of social existence have eroded, it is as consumers, of cars in this instance, that young people claim and affirm membership in the larger community, helping to drive an ever-expanding consumer market, reshaping how families live together and apart, influencing how communities are planned and how local economies unfold. It is as consumers that they come to see themselves as individuals, and it is also as consumers that they struggle to realize the cherished but elusive American values of freedom and independence. "Like, life it's hard when you don't have transportation. You're always waiting for a bus or asking people and it's, I think, if you have a car you're more independent," one young woman remarked. Indeed.

In the preceding chapter, I explored how teens' varied and complicated negotiations with parents around getting a car were shaped by gender and class. In this chapter, I consider the meaning of cars as young adults in their teens and twenties move beyond family and into a public world where the life of communities play out. Like the preceding chapter, this one is concerned with youths' engagement with the broader American car culture. I begin with the idea of freedom, exploring its various invocations by kids themselves, since it is through the car that young people see themselves as fundamentally free. But, as much as the car offers what might be considered a quasi-personal freedom, it also draws young people into a culture of spending where they face a set of irreconcilable contradictions, since their desire for freedom more often than not carries significant social and financial costs, as Kenny and Tom so clearly demonstrate. Our setting is San Jose, a community where cars are as numerous as the people, where signs of a rapidly changing economy are visible everywhere, and where an economic cleavage between young people continues to grow.

Freedom

The promise of freedom that cars represent to youth on the surface seems obvious. As one young woman declared just weeks after getting her license, "You feel kind of liberated." But, from what? In the first instance, the car ensures freedom from parents and home. Youth want freedom from the ever-present parental gaze, the yoke of parental control. "It's three o'clock in the morning, you have a video game you want to play, and it's at your parent's house, and you're going to sneak over there and come back without them even knowing. You're supposed to be somewhere else when you tell them you're there," says Mike, a nineteen-year-old who has lived on and off with his parents since graduating from high school and now attends a community college part-time.

James Kunstler, author of *Geography of Nowhere,* claims that the car promises "liberation from the daily bondage of place."[1] This has distinct appeal for kids on the cusp of adulthood who are slowly gaining access to a number of public spaces once closed off to them as they move beyond the worlds of school and home. But it is the newfound freedom of movement *between* places that perhaps matters even more. Allison, now twenty-two but living at home while she finishes college, recalls the initial allure of having a car:

> When I got my driver's license, I looked at it as freedom, getting out from my parents, going places you couldn't get to before because you

had to have your parent's permission . . . not having to be worried about being dropped off and being picked up. Going to the library even or a dance club or a party and not having to worry about, I don't know, your parents having to come pick you up. Not necessarily, it wasn't embarrassment for me, it was more, just like okay, I make my own choices I can leave when I want to, you know, I made this decision to come here you know I'll drop you off. I felt more like an adult but, um, I don't know, I went to the beach, to people's houses, friend's houses, the movies.

The ability to exercise control over her life, where she goes and when, to make her "own choices," to no longer be subject to someone else's schedule, is deeply cherished by Allison because it is something few youth regularly enjoy. The ability to spontaneously move beyond a setting that suddenly feels unsafe is perhaps particularly significant for young women. Having a car can be a resource protecting against sexual dangers.[2] Yet, the desire for this type of control also seems to reflect a much larger attempt to play with and even control the unfolding of time, to speed it up or slow it down, since the car opens up the possibility of endless spontaneity, immediate gratification, and the means to overcome the boredom that overwhelms so many of us in our youth and beyond. Mike elaborates:

I spend a lot of time in my car inadvertently. Like at night usually. But at night I'm going to be moving around from other people's houses just to be out sometimes and a lot of times just because like okay there's a fun thing over here, we'll go there and later on and I'm bored with this let's go over here and then like picking up people. Doing missions, like let's go get some food.

Mike is among countless youth who spend hours driving around with little purpose. No destination beckons him, he drives just to be out doing something, anything.

For Kenny and Tom, who between them have owned eight cars, the freedom they gain seems to be as much about freedom from self as freedom from place. For Tom, who has never had a car for more than seven months, there is a sense of his trying on different selves, or, as the sociologist Todd Gitlin says, "trying frenetically to find himself by abandoning himself."[3] Fashioning a new image of oneself with each car one has, trying to prevent the sense of being locked into one permanent self—such is the status of the self in a postmodern world.[4]

For Richard, a student at the state university, who moved to the United States from Taiwan when he was ten, the much-sought-after freedom pursued by many youth had to be put on hold until he was well into early adulthood. Explaining why he postponed getting his license, he offers, "I was living with relatives. I didn't have a lot of resources. Like most kids have their parent's car to practice on. I didn't have that luxury." Now twenty-one, Richard recently bought a Kia Rio after finally securing his driver's license a few months before. He admits to me, "Owning a car was scary on a financial standpoint in terms of how much it was going to cost me and the implications on, um, my finances for my education, um, and maintenance and a lot of things that go into it that I didn't want to deal with. Now I'm pretty much in debt." But ultimately Richard decided that the time had come. "There was a lot of pressure in the family because they believed that in America, you should be independent. You must own a vehicle." Most of the time Richard counted on his cousin to get around. In the end it was his Mom, who resides in Taiwan but tries to visit every few years, who pushed him to get a license and then a car. "She was thinking that being independent in the United States means having a car and autonomy and all. I guess to her that's kind of a sign of me becoming an American."

Fully absorbed into an American way of life that values independence over interdependence, Richard, like many kids I spoke to, grew tired of having to depend on others. "It became really inconvenient having to rely on other people. I don't like to feel like I owe people and have to ask for favors, it's not really me. I try not to as much as possible." Now a car owner, he too enjoys "the whole sense of freedom" a little more than he thought. "There's this power that I have to be wherever I want to be, not having to compromise and accommodate other people's schedules." The disdain shown by Richard and other young adults toward dependence is as much a sign of the times as a symptom of their age. "Self-sufficiency, that most tempting and expansive of modern motifs, feels like a sort of liberation—until it becomes banal and we have need of the next liberation," argues the sociologist Todd Gitlin.[5]

But, for Richard, an immigrant newcomer, the desire for a car has as much to do with the desire to overcome the paralyzing social and geographical immobility that many residing in the United States face—the old, the young, and the poor. Through his car, he is free; he is free from social constraint, free to experience upward mobility. The ideal of easy mobility stands as a pillar of the elusive American Dream. Perhaps that is what makes the car so desirable for Richard in the first place.

Trading In and Trading Up: Freedom Ain't Free

But at what price? We are a culture that values mobility and autonomy. The unquenchable desire for independence is part of the modern condition, what Gitlin refers to as nomadicity—life lived on the fly. And it comes at a significant financial and social cost. The all-important independence so valued by youth is as much a symptom as it is a cause of splintering communities, a fracturing and weakening of public and social ties that has vexed sociologists for the past century. Our lives are largely spent alone and on the move, and the social bonds we maintain are primarily instrumental as our emotional ties are reserved for our most intimate and private relationships.[6] With the exception of city dwellers, without a car we realize our isolation. Seventeen-year-old Cesar's story is revealing in this regard.

> *Cesar*: I got stranded in the east side, the ghetto. Bird [a cop] straight up flashed the light in the back yard and everyone just fucking took off running, right? I was talking to this chick, just chopping it up and stuff I was like, I have to go find my friends, you know what I'm saying, I have to go to work tomorrow. She was like, no, no come with me, come with me, and she took me inside the house, 'cause she was close friends with the person who was throwing the party and I look out and everyone is gone and I was stranded in the house with this chick and I was all "fuck."
>
> *Maria*: So, what happened?
>
> *Cesar*: Some other girl ended up paging me and I was like, Dude, come pick me up.
>
> *Maria*: So, she came and picked you up? That's how you got home?
>
> *Cesar*: Yup. Yeah, she didn't know what I was doing. I was like, I was with some homies and I got stranded. I had to give her gas money, but that was a ride home. You know what I'm saying?
>
> *Maria*: Yeah, what about your friends, they took off, did they call you?

Cesar: No, I told them like, Don't leave without me! Like, but I don't
know. I kind of expected them, you know the cops were there. I
wouldn't have waited either.

It is perhaps most striking that, despite his desperate plea, Cesar had little to no expectation that his friends would wait around for him since,
as he admits himself, it's unlikely he would have returned the favor.

Beyond the social cost is the financial one. Kenny may be free to
drive himself where he wants to go, but there is no escaping his $700-
a-month car payment. Clearly, a large price is paid for this freedom,
which raises the question of whether Kenny is really free. Long hours
working at minimum-wage jobs and mounting debt are the price for
many. The extension of credit lines to youth and the widespread avail-
ability of zero-down financing (often at very high interest rates) and
long-term loans helps to explain the rising car ownership rates among
youth.[7] But there is no escaping the accumulation of debt they exchange
for their freedom. Instead, they join the ranks of people living beyond
their means in the United States, where the average unpaid credit card
balance for a household in 2002 was more than $8,940 and where rates
of personal bankruptcy have climbed steadily and rates of households
saving have declined.[8]

Consider Olie, who at the time of our interview had only "eight dollars to my name." He works installing stereos, making just above minimum wage while going to college full-time. "If I bust my ass, then I can
make a thousand dollars every two weeks." He too lives at home but
lets me know, "I pay for everything. I pay my own insurance, pay for
school." Like Kevin and Kenny, he has owned several cars. "The first
car I saved up like a thousand or something, my sister saved up a thousand, and we both pitched in to buy our first car. I sold it . . . and then I
took out a student loan for almost $3,000 to buy a car so I actually had
about $4,000. I got a '92 Integra, and it was actually almost $7,000."
He borrowed $3,000 from the man who sold him the car. "I had to pay
him interest, too. I was working at Macy's, so I paid that off." But as
luck would have it, Olie's Integra was stolen. Thanks to the insurance
payment, he spent about "thirteen-five" on a Honda Civic. "I was actually looking at Beemers, I was looking at Legends 'cause I could have
easily gotten one and just you know paid like twelve down and just do
payments." Ultimately, Olie decided against the double payments of a
car loan on top of the student loan whose proceeds he originally used

for the down payment on his second car, which, he reminds me, he still owes. When Olie graduates from college, he will owe the money borrowed to finance his education on top of the money borrowed to finance his car. Olie is not alone. In 2002, the average student graduating from college was $22,000 in debt. This number is expected to rise as the costs of higher education grow.[9]

Ava's situation is also revealing in this regard. Ava is twenty-two and lives at home in a lower-income area of the city. She is a full-time college student who also works full-time at a bank. She drives a brand-new sparkling white BMW 3-series. Though she has expressed a keen interest she has decided to postpone graduate school indefinitely, mainly to help support her working-class parents. They, after all, let her live at home through college while covering the cost of her room and board— a significant expense for them. She knows there is no way she can help out her parents, attend graduate school, and still keep her car.

It is not uncommon for young adults today, even well into their twenties, to live at home, especially in San Jose, where the cost of rent is so high. Many of those I spoke to are doing so in order to pay the sizable car expense for a high-priced car.[10] Ironically, just as their freedom seems to be finally gained, it just as quickly slips away. Banji, a young woman soon to graduate from college, has had her eye on the Audi A4, whose base list price is $27,000. Recently she has been pressured to move home. "My Mom really wants to teach me to cook and stuff and keep an eye on me and teach me how to be a good future wife or whatever." But Banji also *wants* to move home. "Once I get my bachelor's, I want to move back home because if I live with them then I won't really have to pay for rent. I'll have money so I think maybe I could buy it."

In some ways, the desire to have a nice car and not some "old bucket" reflects a broader pattern of competitive spending that is fundamental to the consumer ethos of American culture and constitutes the engine behind a kind of economic growth and prosperity that rarely translates into tangible improvements for most. Juliet Schor, author of *The Overspent American*, sees the "ever-escalating consumption norm" and "the pressures to spend"[11] as reflective of a larger trend toward social inequality and as part of a new consumerism defined in terms of "upscaling of lifestyle norms: the pervasiveness of conspicuous, status goods and of competition for acquiring them: and the growing disconnect between consumer desires and incomes."[12] A case in point is the fact that some young men who cruise Santa Clara Street rent high-end luxury vehicles, presenting them as their own.[13]

Those young adults who take the leap to purchase a nice car very quickly find themselves in situations where they cannot afford unanticipated car expenses. "My insurance premium is $121, and car payment is $375 a month. It's starting to hit me in the pocket," Anthony offers. Nineteen-year-old Chris admits, "Car payments are killing me as it is." This was also the case for Jack, seventeen, who now drives a used Caprice, which he bought from his stepfather only after first having had a brand-new Honda Civic. "I had a nicer car," he explains. "I had decided to try to pay it off, but I couldn't afford it. I had to give it back, which was a big mistake because I ended up losing thousands and thousands of dollars." Jack's situation is not altogether uncommon. A number of youth found themselves overwhelmed by the expense of a car and with few avenues out of the mess. Jack's parents "don't like to pay for things," he explains. "They figure I work, so I can pay for it." As the youth culture of spending intensifies in the new consumerism, many young adults, even before they are done with school, are locked into what Schor calls "the cycle of work and spend." They are hardly free.

Some of this may be explained by the fact that for suburban high schoolers, status systems play out around cars. As sociologists of education have noted, the wealthiest kids also tend to be the most popular kids because they have the material resources to enhance their visibility within the school, which serves as the basis of popularity.[14] Having a nice car provides one with the means to be elevated in the school's status structure, thus providing greater visibility.

As much as the desire to have a nice ride relates to status concerns, this is perhaps only half of the story. Cars are as much about being individuals, distinguishing oneself *from* the group, as they are about keeping up *with* the group. As so aptly captured in the edgy "Drivers Wanted" advertising campaign launched by Volkswagen of America, "On the road of life there are passengers and drivers."[15] A nice ride provides opportunity to fashion and communicate an image of one's self as unique and in charge of one's own life. The social philosopher Gilles Lipovetsky explains that "in a society of individuals committed to personal autonomy . . . the new offers such a lively attraction: it is experienced as an instrument of personal 'liberation', as an experience to be undertaken, an experience to be lived, a little adventure of the self."[16] Recall Olie, a college student who bought a Honda Civic, a desired car among youth. Outside school and work, Olie spent much of his time, energy and disposable income transforming his Civic into a complete original so that it would look nothing like its former self, that is, a stock Civic bought off the line. The interior and exterior were radically transformed; Olie even renamed the car in the hope of expressing something unique about himself through his car. His car generated a lot of buzz when he drove it because of its appearance and thus provided him with recognition and visibility as an individual apart from the crowd.

In today's society, where status systems are no longer fixed, identities are projects, things we must construct on our own.[17] As traditional institutions and social roles have come to mean less in terms of who we are, it is in the consumer market that these "identities are designed, tried on, worn for the evening and then traded in for the next," the sociologist Don Slater explains.[18] Youth are increasingly drawn into the consumer market and into a culture of spending to forge their identities as individuals as much as to gain membership in specific status groups. Thus, Amanda can say, "I'm more of a sports car person; [my sister] she's more of an SUV-type person," with the expectation that I will understand precisely what she means. It is in this context that cars can be conceived of as our "extended selves" and also part of what Juliet Schor calls the "new essentials," those things we simply cannot live without.[19]

When Any Car Will Do: Life without a Car and Other Tales of Woe

In many ways, car ownership patterns parallel the much-lamented "digital divide," since they reproduce the very class inequities they reflect, revealing and amplifying the fault lines between the "haves" and the "have-nots."[20] Allison, now twenty-two, recalls growing up in a wealthy community where everyone seemed to have been given a new car upon turning sixteen. "One friend got a Jetta, another one got a Jeep, another one got a little convertible BMW . . . depending on where we were going, we would decide which car we were going to take, you know, if we were going out dancing or something, we would take my friend's convertible car and if we were going to the beach, we'd take the Jeep." The ability to accessorize one's activities with a rotation of nice cars surely is a luxury available to very few. Jorge, a young Chicano student who attends an all-boys private school but resides in a lower-income neighborhood close to Freedom High School, described his school as having "a lot of rich white guys. Sixty-six percent white . . . most of them are pretty damn rich. So, you know . . . SUVs are popular, um, you'll see your, there's a good amount of luxury cars." Indeed, a visit to Bernards High School, Jorge's alma mater, revealed a student parking lot full of new cars and SUVs. "The only people who don't have cars are poor kids, to be honest with you. Not to be like financially racist or whatever but I went to St. Joseph's, so everybody had like Beemers and Mercedes and Land Cruisers," Mike explains as he describes life at his private school.

Wealthy kids often are given cars without a hitch. This was the case for Amanda, a young woman of twenty-one whose parents surprised her with a brand-new Pontiac Grand Am GT when she turned sixteen. "It was like a sports-car red, my favorite color, with gray interior," Amanda recalled with obvious pleasure as the two of us talked over coffee one afternoon. "I didn't know, I had no idea, when I came home from volleyball practice there was this new car and I said, 'Oh, who's over?' and my mom said, 'No one's over, that's your car.' So we pulled up and my mom stopped and I ran out of the car, you know. I was astounded 'cause every time my cousins got cars I was thinking, 'God, I wonder if my parents are going to get me a car?'" To Amanda's delight, they did. But she also knows that this was something her parents expected to do. "Both of my parents grew up in the '60s and my dad's parents were pretty well endowed so they gave my uncle and my dad brand-new cars when they started to drive, and the same thing for my mom, they all got brand-new cars. So my parents wanted to do the same for us." Lucena, a college student at one of the state universities in the Bay Area, recalls, "I knew a girl who had a car by her sophomore year [in high school], and she had like the new Mustang and I was like, Okay, go ahead, girl. If you're going to get a car, you need to get a *nice* car because people talk crap, you know, they'd be like, you've got a piece-of-shit car hooptie, you know what I mean?" This—not wanting to have a hooptie, that is—helps explain why middle- and lower-income kids, at least those who participated in this study, were willing to work long hours after school and on weekends, accruing sizable debt, to afford a nice car.[21]

However, kids who are among the working poor and the poorest of the poor are immobilized and often trapped because they are unable to afford a car in a culture whose dependence on cars is absolute. In a number of instances, they can't afford even to get a license, a cost most middle- and upper-class kids consider incidental. Such was the case for many kids I spoke with at Freedom High School, located in a low-income area of San Jose. "No point," explains one eighteen-year-old Freedom High student whose only disposable income came from the lunch money provided from home (and who passed on lunch each day in order to save that money for the weekend or to buy things over the Internet). "I don't even have a car to drive," Natasha offers. Natasha is one of the many sixteen-year-olds in this California community who has yet to get her license, despite being legally of age to do so.* "That's why I'm looking for a job," she explains. Her plans are "to save up for a little car, a bucket that can get me from here to school." Few kids at her school seem to have cars. "Everyone wants the 'Maro but I only knew a couple people. And there's one guy who just bought a Celica and some other guy has a Civic and some other people just have old Civics and buckets. So I guess whatever they could afford." Richard's words echo Natasha's: "In high school I had some friends who had cars, very few, um, most of my friends were immigrants like myself, most of the popular kids did drive, not a lot of the immigrant students drove, understandably for economic reasons and, um, or maybe some of them were deterred by language barriers."

Adriana is nineteen, a student at a local community college. She has neither a license nor a car. "I'm like nineteen years old, should have my license by now. I have two kids," she says, but she has not gotten her license "because I haven't had a car to go take the test." Her mother's car, shared with three other adults, has a standard shift, and Adriana knows how to drive only an automatic. To get around, she relies primarily on her mom or her brother. But this presents some problems for Adriana, since her mother "works all the time," and her brother is also unlicensed. "My brother could do it, I mean, he just needs to take driver's training, do that $200 program." Though Adriana claims her brother is lazy, I suspect it is the lack of money that prevents him from getting his license. Adriana's friends are also largely without cars, as she explains. "I went to a teen-mom school so I know that there, shit, well, teen moms we don't have a dime to our names, can't even pay for our

---

* The Insurance Institute for Highway Safety notes an overall decline nationally in drivers getting their licenses at sixteen since 1993. Available at http://www.iihs.org.

own kids. My best friend . . . she had a car and it was her and maybe three other girls that were students at my school who had cars. They were the cool ones and the rest of us rode the bus." Adriana finds traveling by bus with two young children nearly impossible and thus has little choice but to stay home much of the time. Cesar, a seventeen-year-old who also grew up in San Jose and is without a license, offers, "I'm saving up right now. I'm trying to spend like two or three thousand on this old car. There's a Thunderbird for sale over here on Seventh Street. It's like a older car, it's like a '56 or a '55, that's too old. They're selling it for like $4,000. That's too much."

These class inequities are transparent to those kids who go without cars. "The rich kids, freshmen year, those fuckers have cars. I went to Mitchell, you know what I'm saying? Nice-ass neighborhood. These kids are like fifteen driving big old Broncos and, yeah, they had it good, they had some nice rides," Cesar offers. "This is the 'hood, no one here gots cars, dude. Hey, no one here has, seriously all my close friends, none of them have cars, I can't think of one right now that has a car." Cesar is clearly tuned into the nuances of class, as were other middle- and lower-income young adults. Yet Cesar's comments also reveal that there is not a tidy class correspondence; class does not always determine one's ability to consume or how one consumes. Thus, while adamant that "the rich kids just get shit handed to them," Cesar also holds out for a slightly different version of reality: "Those little poor kids that work like crazy for their cars, those are the people with the rides." Alex Kotlowitz also observed the sometimes odd disconnect between class and consumption, noting, "the urban poor, a group despite its economic difficulties, represents a surprisingly lucrative market."[22] But, in the end, the story does remain the same. A small number of kids enjoy the freedom and mobility that come with a car, no strings attached. Unlike "those poor kids that work like crazy for their cars," they do not have to toil away in dead-end jobs to avoid a fall from a financial tightrope.[23] Others, like Natasha and Adriana, remain bound to place, unable to fully participate in the cultural and public life of the community. Recall Cesar's situation of being stranded, discussed earlier. Cesar had no easy way out of the mess he was in, largely for reasons that might be explained by class. Cesar is not a rich kid; in fact, he is without the amenities that are part of middle-class life, most important in this instance a car. Members of the middle class and the upper class have long used the cultural and economic resources within their grasp to navigate and resolve, even if only personally, the conflicts and troubles of modern life.[24] (Consider parents who place their children in private schools to escape a failing public school system.) They also use these resources, many drawn from a consumer market, to participate in public life. But, for those without, such possibilities are precluded. As Juliet Schor insightfully observes, "In a culture where consuming means so much, not having money is a profound social disability."[25]

Life in Silicon Valley

In more ways than one, the economic and social context of Silicon Valley, the community where all these young adults reside, is important for understanding the car's cultural significance for youth as they transition into adulthood, as they construct their identities as individuals and think about cars as status markers. As I began this chapter, I argued that, for a growing number of young adults, the car is central to the very essence of social existence. Literally an extension of its owner, the car serves as a bridge between the owner's inner and outer worlds. I also argued that through the car, young people see themselves as free, but they also must deal with the contradictory elements of this so-called freedom, a freedom that is unavailable to many young adults whose participation in the consumer market is limited. But to understand why the car assumes such significance in the first place, one must also appreciate the culture and character of Silicon Valley.[26]

Whether one is eighteen or eighty, everyday life in Silicon Valley is difficult without a car. As in a host of other urban areas marked by rapid development—Dallas, Atlanta, and Los Angeles come to mind—in Silicon Valley cars are as much a part of the physical and social landscape as the people.[27] Fewer than 6 percent of families in San Jose are without a car, and even fewer residents regularly use public transit, in large part due to limited service.[28]

Daily life in Silicon Valley can be aptly described in terms of nearly constant change. "Engendered by incessant innovation, consumerist frenzy, economic spurts and sputters, sharp social contradictions" is how one local publication described San Jose.[29] The pace of life at home, at work, and on the road borders on the frenetic, and there is a tangible sense of time spent on the move. San Jose is marked by rapid transformation, deepening social and economic polarization, and high levels of residential and occupational segregation among its various ethnic groups.[30] All can be tied to the expansion and concentration of the high-tech industries in the area.

The epicenter of the technological revolutions of the past quarter century, today San Jose stands as the third largest city in California and the eleventh largest in the United States. San Jose's increasing involvement in a rapidly changing capitalist economy, organized by local and global capitalists over the past several decades, has generated a tremendous concentration of wealth in San Jose and in greater Santa Clara County. San Jose has experienced immense economic growth that has transformed social and economic life, including the cultural and physical landscape, in dramatic ways.[31] Long-time residents have witnessed rapid residential and commercial expansion. Housing, retail, and office space have replaced once seemingly endless fruit orchards. Many residents in the area have enjoyed an unrivaled prosperity in the new economy, and this can be seen in the types of cars on the highway, the real estate development, the influx of upscale retail chains, and the expansion of retail space. At the height of the economic boom, in 2000, one in nine households had a net worth surpassing $1 million.[32] The astonishing wealth created by the "dot.com" boom gave rise to a highly visible and seemingly pervasive culture of wealth and conspicuous consumption that the cultural critic John de Graaf has aptly termed "affluenza," a condition characterized by "stress, overwork, waste and indebtedness caused by a dogged pursuit of the American Dream."[33]

As a result, the young men and women of Silicon Valley are part of a culture of wealth and spending even if they themselves are not affluent. This culture of consumer affluence seeps into the crevices of everyday life, embedding itself in the fabric of this community's most banal routines such that the truly wealthy become the primary reference group to the larger community.[34] The consequence of this is a consumer desire that is far afield from the reality of most of these young people's lives. Perhaps only in this context can Kenny claim with a surprising assuredness that he would be willing to dedicate two-thirds of his income to his car.

This culture of wealth and consumer spending, while failing to either improve or reflect the lives of the majority, obscures the poverty that has also taken root in San Jose. The economic shifts from a solid manufacturing base (primarily canneries) to an economy based on information technology and electronics in the 1960s and 1970s and San Jose's increased participation in a postindustrial economy over the past three decades has contributed to huge disparities in wealth, since a decline in manufacturing has also meant the disappearance of unionized wages. Much like other cities of the twenty-first century, San Jose is marked by widening economic and social polarization stemming from a two-tiered labor market.[35] According to the 2000 U.S. Census, three out of ten families could boast yearly incomes exceeding $100,000, though two out of ten households had incomes less than $35,000.[36] As the historian Glenna Matthews remarked in her recent labor history of Silicon Valley, "In the early twenty-first century, Silicon Valley's rewards are so disproportionately going to the haves at the expense of the have-nots that it may take another shakeup of some magnitude to extend the benefits of the California Dream of prosperity more broadly."[37]

The decline of economic opportunity for the broader community in San Jose has been compounded by a staggering increase in the cost of living. Despite declines in real wages over the past several decades, housing and rental markets remain extraordinarily inflated. In 2001, rent was twice the national average; more than 40 percent of residents paid more than one-third of their household income in rent.[38] The shortage of housing during a period of extraordinary economic growth has also created a devastating rate of inflation in housing prices. Today, the housing market remains beyond the reach of most of area residents. In 2004, the average single-family home in Santa Clara County cost $599,000, and the average-price condo in that same year cost $385,000.[39] Importantly, more than 50 percent of homeowners carry mortgages with monthly payments that exceed $1,500.[40] With the affordability index hovering just above 20 percent, home ownership is increasingly remote for many area residents;[41] this index means that only 20 percent of all current residents would be able to buy the median-price home if they were to attempt to purchase it today (in fact, more than 60 percent of residents live in owned homes, purchased years ago). This is significant on several different levels. It has consequences for the ability of the middle class to maintain itself across generations since home ownership has long been central to the reproduction of socioeconomic status. The remoteness of home ownership also has consequences for immigrant families and the new working class, since, historically, upward mobility and the accumulation of wealth, at least in the twentieth century, were secured in large part through home ownership.[42]

Youth are especially challenged by the changing economic and social reality of Silicon Valley.[43] They are the least likely to be able to own homes (even if they grew up in one) and also the least likely to find a secure, well-paying job. They are less likely to be able to afford the rising cost of higher education, yet they are likely to need it more. As one particularly perceptive middle-class seventeen-year-old remarked, "Hope my parents leave me the house or something. Housing costs are a lot, and, being a teacher, I probably wouldn't be making too much."[44]

The remoteness of home ownership (despite a national housing boom), and the visible and seemingly pervasive culture of wealth and conspicuous consumption in Silicon Valley, combined with the fact that this California community was designed around the car, create a situation where cars carry tremendous importance as consumer objects. The car has replaced the home as the measure of having made it, and is perhaps the ultimate mark of one's success in the eyes of the larger community. As members of the community, youth, too, feel the pull of consumer desire as they struggle with an economy that in the long term seems to promise them only growing economic marginalization and uncertainty. For many youth, the car is a means to manage this economic uncertainty and, for some, to postpone having to face a worsening economic reality.

Further on Down the Road: Dreams Deferred and Other Futures

Whether rich, poor, or somewhere in between, Silicon Valley's youngest live in a world where wealth appears to be just beyond the next turn, ultimately within their grasp. Perhaps this explains why nearly all of the more than one hundred youth whose voices fill these pages characterize their futures in terms of financial success and stability, squarely within the middle-class fantasy of "having arrived." When asked to imagine their "possible selves" twenty years down the road, that is the version of themselves, projected into the future, that inspires action, most see themselves eventually professionally successful, married with children, settled in nice homes, and driving nice cars.[45] Consider Anthony's remarks:

AO: Hopefully, God willing, I'll be married, have a kid or two, hopefully.
AB: Why would you say hopefully?
AO: I don't know. Hopefully, I mean cause I can't tell the future, I can't

control the future but that's how I envision it. I'll be a lawyer by then, a successful lawyer, driving around in a Mercedes or a BMW and just on the weekends having my hot ride and just driving that for show, pretty much.

AB: Will you be living in San Jose?

AO: San Jose, L.A., or somewhere in the area, Fremont, Milpitas, something like that.

AB: So why a BMW or Mercedes?

AO: I don't know, it's a, the status that comes along with that, would be within my range, it's not too showy, it's just the perfect fit for me, I would think.

AB: What would be too showy?

AO: Um, pretty much nothing. Nothing would be too showy.

Others, as they responded to my question about what the future held in store, followed suit. By and large, the majority look forward to futures replete with the accoutrements of an upper-middle-class life.[46]

Well, hopefully I'm making money. I'll be thirty-nine; probably a big SUV cause hopefully by then I'll have kids. Probably a nice Expedition or you know a Suburban or a Yukon, probably a Yukon. —*Lucena, 19*

Hopefully a Beemer. I think a four-door but I don't know the exact model yet . . . I've just seen it, silver because that would be my family car, hooked up with everything . . . top of the line. —*Karen, 21*

You know when I'm thirty-seven, I'll have some money then. I want to be an art teacher, like a high school art teacher. You know right now what kind of family car I like, right. I like the Chrysler, the 300 series. . . . Those have some rims, you know what I'm saying? Those are huge, dude. Yup, that would be a cool-ass family car [laughing]. —*Cesar, 17*

I'd like a Range Rover. I think they're nice cars and they're good-looking cars. I don't know if they're necessarily economic or like, environmentally sound, but I think they're nice. —*Allison, 22*

My Sunday car would be the Cobra R. Annnnd my regular day-to-day job . . . car would be my Mustang . . . my Ford Mustang, that would be my day-to-day car. —*Gustavo, 19*

In twenty years . . . I'm probably gonna be a soccer mom. I'll probably
have numerous vehicles. I'll probably have like a minivan to transport
kids and . . . probably transport soccer balls, I don't know, whatever
sports they want to play, whatever they want to do. And then I'll have
like my truck or something that I can drive on my own.   —*Helen, 20*

No doubt a number of readers will see the gap between aspirations and
attainment as a reflection of the fanciful, if not unrealistic, imaginings
of the young. But context also matters here. Their seeing themselves
having "nice rides" has as much to do with the culture of wealth and
conspicuous consumption in Silicon Valley and elsewhere, and their
desire to spend, as it has to do with the impractical expectations of the
young. Significantly, I also asked participants to identify their dream
car: "If you could have any car, what it would be?" In almost all cases,
the car they dreamed of having and the cars they expected to have as
adults were different. Dream cars included the rare and the enormously
expensive: the Lamborghini, the Ferrari, the Viper, high-end BMWs and
Mercedeses, Bentleys and Rolls Royces. In this sense, these young adults
distinguish between their dream cars and the car they expect to have in
their adult lives. The majority of cars they expected to have range in
price, though most fell between $35,000 and $60,000—cars considered
part of the "near-luxury" or "luxury" market by industry insiders. Certainly, some of the youth in this community will have the sort of future
that will allow them to own such expensive cars; others, unable to afford such luxury, will readjust their goals. Yet, if today tells us anything
about tomorrow, a large number will overextend themselves to achieve
what is increasingly the unachievable.

The majority of San Jose youth, who might have at another time in
U.S. history and under a different set of conditions sought a secure living as unionized workers in the canneries that once dominated the area,
face uncertain and unstable futures. Silicon Valley's youth today, like the
youth of other U.S cities, will be forced to confront not only the loss of
manufacturing jobs and a dwindling union base (as older family members have faced) but also global corporations that have outsourced
much of production and a so-called recovering economy that has failed
to create any real job growth. They will meet head-on the escalating
costs of education and housing, a marked increase in unemployment,
and ever-growing income disparities as they assume the responsibilities
of adulthood.[47] Many will hold down two jobs, as they do now, as part

of a growing underclass. If not already, they will become members of what Saskia Sassen has called the new "serving classes" that support the economic life of cities.[48]

In only a few instances was there concern about what lies ahead. Some spoke about what California's astonishing budget crisis will mean for them in terms of their ability to afford and ultimately complete college in a state where public higher education was once free. Some expressed worry about opportunities to secure a living wage. For young adults like Eve, there was far less confidence in what the future held for them. Perhaps Eve's realism stems from watching her parents, poor Mexican immigrants, labor in both factory and field for much of their lives only to end up, ultimately, without jobs. Her mother is now on disability. When Eve finishes college, she hopes to become a probation officer and have two or three kids. She sees herself always having to but also wanting to work. She knows she has to finish school but at twenty is tired from both going to school full-time and working full-time. "That's why I took out the loan," she explains. "I know that if I don't finish school, it's not going to take me anywhere, and I need to finish school to do what I want to do. My dad always use to tell me, don't end up like me, you know—never-ending job." She tells me, "I don't give cars my priority. I'd rather spend my money on what I consider as something more useful. There are bills out there." Yet she does offer that "when I have my kids, I want to start their own savings account, not towards college but for a car," suggesting that cars are not as much outside her purview as she first proposed. For her own future, however, she suggests that "I'm not expecting anything fancy." But even Eve, who longs for "just living a comfortable life . . . without the stress that I'm facing now," who also wants to stay in Silicon Valley "because of my parents," even though "everything's so expensive," imagines for a moment, "maybe the BMW, who knows." Lucena, who bought her Honda Civic because it is "reliable" and gets "good gas mileage," offered, "I didn't want like a flashy car or whatever, showoff, because for what? First of all, I'm going to college; second of all, that could come later because I'm going to college to get a good job to buy whatever I want." She has complete faith that her education will pay off in the form of a good job, perhaps a nice car, too, and additional expressions of material success.

For most of these young adults, much attention is paid to what they "might" have relative to what they have now. Many of them seemed to delight in thinking about their futures as far off down the road. Perhaps the stable futures they imagine for themselves are what enable them to cope with a transforming social world in which where one is going is far from clear and the social roles that once provided direction are both less appealing and less possible. Cars are likely to continue to grow in importance as other means to assess one's place in the world (e.g., buying a home) move increasingly beyond the grasp of the majority. The middle-income kids of San Jose, with rare exceptions, are unlikely to be able to buy homes if they stay in San Jose. If they are anything like other young adults today, they are likely to postpone marriage and having children, since they will be unwilling to assume these financial responsibilities on top of the debt they already carry. But they are likely to continue to buy cars, seeing them as the means to find their way in a changing world and as a way to participate in the quickening pace of daily life where speed and mobility are more and more valued.

Our current economic system has subverted the grand narrative that has traditionally directed our lives.[49] Gone is the sense of security that one will marry, have children, buy a home, hold down a stable and permanent job.[50] This instability is a symptom of the postmodern condition. The erosion of this master narrative may help to explain the wholesale turn to the consumer market as a place where meaning is created.[51] As consumers, young people come to see themselves as individuals. This is perfectly captured in Allison's remarks as she talks about her life down the road: "I never wanted a minivan. I always wanted like a Range Rover instead of a minivan." When I ask, "How come?" she is initially slow to respond. "I don't know, just the minivan and everything that's attached to it like, soccer mom. I'm not into that. I don't know why. I think it's so much like pack the kids in and rush, rush, and do everything. Where the Range Rover, maybe you can still sort of maintain some sort of identity, like with the minivan, you don't have an identity. You're a mom if you have a minivan." Allison contemplates what it would mean for her to drive a minivan as she constructs and imagines the sort of womanhood she will embrace in her adult life. The minivan is defined as a marker of a woman's relationship to the home. As she refuses to imagine herself driving the minivan, Allison essentially rejects a model of womanhood tied to a middle-class, suburban home and domestic life (even though she does assume that these domestic responsibilities will be hers). To be a soccer mom is to lose one's sense of individuality, to be engaged only in activities that serve the needs of others, and to be closed off from a more public world. Without question, her relationship to cars is a relation mediated by wornout gender notions that often narrowly construct the possibilities for mothers and young women. But this is precisely the point. It is through the consumer market, through her choice of cars, that she finds her way out from under the weight of conventional gender scripts. Through her consumer choices, she crafts an identity outside social constraints. Just like Kenny and Tom, whose stories you'll recall from the beginning of this chapter, the car is her means to an end.

And at that end, the freedom these young adults desire through the car slips away from them as they become entrenched in a culture of consumption. The basis of their individuality is increasingly dependent on what they consume, and the means by which they find their place in the world is inseparable from the market place. Certainly, there are many young adults who forgo the trappings of consumer desire and buy used cars that offer basic transportation. But even many of these young adults, like Eve and Lucena, hold onto dreams of brighter futures and shinier cars, their success in life given expression through the car. These young adults seem to be stuck in a no-win situation. They know, as I do, that to reject the car is to forgo the mobility so valued by American culture and to be trapped, bound to place, and unable to participate in public and cultural life. For youth in large cities, where public transportation is widely available, these problems are probably remote, but they are not for young people in communities like San Jose, where daily life plays out across large stretches of space. Many other cities are laid out like San Jose. In this sense, the points I raise in this final chapter have consequences for young adults across the United States.

In 2004, I moved from California to northern Virginia, just outside Washington, D.C., settling in an area that has some similarities to San Jose. There is a large concentration of wealth generated in part by the expansion of the tech industry in northern Virginia and a culture of consumption that is visible in the cars people drive and the importance of shopping as a popular pastime. There is a stunning number of two-income, professional families and a large immigrant population. Life in northern Virginia revolves mostly around the car. People spend hours sitting in traffic, complaining endlessly about it, just as they did in San Jose. Housing prices are seriously inflated, and many people's work lives and family lives play out in different communities. I see here in

Virginia that a cultural importance is attached to cars by young people (and those in other age groups) in a way that suggests that cars' significance for youth in Silicon Valley is repeated elsewhere in the country. The car is an object that carries much meaning and that is essential for the way youth convey a sense of who they are and where they are going to themselves and to others.

Conclusion
The Ride of Your Life

Christine lives with her grandmother Jessie and her two Chihuahuas, Sugar Baby and Sassy Girl, in a small house in southern California. She drives a beatup 1992 Civic that was once red but is now white with an eyesore of a dent just above the rusted rim of one of the back wheels. "Things are popping out all over the place," she laughingly explains as she struggles to push the center console back into its rightful place. Her friends call her Civic "swamp thing" because of the puddles of dirty water that accumulate on the floor of the car after it has rained. She is "the last person on earth who owns a cassette player," she declares as she points to the dated stereo system in her car, and her car alarm, which seems to work only when she doesn't need it, is decidedly "possessed." Though grateful her granddaughter is willing to drive her to her doctor, Christine's grandmother confesses that she is more than a little afraid, and Christine's boyfriend admits his concern when Christine must drive alone on the highway. That is why Christine has asked MTV to "pimp my ride."

When the host of the popular MTV reality show *Pimp My Ride*, the rapper Xzibit, shows up at Christine's door one afternoon "to make her Civic bling," all she can say is "Oh my God, oh my God," as tears of elation stream down her face. "Swamp thing" undergoes a radical transformation when it is taken to West Coast Customs, a high-end custom auto shop. With sleek seventeen-inch chrome rims, low-profile BMG tires, a new sunroof, $6,000 vertical doors, and a robotic wing, Christine questions if the car is even hers. Assured that it is, she takes a look inside. The car's interior has been outfitted with custom-tailored purple racing seats and an interior to match the car's new exterior, an updated dashboard and controls, a ten-inch flip-down monitor, a Play Station II, the new "bazooka fake nitrous oxide woofer boxes," a six-disc CD changer, and a custom car alarm featuring Xzibit's booming voice warning, "Yo, back up."[1] In the passenger seat is a one-of-a-kind massage chair that "not even Mercedes, Rolls Royce, or Bentley have." Installed in the car's trunk are two small removable doggie dishes so that Christine can feed Sugar Baby and Sassy Girl when on the fly.

Danelle, a busy college student from the California coast, was also selected to have her car pimped by MTV's *Pimp My Ride*. She drives a 1981 Trans Am, a car that was once an American Muscle car classic but is now a wornout bucket of a car. Her father had bought the Trans Am years ago with plans to restore it. But he was short on money and time, and that soon became a distant dream, and the car was passed to Danelle as is. The rearview mirrors are attached to the car with electrical tape. The seat covers are cracked and ripped with more foam exposed than not; the metal springs jab Danelle in her backside whenever she gets behind the wheel. Her windows and T-top roof leak, and the car's exterior is painted with five shades of fading black, "all ugly." Danelle's friend says, "Danelle is glamorous, but that car is not." Perhaps that's why she gets "the look . . . eyes staring at my car, like, 'Is she serious?'" as she drives to school. Explaining why she thought her car should be made over by MTV's *Pimp My Ride,* Danelle offers, "I feel that I am a strong, professional, intelligent young woman. I want my hot rod to be even hotter." The folks at MTV agreed: "A fancy girl deserves a fancy car."

A fancy car is what Danelle, "a busy girl on the go," got. Giovanni twenty-inch chrome rims, high-performance Pirelli tires, and a Clarion CD player with 6.4-inch display were among the $30,000 worth of accessories that enabled Xzibit to put "the smoke back into this bandit." Danelle's Trans Am's radical transformation also included a small crystal chandelier in place of a standard dome light, an espresso machine to "help her through finals," and a state-of-the-art, miniature Sony laptop computer installed in the glove compartment. In the trunk of Danelle's Trans Am has been installed a vanity mirror, a coat rack, a makeup case filled with MAC cosmetics, and a working steamer to enable Danelle to always be at her most glamorous, "to always look good going to class" even when on the go.

The success of MTV's *Pimp My Ride* is revealing. This reality TV makeover show, which transforms jalopies into pimped-out dream cars, as farfetched and fanciful as it is, provides meaningful clues about the changing world in which young people are becoming adults. Both Christine's and Danelle's stories zero in on a key aspect of life in an rapidly changing and increasingly mobile world in which large chunks of our time are spent in cars. That a car's interior might be outfitted with a TV, a massage chair, a Play Station II, an espresso machine, and a laptop signals the ascendance of a car's interior as an important social space—a lived space. These stories also highlight a deepening connection between one's identity and one's car. The changes made to Christine's and Danelle's cars were tailored to express what was unique to them and, in this sense, expressed something entirely individual. *Pimp My Ride* makes clear that cars serve as moorings to help anchor identities. This is increasingly the case as the routines of everyday life play out in the trenches of a frenetically paced consumer society.

Kids' relationships to cars involve far higher stakes than simply debating the merits of having a convertible over a hard top. For decades, cars have been important sites for cultural production, self-representation, socializing, and peer interaction for young adults. Indeed, the car carried significance for America's youth long before most of them had one. In the 1950s, few people under twenty owned cars of their own, but Friday and Saturday nights often revolved around them, anyway. Today, a growing number of youth own their own cars, and many more borrow a parent's car in order to engage a public world beyond home and family. For youth today, a very large part of their sense of their being in this world, their ability to participate both physically and symbolically in American cultural life, depends on the car.[2] Cars also provide opportunity to explore a number of social themes of contemporary relevance: individualism, freedom, and the formation of modern selfhood, consumption, mobility, visibility, status, and changing meanings of public life.

Today's kids live in a world "of changing relationships between public and private, between local and global, between structure and movement, between bodily experience and subjectivity, between self and other."[3] They live in a world organized by what the sociologist Anthony Giddens has called a "posttraditional order" where time and space are radically altered and abstract systems increasingly mediate local life, transforming our most enduring relationship: the relationship of the self to society.[4] Writing about modernity and consumer culture, the sociologist Don Slater has argued, "Modernity dismantles a stable social order which provides fixed values and identities . . . the individual's boundaries, sources of meaning, social relations and needs become blurred and uncertain. This is the context of consumer culture: it floods modernity with a torrent of values, meanings, selves and others, both filling in the cultural deficits of the modern world and constantly intensifying and exploiting them."[5] Advanced capitalism has subverted the grand narratives that have traditionally directed the shape of our lives. As discussed in the preceding chapter, the certainty that one will marry, have children, buy a home, and hold down a stable and permanent job belongs to an era different from the one in which today's youth are becoming adults.

The erosion of this master narrative explains in part the turn to the consumer market as a field where meaning is created. Youth live in a world where the social roles, norms, and institutions that once anchored individual and collective identities (many social roles are less appealing than they once were) have given way to alternative forms of social existence arranged in terms of the "individual as consumer."[6] As Slater has argued, "consumer culture is the privileged medium for negotiating identity and status within a post-traditional society."[7] The consumer culture has increasingly become a primary site of importance where youth give meaning to their lives and identities, as the logic directing a culture of consumption seeps into the consciousness of the young (and the old). Certainly, the car's ubiquity in American life speaks volumes about our identities as consumers and the triumph of consumerism over other modes of existence as a way of life. Youth, even if they do not always have wheels of their own, are firmly a part of this social arrangement. Today, cars serve as "extended selves," part of "the new essentials" that are increasingly difficult to live without.[8]

How are the young making sense of the world in which they are becoming adults? How do they see themselves in this world? What clues might cars provide? These are the questions that inspired this research project. I have tried to answer them as I've worked to unravel the tangled threads of social life that swirl around the car in San Jose where life is lived on the fly. Understanding the culture of San Jose is important for understanding the car's cultural significance for youth as they transition into adulthood, as they construct their identities as individuals and think about cars as status markers, as they participate in a culture of spending, and as they create a set of moral and aesthetic boundaries of distinct car scenes.

I have explored how kids engage with American car culture as they navigate community and family life and the youth car cultures that arise in these contexts. I have been concerned with mapping the quotidian and varied meanings that arise out of youths' encounters with a changing world order and what these meanings might reveal about the physical and symbolic boundaries organizing young adults' inner and outer lives. I have been concerned with the place of cars as youth articulate a distinctive youth politics, solidify their identities, participate in a culture of consumption, pursue the elusive American dream, lay claim to public space, and struggle against the structural limits in which they find themselves.[9] And, I have argued, deeply entrenched relations structured by gender and sexuality, race and class, nationality and citizenship status inform how youth make sense of and use cars as they negotiate the perimeters of culture and public life.[10] I have argued that through their cars, young people see themselves as essentially free, yet recognize the contradictions inherent in that freedom.

Road Tests

I have argued that identity is a central point around which these negotiations play out and can be seen. A few things can be said about youth identities in a posttraditional context. Identity formation today occurs in a context where "the self is seen as a reflexive project for which the individual is responsible," argues Anthony Giddens.[11] "Identity moves from a 'given' into a 'task' . . . such that needing to *become* what one *is* is a feature of modern living," explains Zygmunt Bauman.[12] In this context, youth are called upon to fashion their own identities, to think of the self as a willful project of inventing, reinventing, and refining. There are visible signs of these undertakings everywhere. The dramaturgical work of crafting a self becomes increasingly elaborate as young adults are drawn into the folds of a culture of consumption, where possibilities for self-refinement and reinvention abound.[13]

Youth try on different identities through cars. Through and around their cars, kids engage in a form of identity play. Recall Tom, who in two short years had owned five cars, each representing an aspect of his identity he'd hoped to signify to himself and to the world. This sense of identity play can also be seen as young women imagine the kind of car they will drive in adulthood. Recall Allison's desire for an SUV over a minivan and the extent to which it was bound to her sense of being free from conventional gender scripts. The possibilities for identity invention and reinvention appear limitless, largely because there are so many choices available to consumers. This perhaps explains the popularity of *Pimp My Ride,* where almost any kind of renovation can be done to the car—a flat-screen TV that emerges from the trunk or a tail pipe that emits streams of bubbles. This belief provides youth with a sense of freedom, an especially important option given the restrictions under which most of them live.

Both the racing and the cruising scenes engender fields of play; the moral and aesthetic boundaries of these scenes are fluid, and the actors and actions in flux. As young men and women cruise up and down the several blocks of Santa Clara Street where cruising is concentrated, they try out and on different identities. Young women try on different ways of being girls, loud and raucous, having a laugh, getting one over on a guy, giving out their numbers, hanging out of their cars, all in an attempt to be seen, to gain visibility, and to win public acknowledgment of these identity plays and displays. There is far more flexibility for girls today as they construct their identities as young women than existed at most other historical moments in America. Clearly the young women who made their way down Santa Clara Street enjoyed the chance to try on different ways of doing gender, of performing different sexual selves, and of testing out different rhetorical and interactional styles.

Still, believing in limitless options to construct identity requires young women to navigate the slippery slope of contemporary femininity —the new girlhoods, where young women are supposed to have power and be self-determining and in control of their lives and destinies. Young women, too, are responsible for the project of the self, after all. Perhaps this explains why young women so fiercely demand access to this space, delighting in the outrageous and decadent play of identities as they transgress the moral boundaries that exist elsewhere. Yet, young women who choose to cross the perimeters of this masculine space must carefully manage and negotiate their presence in it. For these girls, the negotiation hinges upon their ability to creatively push and pull, invert and invoke the cultural codes that define femininity and female sexuality. They attempt to maneuver around these limits, at times stretching them, other times upholding them. These young women negotiate around changing meanings of girlhood, rejecting the "good-girl code" while also invoking it as they rein themselves and other girls in. Their actions cast doubt on the possibility of a resistance that is truly trans-formative, inviting us to revisit how cultural studies scholars and sociologists have understood the relationship between power and resistance, structure and agency, among youth.

The endless possibility of refashioning identities through what we consume creates and reflects a situation where identities are less clear, less certain, and less stable. This creates a type of existential angst about who one really is. Youths' struggle for authenticity—to be authentically men or authentically Chicano, for example—plays out around the car. This can be seen in young Chicanos' search for a concrete place to anchor their ethnic identities through cruising. Young Chicanos/as who cruise Santa Clara Street are engaged in the active reinvention of ethnicity as they invest this activity with meaning about who they are as Chicanos/as. Through cruising, they imagine a sense of ethnic solidarity. But the community they search for is not place-bound but time-bound; it is a community that exists in the past, thus making their search all the more difficult. These young Chicanos/as retrace the steps of those who came before them, engaging in a set of cultural activities that their uncles and older cousins once performed in an attempt to bring into being a community in struggle and to anchor their identities as Chicanos/as therein. They encounter a set of struggles that fortifies their links to the generations before them; recall the police harassment these young folks detailed. But they also face new struggles; the gentrifying transformations in the downtown have made cruising and the symbolic connections it once provided more difficult to create.

There is also a struggle for masculine authenticity that plays out through cars. As social roles are less likely to serve as guides for action and identity formation, young men must craft other ways to recognize themselves as masculine, lest they face a crisis of being.[14] As I argued in chapter 3, young men's participation in the world of cars and car racing provides a space to manage the existential dilemmas of masculine authenticity as they create a set of boundaries through which masculinity is reaffirmed as a position of power and autonomy.

The car-racing scene is a significant site where young men construct accounts of who "we" and "they" are and in this sense serves as a space through which racial ideas are formed, circulated, and recycled in ways that have consequences for youth identity formation.[15] As these young men construct their own identities, they rely heavily on notions of the hypermasculine "other" and the feminized "other," both constructs recognized by the group as masculine imposters. The strategic use of racial terms that discredit other young men is one avenue of becoming authentically male. A legacy of race and cultural racism becomes important for the boundary pushing these young men undertake as they attempt to draw both symbolic and moral distinctions between real racers and imposters, between "real" masculine men and mere posers. Thus, young men, as they struggle to gain recognition and visibility as authentic men, re-inscribe a racial order of masculinity.

Struggles for visibility and authenticity also explains young men's search for an intense experience through racing and risky driving. The intensity of experience young men draw from racing, being at the edge and making it back, affirms the self as something that is authentically real. They race to *feel* the intense sensation that provides the means to anchor themselves within a physical world where one's existence is known because it is felt.

In many ways, these points reflect concerns that early sociologists, Emile Durkheim in particular, raised about eroding mechanisms of social integration for individuals in the context of rapid change and the internal struggles they engender. For Durkheim, the rapid transformation brought on by modern society produced a sense of boundlessness captured in his concept of anomie. Young Chicanas'/os' efforts to construct an imaginary "us" through cruising might be understood as an attempt to ward off a creeping sense of anomie as external forces provoke a variety of internal changes in the Chicano community.[16] Parallels might also be drawn between youth's pursuit of intense experience through which they construct identity and the early modern sociologist, Georg Simmel's discussion of the "blasé attitude."[17] For Simmel, the blasé attitude is an ironic, indifferent stance that individuals adopt to cope with the emotional emptiness that modern life demands. As all social relations are subject to increasing rationalization, thereby becoming increasingly impersonal, *real* feeling created by *deep* emotional connection is threatened. Individuals adopt a blasé attitude in order to protect their inner worlds where feeling is expressed, but, paradoxically, this produces a desire for more intense feeling. This longing for intensity helps to explain young men's desire to experience the rush of driving at breakneck speeds and the rush young women feel as they transgress the boundaries of everyday life and soak in the excess of fanciful parade as they cruise.

In a context where the possibilities of constructing who one is appears to know no bounds, the pressure to generate identity is more intense, yet the traditional moorings around which this is done are less secure. The blurring boundaries between the real and the imagined also arise in a posttraditional context, creating a struggle for authenticity that appears to have no immediate resolution. For youth, this is further complicated by the fact that public life is where identities are formed, performed, and played out. As youth move into public spaces, they confront other problems, having less to do with their inner worlds than with the external world they inhabit.

Proceed with Caution

Kids' engagement with cars demonstrates the struggles they encounter as they attempt to participate in public life on their own terms. These struggles arise from boundaries of definition—that is, who youth are as person/nonpersons, citizen/noncitizens, actor/nonactors. Much has been written in recent years about the social organization of youth, with attention to the new realities they confront and the meaningful economic and social changes responsible for these new realities. Yet mainstream accounts of youth continue to define them with little sense of history, without the quality of mind C. Wright Mills defined decades ago as "the sociological imagination." Many adults have little appreciation of the ways in which biography and history collide in the everyday realities of youth and too willingly accept the familiar refrain that youth, teens in particular, really are a "tribe apart," naturally cut from a different cloth than adults. Surely readers are familiar with recycled images of youth overrun by the swell of hormones, bereft of rational thought, obsessed with trifling preoccupations such as high school popularity and who's dating whom. For youth in their early twenties, images abound of a shiftless, hyperindulged generation without moral anchors, direction, or aspirations. Anchored by a model of "youth deficits" that has now extended to the entire under-twenty-five set, these images pigeonhole youth against images of adults as moral, reasoned actors, exercising full self-control. Despite historical and empirical challenges to these views, they have tremendous currency in popular thought and are shared among parents, educators, and policymakers—the omnipotent "experts" on the young.[18] They give rise to policies such as curfews, anti-cruising ordinances, and the recent graduated driver's licensing laws, that narrowly construct youth identities and limit youths' engagement in public life as emerging citizens and community actors.[19] These policies criminalize youth for engaging in commonplace activities that adults are permitted to engage in freely, while also serving as a foil for our anxieties and concerns about other things. According to the National Highway Traffic Safety Administration, 3,657 drivers ages 15–20 died in traffic accidents in 2003. Yet they received far more media attention than the nearly 40,000 other drivers who also died that year. Societal concern for the destruction caused by modern car culture focuses too narrowly on youth.

Panic about youth and risk on the road reflects concern over the status of youth and the extent to which adults see them as being entitled to participate in public life. Youth struggle to remain visible despite concerted efforts by the state and policymakers to render them invisible, relegated to the sidelines of public life. These policy actions ironically occur within a context in which adults bemoan declining rates of civic engagement among youth. While it remains unclear whether our complaints about youths' political apathy are warranted, what is clear is that this generation of young adults has been brought up in a world that actively works to position them on the margins of public life. Not only are their voices censored but their bodies are refused and removed from public centers. Efforts to "keep kids off the street" in downtown San Jose is but one example of this. There has been a widespread adoption of curfews and anticruising ordinances across the United States in the past decade. The sociologist Mike Males argues, "Californians continue to believe today's youth perpetuate unheard-of savageries and require harsher policing. Not just delinquents but average teens increasingly are shackled with daytime and nighttime curfews, curtailments on driving."[20] These policies affect the way young people assess their value in their own communities. It is hardly surprising than fewer than 15 percent of youth in Santa Clara County reported that they felt valued by their community, according to the Cornerstone Project, a nonprofit organization dedicated to fostering youths' resilience in the face of the current economic and political assault facing them. Rather than finding ways of fostering young people's attachments to community and to place, we as a culture isolate youth from a dynamic, albeit contested, public world where community life is formed.

While policymakers and legislators fail to listen to the young folks in their communities, marketers are tuned in, dedicating countless hours of market research to recording what young people have to say, all in an effort to extend profits. In this "age of accelerated meaning," where streams of images swirl around us, it is the meanings created within a consumer sphere that carry youth along, mobilizing them as much as immobilizing them, largely because these meanings resonate with them.

Of course, none of this happens without a fight. Youth continue to struggle to claim physical and rhetorical spaces against their relegation to the overflow of nonplaces (malls come to mind) that pepper the contemporary modern landscape. Santa Clara Street serves as a tenuous place where Chicano/a youth reconnect to community life as they search for a community to anchor their Chicano/a identities. Here economic processes shape the cultural landscape in concrete ways. The influx of upscale restaurants and clubs and housing and the creation of San Jose Police Department's Cruise Management Division to control and contain this commercial space, drawing wealthier young folks mostly from outside the downtown, both reflect shifts in the economic life of San Jose.

There is also a distinct racial cast to these struggles over public space that are not specific to San Jose. "Driving while black" has been at the center of much discussion and debate about the status of race and the persistence of institutional racism in contemporary U.S. society. In many ways, this debate raises fundamental questions about the very nature of everyday racial struggle for everyday folks as they travel beyond their homes, staking claim to public settings.[21] As youth move beyond the private space of home and institutional spaces such as school, they encounter repeated attempts to curtail and limit their movement and mobility. While this is perhaps most pronounced for teens, especially young men of color, young adults in their twenties also come up against efforts to limit their free movement in and between public spaces.

Dead Ends

Youths' engagement in car spaces sometimes inspires them to think more critically about the world and their place in it. In 1996, a group of black youth in Oakland, California, organized a "Take Back the Lake" protest rally against the city's newly adopted ordinance against cruising around Lake Merritt, seeing the ordinance as racially inspired. Led by the hip-hop artist Boots Riley, of the Coup, a group of protesters stormed a city council meeting and were successful in having the ordinance repealed. A group of high schoolers staged a walkout at their high school after a demolished car was placed on the front lawn of the school by an organization that opposed youth drinking and driving. The students were told that a student at their high school had died in that car in a drunk-driving accident, even though that was not true. Unimpressed and incensed by the outrageous shock value and insensitivity of the display, students took matters into their own hands, refusing to attend classes until the car was removed.

But can cars themselves have a transformative potential? Can cars be attached to a transformative politics? In the beginning of this project, I felt far more hopeful than I do at its end. For decades, scholars saw youth culture as an oppositional one, reading young people's actions as positioned against the dominant culture. Countless studies detailed how youth disrupt business as usual in various ways, aesthetic, cultural, and economic. Yet many of the defining features of youth car cultures are not oppositional in the more conventional subcultural sense. Youth car culture is not something youth themselves create apart from or necessarily in opposition to the dominant culture. Within the car-racing scene, for example, tuners largely depend upon a consumer market to fashion or modify their cars and thus play an important role in bolstering what has become a multibillion-dollar industry in after-market car parts. Consider the following monologue from an independent film called *The Debut,* about a Filipino American youth's struggle to reconcile the dual ethnic loyalties of being Filipino and being American.

> I can't believe you guys. You're just two more Filipinos selling out to the man. You're just another brown brother and sister playing into the hands of the car conspiracy. The conspiracy is a plan by the man to distract us from the problems of our brown brothers and sisters around the world. They're happy we people of color are wasting our time changing our mufflers and lowering our cars. They don't want us to learn about the war the Philippines had with the U.S. or the how the Mexican and Filipino Americans fought side by side to unionize farm labor. Yes, it's true, you guys were just too busy adjusting your carburetors and intake valves.

While I would hardly agree that an actual "car conspiracy" is in place, I do think cars lack the transformative potential that other objects in youth culture carry. True, the car is rich in meaning, an empty sign filled with the promise of ever-changing significance. But cars are not simply signs. They belong as much to a material world as to a symbolic one. They belong to a physical world of escalating waste and declining green space, a world of environmental degradation, an asphalt nation in which we live and breathe. Car culture is forever bound to the historical relations of modern capitalist production and consumption; cars are in the first instance commodities. And because they are commodities, they carry high price tags that many kids are all too eager to pay. The price of this freedom, as I have argued, is a steep one, sometimes keeping kids from leaving their parents' nest as rent, insurance, and car payments overwhelm their modest budgets.

Most of the political action led by youth has been *against* cars. Consider the radical action of one young man in his early twenties who planted a number of bombs at a Hummer dealership in California, setting it and some of its stock on fire. His action was aimed at SUVs and the environmental degradation they cause. Cultural jammers, young activists who protest the corporate control of everyday life, have been successful in disrupting the flow of information from auto giants to the people. For example, one graffiti group "jammed" a Hummer advertising poster campaign that featured a large Hummer set against open blue space and the sun. The jammers crossed out the "H," replacing it with a "B" so that the copy read "Bummer" instead of "Hummer," and they also blocked out the sun with the black spot that signifies opposition to the pervasive commodification of culture. But these activists seem to be the exception, not the rule.

In the end, I feel far more hopeful about young adults than about cars themselves. My hope is that youths' engagement with American car culture will inspire a more critical assessment not only of young people's roles as historical actors but of history itself, this historical moment, and the social and economic forces that have created it. My hope is that their engagement with cars will inspire a set of questions about cars —beyond price, horsepower, and bling—different from those we usually ask.

Appendix

From the beginning of this research project, it was clear to me that cars are situated at the intersection of several threads of social action and thus provide an opportunity to take up multiple lines of inquiry. Many readers may have noticed this in the organization of the chapters; each of the chapters, though all address youth and cars, is distinct. Each chapter has its own line of inquiry, drawing from different sociological traditions. My purpose in these chapters has been to demonstrate how these different social threads are deeply entangled; taken together, they reveal significant changes in the social organization of young people's lives, with real consequences in how youth construct identities and make meaning.

My primary aim in *Fast Cars, Cool Rides* has been to show how the everyday worlds of young people and the identity work they undertake in those worlds are shaped by social relations that originate elsewhere. In this way, this project has direct links to a type of feminist inquiry first initiated by Dorothy E. Smith that is referred to as "institutional ethnography."[1] Smith's project, which emerged from a critique of standard sociological research practices, is concerned with explaining how our lived, everyday worlds are socially arranged by a complex of abstract, professional, and administrative forces (e.g., corporate capitalism, schooling, the medical profession, policy, science) that support what Smith broadly refers to as the "extra-local relations of ruling." Her project's purpose is to explain what she terms as "the extra-local organization of everyday experience." Smith calls for a method of inquiry that emerges from the actual site of social existence, where people actually live and breathe, arguing that sociological concepts and categories for analysis that originate outside the everyday world in the end distort and objectify more than they explain. Smith resists a line of inquiry that involves applying abstract concepts that derive from the textual worlds of sociology to the worlds of local existence, seeing this as central to sociology's role in reproducing ruling.[2] Smith challenges conventional sociology on these grounds and proposes institutional ethnography as an alternative. Because institutional ethnography is most interested in understanding the complex threads that connect the social organization of the everyday world with a set of extralocal relations, she also writes against a self-contained ethnography, ethnographic inquiry that overlooks various institutional connections that mediate lived worlds. "Locating the sociological problematic in the everyday world does not mean confining the inquiry to the everyday world. Indeed, as we shall see, it is essential to that the everyday world be seen as organized by social relations not observable within it. Thus, any inquiry confining itself to the everyday world of direct experience is not adequate to explicate its social organization," Smith (1987: 89) writes.

Building from Smith's work and what is now a significant body of writing and research dedicated to institutional ethnography, this research project explicates how a complex of economic and social relations (e.g., the social organization of the consumer market, eroding opportunities under advanced capitalism) provides a backdrop for understanding kids' uses of cars, their relationship to public space, and how they make sense of themselves and the world they both inhabit and influence. San Jose, California, "Silicon Valley," served as my site of investigation. It was clear early in this research that the economic and social landscape of San Jose, stemming from a rapidly changing capitalist economy, was organizing young adults' relationships to school, home, work, and public space. The car provided a way to see how these relations fit together, since to talk about cars is to also talk about these other things. This study begins with the local and ongoing relations that constitute young people's everyday worlds, but with attention to the relations that originate outside their everyday worlds. Toward this end, this project situates the everyday activities of youth formed around the car against a bundle of abstract forces—the hypermobile, trans-national flow of capital, bodies, ideas, production, and consumption under advanced capitalism; the expansion of increasingly sophisticated media, advertising and communication systems; highway transportation policies like GDL laws; statistical reports generated to promote policy change like those produced by the NHTSA; anticruising ordinances; and developmental discourses on adolescence. These extralocal relations are central for understanding the social and self organization of youth and the meanings youth create.

I locate the creation of social meanings within concrete social practices—getting the license, learning to drive, buying a car, driving home from work late at night, cruising down public streets—because of my interest in making connections between the meanings youth generate and the extralocal organization of their everyday worlds, without my having to leave conceptually their practical worlds. It seems to me that this is what Smith means in doing institutional ethnography when she calls upon researchers never to leave the site of local experience in their investigations.

This project, then, is not about explaining youth behavior, making sense of "those crazy things kids do," but instead is interested in the excavation of key social relations that organize young people's experience of the everyday world as they move in and around it. A study of cars provides an opportunity for such excavation; cars are locally negotiated objects but encoded with meanings that originate outside the nexus of local relations. My interest in mapping these complexities directs the methods of research I used and the means by which I collected materials for this project and ultimately analyzed them. The following discussion aims to clarify these methods of research.

Collecting Empirical Materials

Much like other qualitative projects guided by a model of theoretical sampling, this project unfolded as a strange blend of serendipity and careful planning. It was clear to me from this project's early stages that multiple research methods were necessary to draw connections between changes in the local lives of youth and broader social and economic transformations, to flesh out the coordinates of meaning formed around the car and kids' understandings of themselves. It seemed to me that studying a host of forces at work—state licensing, marketing campaigns that target youth, the emergence of lines of credit and their expansion to youth—required a methodology that would enable me to attend to these messy complexities that at first glance appear unrelated. I therefore began collecting materials for this project in 2000, conducting in-depth interviews and doing participant observation and collecting documents that related to kids and cars simultaneously.

Interviewing

At the center of this project are focus group and in-depth interviews conducted with 101 young adults ages 15–23. From the beginning, I was interested in talking with kids whose social experiences varied, and this played a role in the recruitment strategies I used. I had decided I would try to recruit kids from different spaces: school spaces and spaces where they worked or played. The first interview I conducted was with a young man, Mark, who worked at the local video store where I rented videos. At the time, this eighteen-year-old did not have a license, and thus the interview with Mark opened up a range of considerations that I might have overlooked had I begun with someone who had a driver's license. This interview helped to generate questions and themes to be addressed in the interviews to follow. A month later, I interviewed Mike, who worked installing stereos. I met Mike on the job; I watched him work as I waited while another young man installed a stereo in my car. After our interview, Mike referred me to Olie, a twenty-year-old college student who worked with Mike and was into "tuning" his Civic. I interviewed him a few months later. All of the interviews that followed (which were taped and later transcribed) were largely unstructured and lasted between one and three hours. Rooted in the inductive "grounded theory" tradition,[3] I asked respondents to tell me about cars, cruising, car racing, and learning to drive, allowing respondents to move in a range of different directions as the interviews unfolded. Generally, the questions I asked arose from the conversations we collaboratively created, and, in this sense, much depended on the context. In the end, I was surprised by the emergence of a number of unexpected themes across the interviews.

I had originally planned to interview only youths ages 15–18, but it became clear that I should also interview young adults ages 19–23, since they make up a large portion of the youth car scene and share some similarities in life circumstances with this younger set. Whereas at other historical moments these two groups were leagues apart, the same cannot be said with as much certainty today. Many young adults, for example, continue to live at home, and many hold the same kinds of jobs in the service economy as the younger kids. With this in mind, I decided to recruit from the state university, where I was teaching at the time. "Snowball" sampling enabled me to expand what began as a small group of willing participants recruited at the end of a summer course I taught that drew majors from across different colleges at the university.

In total, forty-four semistructured and open-ended face-to-face interviews were conducted with young men and young women ages 15–23 who represent widely different income and racial and ethnic groups. I conducted nineteen of those interviews. In 2003, I recruited three sociology students from the state university who had completed a course in qualitative research methods with me to serve as my research assistants. Maria Flores, Danette Garcia, and Robert Trade together conducted twenty-five additional interviews. To ensure continuity across the interviews, each of the students worked with a loose interview guide that included general probes and topics to cover. My decision to recruit students to help with data collection had two sources. The teaching load at the state university was heavy, and I was responsible for teaching four classes each semester. It was therefore clear to me that this project would be delayed significantly if I collected the material on my own. The second and more important reason was my interest in pulling together a diverse team of researchers in order to complicate the sort of responses gathered from the interviews. I was interested in seeing if researchers in their twenties, both young men and young women from different racial and ethnic groups (Maria and Danette are Chicana, and Robert is Filipino and Anglo) might draw out responses different from those I was able to generate in the interviews I conducted. I advised the student researchers to recruit from their neighborhoods with the explicit purpose of developing a racially and economically diverse pool of respondents. In the end, this did diversify the pool of participants, since the researchers were from different communities in the area. Of the twenty young men and twenty-four young women we interviewed, four were African American, fifteen were Latino/a, ten were East or Southeast Asian American, and fifteen were European Americans. Roughly half of the participants were from immigrant families and were either first or second generation. A range of income groups was represented among interview participants. A small portion of those interviewed (fewer than ten) had parents in high-level professional or managerial occupations. The majority of kids interviewed were from middle-class and working-class families, with six identifying themselves as poor.

There were a few cases where I was unable to determine socioeconomic position. As a number of scholars have noted, assessing class location is complicated. Most of us have multiple class leanings and ties; there is not always a neat correspondence among income, education, and occupation, the traditional measures of socioeconomic status.[4] While I was mindful of the fact that status-conferring objects like cars, clothes, handbags, and jewelry rarely reveal actual class position, I did try to listen for cues about distinct types of cultural and symbolic capital that might reveal class membership. I also relied on other cultural markers to designate class relations and practices, paying attention to the different ways young adults talked about their consumption, their educational histories, their schools' resources, and their family, neighborhood, and community lives. Though none of these is an adequate marker of class on its own, taken together they might serve as approximates of class membership. With these considerations in mind, I have tried to convey a sense of the class and economic diversity of the participants.

Getting these young adults to agree to be interviewed proved to be more difficult than I and the student researchers expected. When we individually approached kids to be interviewed, many said they were "too busy." From this, I began to consider what "being sooo busy" might mean beyond serving as a polite way to decline an interview. The idea of chronic busyness has seeped into our culture's language as a way to talk about everyday life and often serves as a way out of what feels like social obligation; many of these kids had first agreed to be interviewed, only to back out later. But I also I came to see the "I'm so busy" mantra as related to the increasingly frenetic pace of daily existence for these kids. Many of them were working long hours to finance their cars, car insurance, and cell phones, in addition to going to school. There was a concrete sense that many of them were struggling to fit the interviews into their schedule of work, school, family, and extracurricular activities. This was the case with Robert; we rescheduled the interview two times before we actually met. Though this is hardly surprising, many of these young people also take very seriously their social commitments, especially to friends who serve as their primary source of support. This was the case with Mike, who to an adult might appear "irresponsible" on all counts (he was failing out of community college), yet he demonstrated a strong commitment to his friends (ideas about responsibility are largely adult-centered). He spoke at length about maintaining his friendships. Our interview was interrupted several times by friends calling him on his cell phone. He took each of the calls he received as I waited. In the course of the interview, he talked repeatedly about his life as hectic and chaotic. "Hella hectic," he said, but it seemed to me that he used these words differently than an adult might. *Hectic* and *chaotic* seemed badges or evidence of an exciting and unpredictable life spent largely "on the fly," and the interview was an occasion where this could be demonstrated.

These situations were problems in terms of the practical coordination of interviews, yet they also seemed to reveal clues about the social organization of young people's lives. In this sense, these methodological problems led to my asking particular questions of the data as I began coding and analyzing the interview materials.

Focus Groups

In 2001, I decided also to conduct focus-group interviews because I was interested in documenting young adults' collective talk and because group interviews often enable the researcher to witness some of the same social dynamics that organize young people's lives outside research contexts.[5] Through focus groups, I interviewed fifty-two additional young women and young men ages 15–23. I conducted five focus groups in total, each having between seven and fifteen participants. Four of the focus groups were conducted at Weston High School. With an overall student population that is 31 percent Anglo, 49 percent Hispanic, 13 percent Asian, 3 percent Black, and 4 percent other, the district has students who vary widely in linguistic, cultural, and socioeconomic background. The focus groups were ethnically and racially diverse and included Filipino American, Southeast Asian American, Chicana/o, Latino/a, black American, and European American participants. A significant number of participants (roughly one-third) are 1.5* or second-generation American. Students at Weston were primarily from middle-income families; a small portion of the students were either from the professional or managerial classes or poor. This was reflected in the focus groups; only a small number of participants identified their parents' occupations as professional or managerial. In a few instances, I was simply unable to assess a student's socioeconomic location in any meaningful way.

---

* The 1.5 generation refers to people who were born outside the United States but have lived part of their childhood in the United States.

A graduate student, Karen Ranier, helped to coordinate the first two focus groups conducted at Weston. She had graduated from the high school several years earlier and still had a connection with some of the administrators. She facilitated my entry into the school, which enabled me to return the next year to conduct two more focus groups. The first focus group consisted of nine participants: four young women and five young men. The second focus group included fifteen participants, and the two focus groups conducted the following year had eight participants each. Students were recruited during the lunch period a few days before the focus groups were conducted. They were invited for soda and pizza during lunch and study hall with the understanding that they would be participating in a group discussion about cars and driving. The majority of the thirty-six students who participated in the focus groups were first- and second-year high school students, fifteen and sixteen years old, respectively. None of the fifteen-year-olds had a driver's license. The majority of sixteen-years-olds had a driver's license, but many did not have their own car.

The final focus group I conducted consisted of eleven young women, all Chicana, ages 20–23. All were members of the same multicultural sorority at the state university where I was teaching. All were first-generation college students, and all were middle income. Their parents were mechanics, office workers, civil servants, and police officers. Half of the group came from families headed by women, and while the families could now be defined as middle income, many had lived on far lower incomes during their childhoods. Carmen Garcia, another student research assistant, helped organize this focus group since she was a member of the sorority and was a former student of mine who had also completed the qualitative research methods course with me. I had interviewed her the month before, and in this sense she served as one of my main informants regarding the world of car cruising. Carmen had deep ties to the local Chicano car culture, she knew a lot of the history of the Lowrider movement, and she had expressed sincere interest in the topic and offered to help organize the focus group. Jason Yates, a fifth student research assistant, who had also completed the qualitative research methods course with me and had solid ties to the import car-racing scene, conducted a sixth focus group with five participants: four young men and one young woman ages 19–23. The interview was conducted at Sears Point, a raceway in northern California. All the participants

were from Santa Clara County, and all were involved in the underground and organized racing scenes.[6]

Problems arose with the focus groups. The focus group with fifteen
participants was simply unruly and in the end lacked the sort of depth
that the other focus groups provided. However, it did offer an opportunity to talk with a broad base of students and revealed some interesting
social dynamics within high school peer groups. At several points during the focus group, I lost "steering" control as participants clamored to
be heard above what sometimes unraveled into utter mayhem. In this
way, there was a real sense of this talking space emerging as kids' terrain. In these moments, I sat back and listened as members of the group
continued to talk over one another. It was rare that the kids veered off-
topic, since they had much to say about cars. In the end, I learned far
more than I expected from a group that size, though the following year
I made sure the groups remained small.[7]

In the mixed-sex focus groups, the boys tended to dominate the conversation, with one exception. In the last focus group I conducted at
Weston High School, composed of eight people, three of the participants, all ninth-grade young men, arrived early. As we waited for the
others to arrive, we began talking. I turned on the tape recorder, and the
boys, clearly all friends, spoke animatedly among themselves about cars
and car racing, the cars they wished for, and the little driving they had
done in parking lots and neighborhood streets (they had not yet been
legally awarded a license). But as the rest of the group trickled in, they
grew increasingly quiet; the new group of five, three young women and
two young men, all sophomores, dominated the rest of the conversation, despite my efforts to draw these young men back into the conversation. It was clear that the internal dynamics of the school's social
structure, what the sociologists Patricia Adler and Peter Adler call "peer
power," was at work, silencing these young men, who stood in subordinate positions to the other students.[8]

The focus-group interviews produced rich dialogue that was important to the analysis I developed. The conversations were lively, at times
quite raucous. The students at Weston clearly enjoyed the time they
were able to spend away from the normal routines of school, and the
women from the sorority, who shared a deep and lasting friendship,
seized on the focus group as an opportunity to share in the collective act
of remembering and telling that served to unify them as a group. In all

the interviews, there was a clear sense that the participants were using the interviews to pursue their own ends. That people bring their own agendas to the interview encounter is an inescapable fact of doing interviewing research. While this shapes the direction of the research in ways that sometimes runs counter to the researcher's aims, it can reveal the social situations that frame participants' lives outside the research encounter. This was the case with Mark, the first young man I interviewed. We were scheduled to meet for the interview at a coffee house, where I conducted many interviews, and when I arrived I saw a young man who normally wore jeans and black t-shirt (at least to his job at the video store) dressed in a suit. I wrote the following in my interview log after our interview:

> Mark and I met March 5, 2000, at 2:00 P.M., a Saturday, at Java City, a coffee shop, about two miles from where Mark works at a low-wage job at a local video store. The plan was for us to meet, talk for an hour or so, and then I would drive him to work. Mark showed up dressed in black. He had on a black-pressed shirt, buttoned to the collar, and black pants. He wore a black double-breasted jacket that appeared to be two sizes too small. I was surprised to see him so dressed up, given that he would be going to work after. His curly hair was long, parted in the middle and pulled into a low ponytail. I arrived after him, and as he greeted me at the table he extended his hand. I think he thought of this meeting as a professional meeting. Throughout the interview it was clear that Mark was actively working to present himself as mature and not like other kids. It occurred to me during the interview that kids who present themselves as "individuals" and are invested in being seen as autonomous individuals must actively work to present themselves as not kids. To be a kid means to be not an individual but someone who conforms and follows the will of the crowd. A young person then must actively distance himself from other kids to be seen as an individual, and that's exactly what Mark did. Throughout the interview he repeatedly talked about kids as followers, not leaders, as nonthinkers—disparaging and degrading exactly what he is, that is, a kid himself. Mark and I sat down after he got himself a very large cup of coffee, which he remarked he could not live without, and he also refused to let me buy him a coffee. As he sat down, I noticed a pack of cigarettes (Lucky Strikes) in his front pocket and asked if he'd rather sit outside and smoke. He said he would, and we moved outside for the interview.

Interviews are dramaturgical; both researcher and participant fulfill interactional roles and pursue specific lines of action. The interviewer and the interviewee have their own agendas, and this informs how they collaboratively craft this research space as a social space.[9] Interview claims also serve as strategic identity claims. In this sense, the research materials generated through interviews are never transparent. Keeping this in mind, I mined the young participants' responses for clues about their social worlds, attentive not only to what they said but also to how they said it, mindful of to whom it was directed.

A number of researchers have addressed the issue of age as being relevant to conducting research with teens and children. Age clearly structured the interviews and the observations I conducted. On more than one occasion, I found myself adopting what I came to regard as a maternal role. I openly expressed concern for some of the actions the kids talked about, though I felt conflicted about doing so. For example, in the first focus group, I was alarmed to hear one of the boys, JP, say that he refused to wear a seat belt and felt a moral obligation to say something about the risk in not wearing a seat belt (even while recognizing that he might be saying this for effect). At the time I was eight months pregnant, and my comments arguably reflected my anticipatory socialization to motherhood.

JP: Nah, I don't wear a seatbelt when I'm driving.

AB: You don't wear a seatbelt. Why?

Bob: How dumb can you be?

JP: I don't believe in them.

AB: You don't believe in them? Well what if . . . what do you mean?

Alan: I force him sometimes.

AB: [addressing Alan] Do you wear a seatbelt?

Alan: Yeah, I wear a seatbelt.

AB: What about you guys?

Cynthia: I always wear a seatbelt.

Tracy: I wear a seatbelt.

AB: So how come you guys wear seatbelts?

JP: I don't believe in 'em, seatbelts, I feel like they'll hurt you more than anything, you can go like this you go boom whiplash.

AB: Well, it's not, you know, statistically, it's not true actually, you're gonna most likely be injured if you do not have your seatbelt on.

JP: I'd rather go through the window, before I get whiplash or something like that.

AB: So what about for you? [addressing Tom] Tell me, do you wear your seatbelt? Yeah?

Tom: Sometimes.

AB: Sometimes, so when wouldn't, when wouldn't you wear your seatbelt?

Tom: When I am in the back.

AB: Oh, when you're in the backseat?

Tom: Yeah.

AB: So, you know, you can get tickets and the driver can get a ticket if you don't have your seatbelt on in the backseat.

In the course of this research, I came to see a gradual shift in my worldview. This has had consequences for my interactions with these kids, which were perhaps most apparent during the observations, about which I talked in the introduction to this book.

Observations

Observations were a significant part of this research. I conducted "multi-sited" observational research because car cultures are dispersed and mobile and because I came to see distinct car communities operating within overlapping fields of action. It was clear that each of the sites was governed by a different logic. I have already addressed a number of the issues that arose as I observed Santa Clara Street. Here I discuss observations of other key sites and the logic that directed these observations.

To gain a broad sense of the car's significance in Silicon Valley, I attended two car shows, visited three car washes, and spent lots of time walking around grocery store, mall, and convenience store parking lots—always during the day. I was interested in understanding how people in the community feel about cars and how they conduct themselves in and around cars; I hoped people might reveal these through their observable interactional routines. Because these were public spaces, gaining access to them was relatively uncomplicated. The observations in these sites were informal. I went, walked around, took notes, and, when possible, talked to people. I observed three different types of car washes: a car wash organized by students at the state university to raise funds for the upcoming Chicano commencement; a self-serve car wash in a low-income neighborhood, and a full-service car wash in South San Jose, not far from Weston High School. There was a clear and obvious divide in terms of the cars at the car washes: at the self-service, the cars were much older, and there were far fewer SUVs. At the full-service car wash (which costs $30 for a wash, towel dry, and vacuum), the cars were newer, and there were far more luxury sedans and SUVs. I visited the full-service and the self-service car washes a number of times over several years, sometimes participating in the activities of the site, washing my own car, and sometimes just observing. I visited a Volkswagen and a Honda dealership. While there, I was able to talk with the sales staff and collect marketing material that was useful to my understanding of the youth car market.

I also observed three school parking lots after school: those at Weston High School, Freedom High School, and Mitchell High School. I selected these three schools because they are all in the same school district but are differently situated. Mitchell High School is a California "distinguished" school (its academic ranking is well above California's average), and it is located in an established neighborhood with very expensive houses. But it is also a magnet school, which means that its student body is pretty diverse, despite the fact the neighborhood is not. Weston High School is situated in the southern part of the city, well known as predominately white, even though the students did not entirely reflect this homogeneity. Freedom High School, the third school, is situated in a low-income neighborhood, home mostly to Latino and Vietnamese families. Unlike at Mitchell, the student body is drawn largely from the neighborhood and is primarily of color; there are many immigrant students.[10]

Attending car shows enabled me to observe a broader base of young adults for whom cars are centrally important to their lives, whereas observations in high school parking lots provided a window through which I documented how young adults organize themselves around their cars. My presence in the school lots went largely unnoticed by adults and by many of the kids, too. Had I been a man observing and skulking around a school parking lot, my presence would have likely raised some suspicion. But this was not the case.

I gained a more solid sense of the significance cars carry for youth from observing auto shop at Freedom High School, which I attended for the better part of the Spring 2004 semester. The opportunity to observe Mr. O'Malley's class was unexpected. I had been observing the parking lot at Freedom High School and one day noticed a group of young men standing around a car, parked beside a garage that I came to realize was one of several car bays that constitute "autoshop." I decided to return to the school the next day to talk to the auto shop teacher to ask whether I could observe. Mr. O'Malley invited me to sit in his classes. I attended four sections of lab (about five hours total each day) once a week for six weeks.

It was immediately apparent that Mr. O'Malley had excellent rapport with the students in his classes, and this seemed to facilitate an easy rapport for me. Mr. O'Malley vouched for me, and this enabled me to connect with the students, nearly all of whom were young men. There were two young women in one class and three in another, and the time I spent with them was informative. When I asked about being girls in a class full of boys, they had much to say. The five young women talked about feeling isolated and excluded from the groups of boys, among other things.

Most of my time was spent moving between groups of young men who were working either on their own cars or on the school's cars. They spent a lot of time just hanging around, passing the time. It was easy to just stand around talking as they did. The groups were so fluid and changing that it was easy for me to latch onto them. Most of the students were friendly. Many welcomed me each time I returned, with a number asking about the progress of the book. Many were genuinely interested in what I was studying and asked me questions about my focus. It was also clear that my presence provided an occasion for the young men to demonstrate the knowledge they had of cars. Many seized the opportunity to talk to me, though they rarely approached me on their own. Mostly, I approached them.

It was easy to participate in their interactional world, though always as a white woman researcher who looked more like a teacher than like one of them. I did commit a few gaffes that revealed to me the social organization of their world and also served to position me outside that world. Consider my observations, taken from my field notes:

> I arrive to school. I approach a group of boys hovering around a red Civic. Daniel says hello to me and a few others acknowledge me. I remember many faces from the week before and say hello. I check out the

hood which looks different from the car and ask if it's a new hood. This must be a stupid question because this sets them off in hysterics. One says, "Yeah, a special one from Japan." As I take a closer look, I realize it is a hood with only primer and no paint. This was one of several stupid questions I asked during the day that serve to disrupt the flow of interaction, but these boys are mostly forgiving. (May 10, 2004)

Only later did I realize that their laughter was not intended to humiliate me. I witnessed many kids being laughed at for saying or doing silly things. It seemed to serve as a way to let the offender know that a norm violation had occurred without disgracing him. I witnessed no heated exchanges. But I was struck by the fact that these boys didn't let anything slide; everything was subject to comment. The term *bitch* was repeatedly thrown around, hurled at others for the most minor infractions. I remember that the first time I heard "bitch" (one of perhaps twenty times during my first school visit), I wasn't sure whom they were talking about, whether it was directed toward the only woman in the class, me. But I realized soon after that they were talking to each other. These exchanges were all a part of the banter among boys—"Yo bitch," "look at you," "Sick," "You idiot." There was only one instance where a sexual reference, though not directed toward me, left me feeling uncomfortable and I moved onto another group. I was also struck by the succession of the words "shit" and "fuck." Only on one occasion did a boy apologize for cussing in front of a "lady," and I quickly assured him he needn't bother. That apologies for cussing were few and far between indicated to me that my presence was for the most part accepted by the boys.

The time I spent in the auto shop at the tail end of the research provided many of the missing pieces for me in understanding young men and their struggles around masculinity and race.

The Textual Materials

Important to this multimethod project was the textual materials of varying sorts that I collected over the course of five years. Analyzing contemporary and historical documents relating to youth car culture, including films, car Web sites, magazine articles, and advertisements allowed me to identify recurring themes in the relationship between youth and cars. I gathered hundreds of documents, mining them for emergent patterns. I visited the New City Library Picture Collection, in 2001, to view archival documents: mostly print advertisements for automobiles from the twentieth century. The Good Guys Car Show, which I attended in 2000, had hundreds of old magazine advertisements for cars on display that could also be purchased. What I was able to surmise from these two sources was that advertisements for cars directed specifically at teens began to emerge in the 1930s and 1940s. I also reviewed "teen" movies where cars were significant to the story line, including the classics *Rebel Without a Cause* and *American Graffiti* and the commercially successful contemporary films *The Fast and the Furious* and *2 Fast 2 Furious*, and MTV's *Pimp My Ride*.

My search for documents connecting youth and cars began with very basic Web searches. What I uncovered were two recurring kinds of Web conversations and information that had direct relevance for this research. The first was the wealth of statistical reports on driving, traffic accident fatalities, and injuries involving teens that have been completed by various transportation-related agencies—the National Highway Traffic Safety Institute, the Automobile Association of America, the Insurance Institute—and media reports that used these statistics. This led me to Lexis-Nexis, a library database with hundreds of thousands of articles that have appeared in various print media. I uncovered hundred of documents there. Analysis of these statistical documents and the articles in the print media that used them enabled me to investigate how teen drivers have come to be seen as a public problem, much like drunk drivers. The second type of Web documents that were of particular interest to me were bulletin boards dedicated to cars. Over the course of five years, I visited more than a hundred bulletin boards and personal Web pages maintained by young car enthusiasts. That there are so many bulletin boards is perhaps not surprising, given young people's relationship to the Internet. These bulletin boards seem to function as virtual communities, serving as a space where ideas about cars and their cultural importance are (hotly) debated and exchanged.

As I began to write this book, I expected the textual documents I had collected to serve a more central role than they did, especially the statistical data on traffic accidents and youth and the media stories surrounding them. But, as the writing progressed, it became clear that the ethnographic and in-depth interview materials were the most revealing of the social dynamics I hoped to explain when I began this project. As it stands, the documents serve as a backdrop for understanding the every-day worlds of the young adults in this book and peripheral aspects of their extralocal organization.

In the end, the use of various strategies of data collection served to broaden this project's scope, enabling me to explore how a range of social forces, enacted at a local level, organizes the personal realities of young adults, while also attending to the various ways the activities of youth influence the very social forces under which their lives are organized.

Notes

1. American car culture and the car reveal much to us about the expansion of commodity culture, the growth of the leisure industries, the shifts in work and leisure activities, suburbanization, and the ebb and flow of economic production in post–World War II America. See for example Duany, Plater-Zyberk, and Speck (2000); Flink (1988); Gans (1967); Gudis (2004); Silverstone (1997).

2. See Poster (1988) and Baudrillard (2000). See also Hebdige (2000).

3. O'Connell (1998): 44. See also Sharff (1991) for a discussion of women and the car.

4. Miller (2001a): 6.

5. See http://www.letskeepmoving.com.

6. The meanings individuals attach to the car as a cultural object tell us much about their experiences in social life, revealing not just who and where they are but who they want to be and where they one day hope to go. Simon Maxwell (2001) explores how individuals make sense of their car use in the face of social, environmental, and political concerns. He argues that people's sense-making activities largely work to reduce guilt and anxieties about their reliance on cars in everyday life. Simon points to the specific discursive repertoires of utility, freedom, and independence that people use to deflect personal responsibility in view of public concerns about car use in the everyday life.

7. Behind the car stands America's ongoing struggle with democracy, equality, and freedom, principles that have turned out to be much more elusive in our everyday pursuit of them than Ford's Model T, "a car for the great multitude," as Ford's advertising machine had once promised. In 1906, Ford's Model N (which sold for $600) was released, followed by Ford's legendary Model T in 1908. More than 15 million units of the Model T (priced at $575 in 1912) had been sold by the time its production ended in 1927 (Flink [1988]). Using a populist rhetoric common in the early twentieth century, Ford referred to the Model T as a car for the "the great multitude." Indeed it was. The pricing of the Model T, combined with the increasing standard of living from improved wages for the American working class, made car ownership a possibility for millions of Americans. For further discussion of this topic see Flink (1988).

8. See Flink (1988).

9. Ford's assembly line also symbolized the magnification of workers' alienation and a decline in creativity and passion of craft. See Flink (1988).

10. As one example, recall Michael Moore's celebrated 1987 documentary, *Roger and Me,* which chronicled the community devastation wrought by the closing of GM plants in once-thriving Flint, Michigan. One can argue that the prosperity enjoyed by Flint's residents was also a consequence of the car. The relationship between television's popularity and civic engagement is addressed in Robert Putnam's seminal piece *Bowling Alone* (2000). See also Duany et al. (2000); Jane Holtz Kay (1997); and James Kunstler (1993). One might also argue that cars, like television, can play a unifying role in the lives of individuals on a local level. By that I mean that, just as television communities develop, so too do car communities and car clubs. In this sense, cars can serve an integrative role, drawing community members together.

11. Available at http://facts.330.ca/statistics.

12. Holtz Kay (1997).

13. See Cornel West (1994) for a discussion of nihilism within the poor urban core.

14. American-owned General Motors was indicted by a federal grand jury for criminal conspiracy in 1949 for actions to dismantle public transportation, though justice was hardly served since, in the end, GM was fined a meager $5,000. See Kunstler (1993) for a more elaborate discussion.

15. Adbusters (2003): 7. Adbusters is a Canadian magazine founded by Kalle Lasn and published by Adbusters Media Foundation in Vancouver, B.C.

16. This point was made tangible for me recently. While on vacation, my husband and I were traveling between Baltimore, Maryland, and New York City. Since we were without a car, we needed to decide our transportation. Our options were the train and a rental car. The cost of two adult round-trip tickets by train was an estimated $270, while the rental car cost a mere $50 plus gas and tolls. Our decision was an obvious one.

17. Emergence from the abyss of car dependence is unlikely since the federal government seems intent on investing in the so-called energy-efficient smart car over public transit as an alternative to what we have now. Even investment in research and development of energy efficient cars has receded in recent years. See Holtz Kay (1997).

18. See for example Katie Alvord (2000).

19. See for example Crossman and Crossman (2002).

20. See Corrigan's (1975) insightful analysis of "doing nothing."

21. By 2000, more than forty states had adopted some version of graduated driver's licensing, motivated largely by the proliferation and repeated presentation of statistical reports reflecting "alarming population trends" related to the

number of teen drivers. California's GDL law was first proposed in 1997 by Republican state senator Tim Leslie, who authored The Brady/Jared Teen Driver Safety Act, named after two teen drivers, Brady Grasinger and Jared Cunningham, who died in separate accidents in southern California. The California GDL law, sponsored by AAA, requires all drivers under eighteen to hold an instructional permit for six months instead of the thirty days required for adults before they can obtain a provisional license. Teens ages 16–18 must also complete fifty hours of adult-supervised driving, including ten hours at night while holding an instructional permit. A parent or guardian must certify in writing the completion of these hours. Teen drivers may not carry passengers under the age of twenty unless supervised by a licensed driver at least twenty-five years old for the first six months (except in situations of family need). Teen drivers may not drive between midnight and 5 A.M. for the first twelve months. Exceptions to this provision are granted for driving to work or school or in family and medical emergencies. The GDL mimics what are called status laws—laws imposed on youth and children but not on adults. Violations of GDL laws are classified as secondary violations, which means teen drivers will not be stopped solely because they are suspected violators.

22. Furedi (2002): 19.

23. Much scholarship has been dedicated to examining the connections between youth and public life. See for example Cahill (1990); Cohen (1997); Davis (1990); Gaines (1990); Hebdige (1997); Lipsitz (1994); Lucas (1998); Watt and Stenson (1998).

24. The determination of whether a driver is *cruising* down Main Street, USA, or simply circling for the next available parking spot is likely to be arbitrarily based on the drivers themselves and perhaps the type of car driven.

25. One can make the argument that youth have spent as much time working to become invisible as to become visible. Certainly the car provides youth the opportunity to experience a level of privacy they are denied in school, home, and other sites of surveillance. I think that the fact that the insides of cars assume as much importance as they do for youth reveals youths' attempt to be outside the purview of adults. But it is very clear that one of the key struggles for youth that take shape around the car is visibility.

26. See Giddens (1991). He discusses symbolic tokens (money) and expert systems (the emergence of highly technical knowledge) as two central aspects of the abstract systems of late modernity. Giddens argues that an essential feature of the mechanism of late modernity has been what he calls disembedding, "the lifting out of social relations from local contexts and their re-articulation across indefinite tracts of time-space" (1991: 18). The sociologist Dorothy Smith (1999) has also explored the increasingly abstract administrative systems (such as recordkeeping) that form the core of the extralocal relations of ruling that organize our every world.

27. See Giroux (1995); also see Fine and Weis (1998) and Kellner (1997) for discussion of the eroding opportunities for youth.

28. See Macleod (1995). Michael Males (1999) also provides an equally grim picture of the declining economic realities for youth over the past twenty years.

29. A number of scholars have identified a new consumerism. See Klein (2002); Ritzer (2005); Schor (1998).

30. In referring to young people, I use several terms *kids, youth, young adults,* and *teens* throughout the book. However, I do not use all of these terms interchangeably. When I use the terms *youth, kids,* or *young adults,* I am referring to anyone under the age of twenty-five. I use the term *teen* to refer to young people who are under twenty. Some might object to my using the term kid in referring to a twenty-three-year-old. But I do not use this term to diminish them or to disregard the responsibilities young people assume as they transition to adulthood.

31. According to a recent Rand Youth poll, by the time this generation of teens turns twenty, they will have received $33,000 per capita in income and gifts. Youth are also spending more on credit, thus accumulating more debt than earlier generations (just over 10 percent of all high school students have their own credit cards).

32. Chris Woodyard, "Generation Y: Boomers' Kids a Booming Market," *USA Today,* September 11, 2003, cited at www.Teenresearch.com.

33. It was generally assumed that youth owned used cars, "buckets," and "jalopies."

34. Klein (2002): 23.

35. Automobile companies did not pave the way toward the branded America we have become. Once called "lumpy object purveyors," automobile companies are not recognized as innovators of images the way that high-concept brand builders such as Starbucks, which doesn't really sell coffee as much as it sells an "experience," and Nike, which isn't in the business of selling sneakers as much as it is promoting a motto for living, "just do it," are, according to Naomi Klein (2002). Klein has identified a significant shift away from a "commodity-based market" (where automobiles once reigned) to an "image-based one," where the product is subordinate to the image so that the logo itself becomes the new commodity fetish; the objects sold fade into the background. Klein (2000): 14. See also Matthew Sharpe (2003), available at eserver.org/clogic/2003/sharpe/html. See also Goldman and Papson (2000), who assert that in this "age of accelerated meaning," advertising, marketing and marketing research have grown in importance. Today, marketers are equipped with far more information as a larger segment of corporate spending has been rechanneled toward marketing campaigns. The result, among other things, is an enormous inflation in spending for marketing and advertising as companies spend millions to track

the behaviors, trends, and the likes and dislikes of the "net gen," conducting in-house focus groups and deploying "urban anthropologists" into the field.

36. "Today's Image Conscious Youth Embraces Car Culture: Kids Head Back to School in Customized Rides," available at www.prnewswire.com, August 27, 2004.

37. R. J. Ignelz, "In the Lot of Luxury," *San Diego Union Tribune,* June 23, 2004, A1.

38. Valerie Seckler, "Missing the Mark with Millennials: Fashion Industry Target Marketing Teenagers and College Students," *Women's Wear Daily,* February 19, 2003, available at www.lcourse.com.

39. *Wall Street Journal Weekly,* April 27, 2003 (TV news—car news).

40. Matt Nauman, "Scion's Day in the Sun: Toyota Enjoys Success with Its Young Brand," *San Jose Mercury News,* November 14, 2003, 1H, 4H.

41. It was estimated that seventeen thousand would own "luxury cars" costing upwards of $50,000 by the end of 2004. R. J. Ignelz, "In the Lot of Luxury," *San Diego Union Tribune,* June 23, 2004, A1.

42. Corporations long ago seized on educational institutions to sell their wares, to build brand awareness, and to "propagandize for corporate social and economic points of view," according to Molnar (1996): 17. For an excellent discussion of Volkswagen and the meanings attached to it, see Frank (2000).

43. "Gateway Bugs College Students," June 1, 1999, available at www.theautochannel.com.

44. Each year VW sponsors DriversFest, a concert that has featured popular youth bands such as Barenaked Ladies, the Razorbacks, and Econoline.

45. "Toyota Unveils New-Concept 'Echo' Designed for Youth Appeal," January 4, 1999, available at www.autochannel.com.

46. See Klein (2002); Molnar (1996); Quart (2003).

47. See Jameson (2003) and Bauman (2000) for a discussion of culture, flow, and mobility in the postmodern age.

48. Such an open definition of culture precludes fixing culture to any one place, requiring us to recognize the agentic possibilities of culture-making as we also attend to the relations of power that materialize through these meaning-making processes, since meanings are made within a play of forces, patterned by social structures but never fully determined by them. See for example Duncombe (2002); DuGay, Hall, Janes, McKay, and Negus (1997); Hall and Jefferson (1975); Fiske (1989a, 1989b); Mukerji and Schudson (1991); Pile and Keith (1997).

49. Baudrillard (2000) writes, "The empirical 'object' given in its contingency of form, color, material, function and discourse (or, if it is a cultural object, in its aesthetic finality) is a myth. How often it has been wished away! But the object is *nothing.* It is nothing but the different types of relations and significations that converge, contradict themselves, and twist around it, as such—the

hidden that not only arranges this bundle of relations, but directs the manifest discourse that overlays and occludes it" (57).

50. This is a point Miller (2001a) makes. He writes, "Investigations of cars and car culture run the risk of occluding the dual hybrid, and paradoxical nature of the car: either celebrating its humanity through investigations of the varied culture meanings ascribed to it at the expense of investigating its material effect or eclipsing the cultural terrains where agentic possibilities are mobilized by focusing exclusively on the car's materiality." See also Wollen and Kerr (2002).

51. I draw here from Slater's (1997) discussion of the meaning of things and from DuGay et al.'s (1997) insightful analysis of the Sony Walkman, through which they lay out the work of doing cultural studies as the study of meanings, and the conditions for their production and circulation. They write, "Meanings bridge the gap between the material world and the world in which language, thinking and communication take place—the symbolic world . . . cultural meanings do not arise in things but as a result of our social discourses and practices which construct the world meaningfully . . . certain meanings and practices . . . which seem to stand for or to represent a distinctive way of life: the culture of late modern, post-industrial societies like ours" (10–18).

52. Cultural studies frameworks are particularly useful in this regard. Cultural studies scholars have historically defined culture with attention to broad economic processes of production and consumption, establishing the constitutive links between economy and culture. See Paul Willis (1977) for a paradigmatic example of such a framework that examines the connection between economic and cultural practices as central to the reproduction of prevailing social forms. My understanding of discursive space derives from a line of inquiry developed by Dorothy Smith (1987, 1990a, 1990b, 1999). Smith argues against an understanding of ideology and social meanings in the abstract and seeks to locate the production of social ideas and meanings within ongoing, local concrete social relations.

53. Gilroy (2001): 89.

54. Much scholarly attention has been paid to the commodification of culture, demonstrating that virtually no aspect of social life is beyond the reach of commercial forces; even our most intimate relationships bear the mark of commercial influence. See for example Clarke, Doel, and Housiaux (2003); Klein (2002); Schor and Holt (2000); Nava (1987, 1991); Steinberg and Kincheloe (1997). In much literature, "culture" precedes the marketplace; culture is defined as a set of practices that have been hijacked by market forces, appropriated and then ultimately coopted in such a way that its new forms are entirely different from the originals. Car culture is clearly a little different, since cars are in the first instance commodities.

55. Readers will no doubt recognize this second understanding of car culture as more in line with the youth subcultural analysis often associated with the

"Birmingham school" of cultural studies. See for example Hall and Jefferson (1975); Hebdige (1979); McRobbie (1991); Willis (1977). See also Epstein (1998); Gelder and Thornton (1997); Skelton and Valentine (1998); Muggleton and Weinzierl (2003) for more recent engagements with the theoretical work of the Birmingham school, and Inness (1998); Harris (2004a, 2004b); Roman and Christian-Smith (1988) for feminist engagements with the Birmingham project.

56. I draw here on Ulrich Beck's (2000) insightful remarks: "People struggle to live their own lives in a world that increasingly and more evidently escapes their grasp, one that is irrevocably and globally networked. Even the most natural of action of all—the inhaling of clean air—ultimately presupposes a revolution in the industrial world order. . . . In the global age, one's own life is no longer sedentary or tied to a particular place. It is a traveling life, both literally and metaphorically, a nomadic life, a life spent in cars" (168).

57. See Best (2000); Brake (1985); Chin (2001); Eder, Evans, and Parker (1995); Corsaro (1997); Van Ausdale and Feagin (2001); Fine (1987); Giroux and Simon (1989); Gaines (1990); Graebner (1990); McRobbie (1991, 1993); Roman and Christian-Smith (1988); Ross and Rose (1994); Skelton and Valentine (1998); Thorne (1993); Walker (1987); Willis (1977).

58. See for example Lim (2004); Malbon (1998); Massey (1998); Yaeger (1996).

59. Thus requiring new forms of investigation and news ways of thinking about the connections of cultural experience and social identity. This is a point made by many scholars. In relation to changes in the social existence of youth see Dimitriadis (2001); McDonald (1999). McDonald writes, "The demodernisation of advanced societies has fractured formerly coherent ensembles which we can no longer understand in terms of integrated class structures or a shared culture translated into norms and roles. Integrating class hierarchies or culture have given way to the opposition between 'in' and 'out,' mobile and immobile, functional and dysfunctional, individual and non-individual. This weakening of older forms of social structure has meant a shift in intellectual framework . . . to focus on exploring the relationship between globalisation and individualization" (1999: 120).

60. Slater (1997): 30.

61. See for example Halter (2000). See also Slater (1997); Lipovetsky (1994); and Bauman (2000).

62. See Anataki and Widdicombe (1998); West and Fenstermaker (2002); West and Zimmerman (1987) for an excellent theoretical discussion of identity as active interactional accomplishment. See Miron and Inda (2000) for an analysis of the constitutive/performative elements of speech in the construction of race and racial identity.

63. See Omi and Winant (1986) and Guillamine (1995) for a discussion of race and sex as discursive constructions emerging from a discourse of biology.

64. Giroux (1995): 32.

65. The "heart and soul" of immigration in northern California, Silicon Valley is home to a large number of refugee communities.

66. African Americans represent 4.5 percent of the community, and 36 percent of residents are European American. These numbers change slightly when the suburban communities in the larger Santa Clara County are included. Statistics available at www.sanjoseca.gov/Census_2000.

67. Best (2000); Brown (1999).

68. After much thought, I have decided to name the city and county where this research was conducted. Likewise, I did not change street names, largely because of the matter of historical record that I was interested in capturing and conveying. I did change the names of all the young adults who were interviewed, the names of the high schools, and the names of local commercial establishments because I wanted to preserve their institutional and individual confidentiality.

69. The matter of researcher reflexivity is a complicated one that deserves more attention than I am able to give it here, but I raise this issue to situate the observations I conducted and the analysis that developed from them within a particular set of social relations.

Notes to Chapter 1

1. The social meanings attached to car cruising are varied. From a legal standpoint, cruising is defined as driving in a specific area for an extended period without a specific purpose. Like other leisure activities, cruising is a social practice through which youth identities are created.

2. Witzel and Bash (1997).

3. See for example Peter Stearns (2003) for a discussion of autonomy in the context of parental anxiety.

4. Palladino (1996): 101.

5. Long before shopping malls and warehouse-size grocery stores, Main Streets all over the United States were the center of daily living. See Ritzer (2005).

6. Witzel and Bash (1997): 44–45.

7. Skelton and Valentine (1998): 7.

8. Mike Davis (1990), in his social history of Los Angeles, discusses youth curfews, drawing attention to the racial bias in the enforcement of curfews. Curfews tend to be heavily enforced in communities of color, especially in poor urban areas, but not in largely white communities, especially in higher-income suburban areas.

9. See Witzel and Bash (1997) for a detailed discussion of these anticruising ordinances. Many cities in the United States (re)enacted such policies in

the 1990s to thwart cruisers as a leisure culture based on cars experienced a revitalization.

10. See Stanley Cohen (2002) for an analysis of the "moral panics" and collective anxieties that have developed around youth subcultures as they engage public life and public space. See also Lucas (1998).

11. See Sandoval (2003). Sandoval examines the connections among lowrider culture, Chicano identity, and cultural transmission. Sandoval focuses on the intersection of lowrider culture as *lived practice* and lowrider culture as *media practice,* with particular attention to the dynamics of class and gender. Her work highlights the emergence of lowriding as an increasingly middle-class leisure activity (and lowriders as commodified objects), increasingly divorced from the working-class *barrios* from which it sprung. See also Holtz (1975) for a discussion of lowriders and urban youth subculture.

12. Some historical analysis has been given to zoot-suits, the "Pachucos" who wore them, and the zoot-suit riots of 1943. The historian Stuart Cosgrove writes, "The zootsuit's history can be seen as a point of intersection between the related potential of ethnicity and politics on the one hand and the pleasures of identity and difference on the other" (2002: 165). Cosgrove argues that the zoot-suit style is a consequence of a disinherited generation, stripped of its beliefs, cultural practices, and language, alienated from its immigrant parents, who belonged to a different time and different place, and disadvantaged by the racism that pervaded employment and education in the United States.

13. The sociologist Carol Ray remarked that in 1950s Los Angeles, lowriders were generally called "chopped and channeled," which meant that their car's rear or the entire car was lowered. This style was in contrast to that of cars with lowered front ends (usually more traditional hot rodders). This style was called "on the rake." Lowriders were called "taco wagons" by young white working-class men in Los Angeles. Personal communication.

14. Sterngold (2000): 2, available at www.lowrider.com/information/history/nytimes.

15. See Bright (1998) for a discussion of lowriders, aesthetics, cultural production, and zoot-suiters. See also Lipsitz (1997).

16. The term *La Raza,* signifying all Chicanos/as and Mexicanas/os, served as an important organizing and unifying tool in the Chicano movement that emerged in the late 1960s. See Chabram-Dernersesian (1997); Martinez (2000); Garcia (1990); Anzaldua (1987) for feminist discussions of La Raza, Chicano/a identity, and the Chicano movement.

17. I use the term *community* throughout this chapter, even though I recognize the contentiousness and ambiguity of this term as an analytical construct. I use this term because it has such tremendous salience for the young Chicanos/as I studied. People in San Jose regularly refer to "the Chicano community," while also recognizing the splintering aspects of this group.

18. For investigations of youth in urban contexts, the role of place in the formation of youth culture, and youth identity see Massey (1998); Tienda and Wilson (2002); Watt and Stenson (1998).

19. *Lowrider* magazine (April 2001): 7.

20. I follow Pyong Gap Min's (1999) lead in making a distinction between *ethnic solidarity,* defined in terms of collective action for the shared interests of an ethnic group, and *ethnic attachment,* defined in terms of social and emotional ties to an ethnic group.

21. See Paul Gilroy (1993) for a discussion of ethnicity as an ongoing construction tied to place, history, and experience as an alternative to primordial and essentialist notions of ethnicity that prevailed in much of the early literature on ethnic identity and ethnic attachment. Much of the current research on ethnic identity has focused on the redefinitional, emergent, and constructed nature of ethnicity, highlighting the discursive and interactional strategies individuals and groups use to negotiate the structural and historical forces that construct them. See Claire Dwyer's (1998) analysis of young British Muslim women. See also Anthias (2001); Bose (2003); Deyhle (1998); Marquez (2001); Tsuda (2001); Kahani-Hopkins and Hopkins (2002); Valdivia (2003).

22. The intersection of Story and King Roads on the east side of San Jose is also an important site for cruising in the area.

23. *Lowrider* magazine, which plays a vital role in the loosely networked lowrider car clubs across the United States, originated in San Jose in the late 1960s. See "Cruising into the Eye of the Revolution," *Lowrider* magazine (April 2001): 160–162.

24. The mass displacement of lowriders from streets like Whittier Boulevard, in Los Angeles, in the 1960s and 1970s, through anticruising ordinances led to the formation of car clubs and, ultimately, to the Federation of Lowriders, a string of car clubs that organized against the criminalization of lowriders and lowriding. Today there are hundreds of loosely networked lowrider car clubs, most, though not all organized by Latinos and Chicanos. Recently lowriding has become popular in Japan, and lowrider car clubs have been formed there. Car shows to display lowriders occur across the United States. The largest car show, usually held annually in a large convention center, is sponsored by *Lowrider* magazine, a publication that is more than twenty-five years old with a readership well into the hundreds of thousands. For several decades, lowriders have been under attack, treated as criminals, as many Latino street youth mistakenly are. Lowriders have been regarded as "gangs on wheels" (Sterngold [2000]). But members of the lowrider movement have actively challenged this characterization, demonstrating a social action element. In 1968, Whittier Boulevard, in Los Angeles, was the site of a large rally protesting the ongoing violence against lowriders; supporters argued that cruising was a constitutional right protected by the right to free assembly, the right to freedom of movement,

and the right to free speech. See *Lowrider* magazine (April 2001): 161. Low-rider car clubs are often family-based clubs, and many have spearheaded community programs to deter Latino youth from becoming involved in gangs. See www.burnucscd.edu/archives/raza/1997/09; www.LowRider.com; www.lowrider magazine.com; www.firstcut.com; www.BrownPride.com.

25. *Lowrider* is a term used to describe particular kinds of cars *and* people. A lowrider can be engaged in the activity of lowriding in a lowrider car.

26. Restored lowriders can be very expensive. The award winning lowriders showcased at car shows are usually owned by older men. But the events themselves are attended by large numbers of young adults.

27. This perfectly illustrates the draw of the consumer market in constructing the self. See for example Halter (2000).

28. Many educational scholars have written on what is arguably a crisis in Latino education, demonstrating the various ways American schools fail Latinos/as. See for example Fine (1991); Fine and Weis (1998); Darder, Rodolfo, and Gutierrez (1997); Lopez (2003); Moll and Ruiz (2002); Suarez-Orozco (2002); Olsen (1997); Rumbaut (1998); Smith (2002); Vigil (1997). See also Bourgois (1995) for an account of the struggles at work and in the street for poor urban Latinos, and Montero-Sieburth and Villarruel (2000) for an examination of Latino adolescents. See Horowitz (1983) for an examination of Chicano community and family life.

29. Survey data published by KIN: Knowledge of Immigrant Nationalities of Santa Clara County in 2001 reveal that 75 percent of Mexican immigrants came to the United States because of economic hardship in Mexico. From a random sample, 43 percent of Mexicans and Mexican Americans residing in Santa Clara Country had household incomes below $30,000 (53). Because of low wages, many remain without basic medical, eye, or dental care.

30. "Keepin it real" is achieved largely by remaining connected to one's roots and sustaining an authentic self. A insightful analysis of racial identity and authenticity is provided by Carter (2003). Carter discusses the way black students work to maintain a sense of authentic blackness and black cultural capital in the context of schooling.

31. See Vigil (1988, 2002) for a discussion of the Chicano community and street gangs.

32. Thornton (1997): 201.

33. I draw loosely here on Benedict Anderson (1983) work on "imagined communities," even though his discussion centers on the role of the print media in constructing national communities. Anderson argues that nationality and nationness are cultural constructions that emerged toward the end of the eighteenth century. Anderson conceptualizes national communities based on nationality as imagined, largely because most community members don't know the majority of the other community members; yet they feel a sense of solidarity or

communion. Anderson traces the emergence of nationalism and national community as constructions, giving rise to a new form of collective consciousness that moved from a colonial consciousness to a national consciousness for nation-states. He identifies the rise of print capitalism as central to the ability to achieve a sense of imaginary communion among a group of people who often occupied disparate social locations and social realities. Anderson's conceptualization of imaginary community provides a useful way to understand the dynamic of community formation for young Chicanos/as that hinges on the unifying concept of La Raza. *Lowrider* magazine is an important conduit in the formation of national/ethnic identity and for uniting its readership as Mexicanos.

34. Taylor (2004): 23–24.

35. Taylor (2004) argues the social imaginary is created through the stories, myth and legends a people tell about themselves.

36. Sterngold (2000): 2, available at www.lowrider.com/information/history/nytimes.

37. Gender is relevant here. Women were largely excluded from these struggles since they occurred in public places. The emphasis placed on Chicanas' domestic and familial roles in the life and survival of the Chicano community precluded the same level of investment in public life for women until this relegation of women was challenged by Chicana feminists in the 1970s. See Garcia (1990). See also Mirande (1998) for a discussion of Chicano and Mexican masculinity. Chicanas also were not seen as physical threats in the way Chicanos were and thus were not subject to the same level of intense harassment by officers on the street.

38. Survey data published by KIN: Knowledge of Immigrant Nationalities of Santa Clara County in 2001 reveals that only 41 percent of Mexicans in the county felt respected when stopped by police officers. Twenty-nine percent reported they felt scared, 28 percent felt mistreated, and 26 percent felt they did not know their legal rights. Twenty-nine percent of Mexicans in the same random sample identified police officers as among the top five sources of discrimination they faced (55).

39. Almost every young man and young woman of color interviewed talked about "driving while brown/black." DWB is central as they solidify their identities as "of color." Consider Keisha's narrative, which focuses on the ongoing persecution her boyfriend experienced because he is black.

> I've been with Demetrius and been pulled over many times . . . I don't even remember how, but whatever, they told Demetrius and me to pull over and they pulled him over and they asked him to get out the car, you know, ID, you know, asked me for my ID, how old I was, what we were doing, that kind of stuff. And he's like, you look like a pretty cool type

guy, what are you doing out and you know just, I guess 'cause there's like a bunch of drugs dealers that hang out in that area.

40. According to *San Jose Mercury News* estimates, 400,000 attended the Cinco de Mayo celebration in 1998. See Ben Stocking and Becky Bartindale, "Cinco de Mayo ¡Perfecto!" (1989).

41. I draw a distinction between the Cinco de Mayo parade and the cruising that follows. These events are not one and the same, and this is not an analysis of Cinco de Mayo itself. See Sommers (1985) for an analysis of Cinco de Mayo. Etzioni and Bloom (2004) also provides a discussion of Cinco de Mayo.

42. Ethnic distinctions based on appearance are notoriously unreliable, and thus I offer this comment with caution, since I cannot be certain that I did not mistake some Anglos for Chicanos and Chicanos for Anglos. I saw few members of other ethnic or racial groups.

43. I checked the newspapers, and there were no reports to verify the story.

44. Bauman (2000): 199.

45. Using Etzioni and Bloom's (2004) schema of holiday types, one might regard Cinco de Mayo as both a *recommitment ritual* and a *tension management ritual* in that on the one hand the festivities provide opportunity for Chicanos/as to reaffirm their commitment to their ethnic community and national identity (as Mexican) and on the other the occasion provides an opportunity to suspend the instrumental activities and "profane" routines of the everyday world of work and school, providing a release of sorts from social obligation. Etzioni and Bloom argue that the extent to which a society celebrates tension management holidays over recommitment holidays can serve as a measure of the society's "value integrity and enforcement" (13). Using a Durkheimian framework to analyze Cinco de Mayo draws attention to themes of social integration over and against the excessive individualism of modern everyday life, where the individual members of society pledge their commitment to a set of shared beliefs and values and reaffirm communal bonds. The Mexican flag, an object of ritual worship in this setting, commands a deep reverence by participants.

46. The Martin Luther King library, an impressive building, was a joint venture of San Jose State University and the city's redevelopment agency.

47. Quotation from "Discussion Points on Design Proposal for the San Jose Joint Library Art Collection Item #17 Lowrider Tables. Public Hearing 11/18/02," Chicano/Latina Faculty and Staff Association and the Chicano Library Resource Center Advisory Committee, San Jose State University.

48. Yet, it is meaningful that many youth continue to define cruising as an activity for Chicanos. One young white woman, who explained that she has never cruised, largely attributes this to the ethnic organization of this activity. Melissa, a nineteen-year-old white woman, told me:

I've never really done cruising. For some reason, I feel like I'm white and I can't cruise. I'm such a white person. You see what I'm saying? It's such an ethnic thing, I think. This is a stereotype, too. I mean if you do a ethnic stereotype because it's like *Cheech and Chong*. The lowrider cars are more Hispanic, come from like Hispanic origin.

49. Local merchants, corporations, community activists, urban planners, and policymakers are also key players. They are rarely physically present; yet their influence is far-reaching. Different times of the day and night draw different groups. The presence of some, such as the residents of nearby Naglee Park, a stronghold of white Democrats, many of whom are wealthy, with long-term ties to the community and the nearby State University, is fleeting.

50. In this sense, the police officers I interviewed were sympathetic to these youth struggles. They seemed to recognize that part of their work assignment was to remove these youth. My sense from the interviews was that they did so somewhat reluctantly. Many of the youth I interviewed viewed cops as the enemy; yet I observed many instances of an easy rapport between some of the cops and the kids. It was clear that for some of these officers working in the CMD was enjoyable because it provided an opportunity to be a part of the community, instead of an enemy of it. One of the officers, Steve, who was particularly thoughtful in many of his comments, talked about the routine nature of his work, about looking forward to seeing the same kids the following week. He joked that kids at the end of Saturday night would be sure to say goodbye and "see you next week." I walked away from a few of the interviews with the sense that managing the downtown carried the promise of connection between peace officers and community members, though this hope was realized in only very small ways at this time. In thinking about this apparent contradiction between the officers' and the kids' definition of the situation, I am reminded of Handel's (1982) discussion of Bittner's study of routine peace/police officer work on "Skid Row" from an ethnomethodological perspective. This study focused on the police officer's "concern to foster the impression of his authority and control in his district. . . . They are alert to challenges to their authority and bring their resources to bear to maintain it whenever challenges arise. . . . To the policemen, their unquestioned authority is essential to the smooth operation of their tactics" (18–19).

51. The historian Glenna Matthews (2003) attributes the economic decline of the 1980s to changes in the semiconductor industry stemming from growing competition from Japan. Government subsidies, tougher trade policies with Japan, and the growing popularity of outsourcing production led to the economic recovery of several semiconductor companies in the early 1990s. A steady erosion of manufacturing jobs is also responsible for the economic decline experienced in the 1980s.

52. San Jose has been named one of the five safest cities in the United States, according to the San Jose Police Department Web site. See http://www.sjpd.org.

53. Redevelopment Agency of the City of San Jose, 2003, P. A-320. See http://www.sjredevelopment.org.

54. Zukin (2003): 128. Zukin (1995) discusses the reorganization of American's urban core according to a logic of consumption and entertainment, with consumption as the "motor of urban social change" at the end of the twentieth century. This can be clearly seen in the redevelopment of downtown San Jose. However, San Jose did encounter a few snags with this approach to redevelopment. An earlier attempt, the Pavilion, a fairly large retail space, opened downtown but did not succeed, some believe because of the absence of occupied residential housing to support retail of this kind. Over the next decade, the San Jose Redevelopment Agency was successful in creating a residential upscaling of the downtown. The transformation in downtown San Jose might be regarded as a postmodern transformation. Don Slater (1997) regards the postmodern city as "a place of consumption, entertainment and services. . . . Cities are transformed to attract, through consumption, leisure and entertainment facilities they offer, tourists, other international movements of people (for example, business conferences and major sporting events), middle-class consumers who took to the suburbs during late modernity and 'gentrifying' folk working in professional and financial services" (202). The cities Slater talks about are likely large global centers (Los Angeles and New York City), which San Jose is not. But the blueprint for urban social change seems to be largely the same. See also Davis (1990), which examines the postmodern transformations in Los Angeles.

55. For example, the downtown is full of new and impressive buildings that provide office space for corporations such as Adobe, SBC, Earthlink, Knight Ridder, Comerica, and Ernst, Young & Cooper among many others.

56. Traci Hukill, *Metroactive,* November 26, 1997, 6.

57. David Madrid, "'Hitting the Strip,'" *Silicon Valley De Bug: The Voice of the Young and Temporary,* Pacific News Service (July–August 2002): 7–8.

58. This point about "capitalists of place" was drawn from a personal communication with the sociologist Carol Ray. See Logan and Molotch (1988).

59. For theoretical and empirical examinations of the relationship between race and space see for example Davis (2000); Laguerre (1999); Kennedy (2000). For exploration of resistance and place see Moore (1997).

60. For an historical investigation of Mexican Americans and the Los Angeles Police Force see Escobar (1999).

61. When I attended Cinco de Mayo 2004, I drove passed a fleet of fifty or so cop cars parked in a lot just beyond Santa Clara Street early in the day. When I passed the same lot, hours later, the cars had dispersed.

62. See Davis (1990); Katz (1998); Lucas (1998); Massey (1998).

63. See Schlesinger (1992).

64. As Zygmunt Bauman, quoting Eric Hobsbawm remarked, "Never was the word community used more indiscriminately and emptily than in the decades when community in sociological sense became hard to find in real life. Men and women look for groups to which they can belong, certainly and forever in a world in which all else is moving and shifting, in which nothing else is certain" (2000: 171).

65. Austin and Willard (1998): 6.

66. Stanley Fish (1980) uses the notion of interpretive community to refer to different communities of readers of literature. See also Janice Radway's (1984) classic ethnography on the Smithton women, a group of middle-aged, Midwestern romance readers, for an understanding of interpretive community.

67. For example, one white young woman, in discussing lowriders, offered, "We had a Christmas party and everybody had to bring a gift. And it was a gag gift. And so one of the gifts was a redneck car set and it was funny 'cause it came with the Chiquita bouncing dog. The Taco Bell dog. And it came with the chain-link license plate thing and tassels to put around your windows. It was the funniest and best gift." Later in the interview, she offered, "A lot of white people wouldn't put the same kind of tires that a Hispanic person would. Wild wheels, that's what it is, the spokes in some of the tires . . . they're really, like, choppy, but then on some of the white people's cars, you'll see really nice designs like these on the rims."

68. Deyhle (1989): 24.

69. See www.strayrecords.com and www.daveyd.com/bootscomrad.html.

NOTES TO CHAPTER 2

1. Cruising is a staple activity for California youth. Nearly all the young women interviewed for this project had cruised at least once, though only some of the young women were regular weekend cruisers. Girls in this cultural scene represent a range of income groups and educational levels. High school girls and college women both cruise. Girls of different racial and ethnic groups can be found cruising, though Chicanas visibly constitute the largest group. The predominance of Chicanos/as in this cruising scene is most visible on Cinco de Mayo, the most popular day of the year to cruise, as I discussed in chapter 1.

2. Cars themselves are defined in and through a gender meaning system that symbolically serves to maintain young women's marginal place and reconstitutes the world of cars as a world populated by men. Designation of girls' (chick) cars as "bitch buckets," a moniker referring to many convertible cars, or the use of other derogatory labels symbolically serves to maintain young women's secondary place in the male-dominated world of cars. Categories of masculinity and femininity help organize a hierarchy of cars that links cars without

the requisite speed or might, or those with excess frill, to femininity or, worse yet, homosexuality. Consider, for example, the ways in which the Mazda Miata has been coded as a "sissy car."

3. Companies in the business of selling car parts, aftermarket parts, and racing gear celebrate a world where male sexual gratification is central through its sexualized imagery, logos, and narratives. Consider, for example, BLŌ ME, a successful retail business that sells a variety of t-shirts. "Racing Asphalt is for Pussies" is the legend on one of the more popular shirts.

4. *Lowrider* magazine (April 2001). In the September 2004 edition of *Lowrider*, a total of twenty-one young women wearing bikinis were counted. Again, all of these women were featured posing in front of a car, straddling a tire rim, or bending over the car. Straddling and bending-over positions were most common. I counted an additional twenty-nine images of women engaged in the same activities but wearing either hiked-up miniskirts or short shorts. I also recorded a few images of women licking or sucking on car parts. No women were featured behind the wheel in this edition. Less common in both editions were images of women who had not been sexualized. I recorded pictures, usually from car shows, of women standing in front of cars, dressed in jeans and t-shirts.

5. Most pictures were advertisements for cars, car parts, or upcoming car shows.

6. Contradictory images of women do sometimes prevail. The April 2001 edition of *Lowrider* magazine also featured a lengthy article on Dolores Huerta, feminist and longtime activist in the United Farm Workers. Carla, one of the young women whom I interviewed both in the focus group and individually, spoke to the contradictions of *Lowrider* magazine:

> *Lowrider* magazine I would say is more culturally aware of what's going on than other magazines. It gives scholarships to Chicanos so they can go to school . . . they, um, they give a lot of power to women, I would say to Chicanas. And that's really good 'cause then the Mexican culture is just like, a lot of machismo and the females don't get their voice out there and *Lowrider* does it. Even though they do show the women, whatever, dressed like that, they do appreciate them and recognize them.

7. For an excellent historical analysis of the automobile, changing definitions of womanhood, and enduring ideas about men's and women's claims to independence and freedom see Scharff (1991).

8. Logically, this makes an investigation of girls' experiences in this cultural field a theoretical necessity, since to understand how masculinity as a system of meaning operates requires an understanding of the sites where these meaning are inscribed. See Bordo (1993); Brumberg (1997); Butler (1990).

9. See McDowell (1999) for discussion of gender identity and space.

10. See McRobbie (1993) and Willis (1977). Both discuss public streets,

girls, and youth culture. See also Devlin (1998); Gettis (1998); Odem (1995, 1998). All discuss the relationship between concern about young women's public display of sexuality and attempts to curb and contain juvenile delinquency. See Jones (2002) for a discussion of girls and car cruisers.

11. All the sorority women I interviewed are first-generation college students. All middle income, their parents were mechanics, office workers, civil servants, and police officers. Half of the group came from families headed by women, and while most of their families could now be defined as middle-income families, many had managed on far lower incomes during the girls' childhoods.

12. Much of Goffman's writing centers on the ritual performance of self. He sees this performance as central to the structure of social encounters and the ritual maintenance of a specific interactional order. It is through the ritual performance of self that social reality is sustained. Disruptions in the performance of self threaten the structure of the social encounter itself, and, because of this, the performance must be carefully managed. See for example Goffman (1959, 1967).

13. I repeatedly watched the cameras zoom in as young women walked away. Reminiscent of Laura Mulvey's analysis of cinema, the camera, and the male gaze, rarely did the women address the camera head on or engage the camera as subjects.

14. See Blackshaw (2003); Presdee (2000); Young (1997) for discussion of play and performance, deviance and social and criminal transgressions.

15. At times I wondered if this double standard was exaggerated. For example, one young woman remarked, "I've never seen a girl holler at a guy except for like Cinco de Mayo." But in my observations I witnessed several instances of girls yelling at boys.

16. I draw from Goffman's analysis of "face-work" and "deference and demeanor" presented in Goffman (1967).

17. See Goffman's (1967) discussion of "deference and demeanor."

18. See Candace West and Don Zimmerman's seminal piece "Doing Gender" (1987), which examines gender as a ritual accomplishment. See also West and Fenstermaker (2002). See DeVault (1991) for an examination of the ritual family activities like food provisioning and preparation that maintain the salience of gender to women's identity.

19. Lightfoot's (1997) research focuses on adolescence, though I think her arguments can be extended to youth in their early twenties, given the postponing of adulthood that increasingly is common in this changing world. Scholars refer to the period of postponement as "emerging adulthood." See Hollander's (2002) discussion of gender, vulnerability, resistance, and the social construction of identity.

20. The gendered nature of risk cultures is also explored in chapter 2 and 4.

21. Brown (2004): 15.

22. This kind of talk is similar to what Lyn Mikel Brown observed during her time spent listening to rural white working class girls. See Brown (1999).

23. The fact that the term *pimp* is girls' code word for the worst kind of boy and boys' celebration of the best kind of boy is instructive.

24. Schippers (2002): ix. Also see Inness (1998); Leahy (1994); Lim (2004); Roman and Christian-Smith (1988); Raby (2002); Sato (1998); Tolman (1994); Williams (2002) for discussion of young women and the negotiation of gender.

25. There are obvious parallels here between Paul Willis's (1977) working-class "lads" and these young women, who reproduce the very system that contains them as they play within its boundaries.

26. Brown (1999) talks about the pleasure girls take in these disruptions of gender realities.

27. Young women's struggles for freedom are hardly new. Paula Fass's (1977) historical account of 1920s youth reveal college girls' struggle to claim greater freedom through their use of symbols of liberation such as smoking, dancing, dress, and drinking.

28. Carla's story reveals some of the contradictory elements of being and living Chicana. While she indeed had met her fiancé through cruising and was expecting a baby, her story did not end as she had hoped. She gave birth to a healthy baby girl a few months after the interviews and was living with her fiancé at his mother's small apartment. When I saw her months after the baby's birth, she told me that she had left the area and was living with her parents because her fiancé had beat her. She was struggling to stay in school despite the two-hour commute required to travel from her parents' house to the university. Her story is not entirely uncommon. Domestic abuse affects women across different cultural and class communities and is part of Latino culture. But perhaps more meaningful is that she left once the abuse began and was now commuting more than two hours a day to finish college while hoping to transfer to a state university closer to her parents' home.

29. The 1990 U.S. Census noted a dramatic increase in the number of years in school completed by black, white, and Latina women. The greatest spike was among Latinas, and this trend has continued. In 1990, 20.2 percent of Latinas ages 25 and over had completed one to more than five years of schooling, up from 4.7 percent in 1980. These numbers are reflected in the attendance figures for the local state university where these young women attend school. During the fall 2002 semester, 1,950 "Hispanic" females were enrolled and 1,538 "Hispanic" males were enrolled at the university. For the fall 1999 semester, 1,774 "Hispanic" females and 1,411 "Hispanic" males were enrolled there. This gender gap in education is most pronounced among communities of color, according to Nancy Lopez (2003). Lopez notes that "during the 1990s twice as many African American women as African American men earned college degrees."

Lopez points out that these proportions hold true for high school graduation rates. In 2000, 44 percent of Latina finished high school, whereas 35 percent of Latino men finished high school. This is the "quiet revolution" led by Latinas seeking "independence, self-sufficiency, and physical safety" that Fine and Weis (1998) identified in their investigation of working poor and working-class young adults among Generation X: "While the Latinas with whom we interviewed could easily be seen as traditional or relatively conservative in their gender and sexuality arrangements and judgments, it would be misleading to presume that they are un-conflicted about the dance of power/gender/sexuality that unfolds in their homes and in the streets" (217).

30. Yet, it is also clear that these young women are able to move into and out of their home communities with some ease. They attend a local public university close to their homes. Their family members, mostly their mothers, are supportive of their decisions to obtain a college diploma.

31. This point is evident in the historical analysis provided by Witzel and Bash (1997), although it is stated without any remark from the authors.

32. I draw specifically here on the writings of Zygmunt Bauman (2000), particularly in his discussion of emancipation and individuality, in which he details the shift from what he calls "solid modernity," where emancipation is conceived of as a collective project embodied in the notion of the "good society" to be achieved by the state and the public to "liquid modernity," characterized by a new stage in modern life in which governing institutions, the state, and the public have receded in their role in creating a just society and emancipation rests entirely upon individual effort.

33. For a discussion of the idea of new girlhoods see Harris (2004a, 2004b); Brown (1999, 2003).

Notes to Chapter 3

1. These are terms are used widely by youth in San Jose. Concern about "gangs" in San Jose, specifically the Nortenos and Surenos, are frequently articulated in the context of school, youth, and community life. Additionally, there are several "gang prevention" programs in the wider county. However, what actually constitutes a gang has been the subject of much popular and academic debate. I do not address this debate here, but I do resist reifying this contentious term.

2. I hesitate to use the term *subcultural* given the increasing questioning over the value of this term in understanding the social practices that define the experiences of youth in an increasingly global context. The term *subcultural* originates with the "Birmingham School" of cultural studies and signifies youth groups formed in and against the "host" culture. *Subculture* was used to signify oppositional class-based groups (usually working-class young men) who engage

in a sort of cultural and class warfare through style politics. In the past several decades, scholars studying youth culture have identified three problematic points arising from "subcultural studies": class reductionism; the romantic construction of these youth groups; and the limits of aesthetic forms of resistance in a context of rapid market appropriation and cooptation that have led to a reevaluation of this term. For a more comprehensive discussion see Muggleton and Weinzierl (2003).

3. In this sense, the import car scene has a transnational dimension.

4. Namkung (2004).

5. Mike, a bicultural Filipino whom we will meet in chapter 4, also worked at Great America while in high school. And while he travels within the same loosely extended group of import racers, he is an upper-income kid. He attended a prestigious private high school in the area, and his parents, both professional workers, own several homes in northern California. The import car-racing scene appears to be a scene where young men develop loosely formed ties across economic groups. In this instance, being Asian as much as having an interest in imports seems to serve as the basis of their social ties. Victoria Namkung (2004) has argued that the import scene reflects attempts to construct a pan-Asian identity among Vietnamese, Filipinos, Japanese, Chinese, and South Asian youth largely on the basis of their exclusion from "mainstream" or the dominant Anglo youth culture broadly and the hot-rodding car culture specifically. Signs of a pan-Asian identity are clearly visible in this research.

6. Some car racers cruise in the absence of a race. But there are fairly distinct lines between the racers and the cruisers. If there is nothing else to do, racers sometimes cruise, though they generally talk about this activity with some disdain. Cruisers attend races every once in a while but not routinely and usually do so as spectators, not racers. Tino told me that he did not race because he enjoyed the collective experience of cruising. In his words, you get to spend time with "your homies," but when you race, "you're alone." Most of the time racers in these semi-organized races in business parks do not have passengers in their cars when they actually race. While the boundaries between these two groups are sometimes fluid and allow some level of boundary crossing, when it comes to "identity talk," cruisers and racers draw distinct lines between their groups.

7. This has much do with the racial-ethnic composition of the school itself. A majority of the students are Asian or Latino. Hot rodding continues to have a predominately Anglo membership.

8. Namkung (2004): 160.

9. For example, twenty-year-old Melissa explains that her boyfriend, Jake, who aligns himself with American Muscle, "will park next to the lowest car to make his truck look bigger. . . . Jake will not park next to [trails off] he'll park next to a truck that he knows will make it look stupid. Like he'll park next to

the truck that's smaller than his. He'll park next to like a '87 Blazer that's got a 3-inch lift and big tires and he'll park where his car looks bigger."

10. *San Francisco Chronicle,* June 12, 2001, available at www.sfgate.com.

11. The car-racing scene shares particular sensibilities with the underground graffiti world that MacDonald (2001) depicted as "an illegal confine where danger, opposition and the exclusion of women is used to nourish, amplify, and salvage notions of masculinity" (149).

12. McDonald (1999) sees the search for intensity and visibility as central to the project of self-creation in the context of what Zygmunt Bauman (2000) calls "liquid modernity," a period of late modernity that emerged in the late 1970s and was defined by flow and movement, rather than the stability and stasis that are associated with "solid modernity." Drawing from their insights, I see racing as an attempt to disassociate from the self on the one hand and an attempt to know the self through intense sensation on the other. It is as if the racer steps outside himself in order to step back in at some other point of entry. In some ways, I conceptualize the structure of the self along the lines of how George Herbert Mead conceptualized the self as made up of its component parts, the "I," the part of the self in action, and the "Me," the reflective self that allows for an awareness of self and also social control.

13. See Lightfoot (1997).

14. Bearing witness to dangerous scenarios and crazy situations is also central to constructing their world as a world of danger, daring, and peril. One morning I learned that Jason, who now drives a green Jetta, had originally had a Mustang until it was stolen, right out of the parking lot at school during fourth period. I responded with visible shock, since I was amazed that a car could be stolen from a high school parking lot. I could tell he still found the whole thing slightly bewildering. His was not the last nor the first story I heard about stolen cars. The boys seemed able to easily recall stories of theft in the neighborhoods where they live around the school, which is partly a function of their living in low-income neighborhoods. Thuy Vo, on another morning, showed me where someone tried to jimmy the lock on his Civic. His car had been parked outside his house in the driveway when this had happened (during the day, no less).

15. In talking with these boys and others in the class, I consciously directed the conversations toward future plans. I had the opportunity to speak with almost all of the 125 or so students in the four classes I observed. Only a handful (fewer than five) intended to move on to four-year colleges. Among this handful, all were in advanced placement classes and had decided to take this class to be either more "well-rounded" or because they saw the class as an easy "A." A much larger group planned to move on to community colleges or technical schools, where they hoped to gain career skills in graphic design or as auto

technicians. About half of the racers with whom I spent the majority of my time planned to move on to community colleges because they weren't quite sure what else there was to do. A few talked about moving on to community college because it was a more affordable alternative to a four-year school. None (among this group of racers) talked about plans to move on to a four-year college after community college. All assumed they would continue with the jobs they currently held. It is likely that some in this group will move on to four-year colleges eventually, but this clearly was not on their immediate horizon.

16. Blackshaw (2003); Kimmel (1997); Horrocks (1994).

17. The declining significance of physical strength to masculine dominance in the Western world might also help to explain the proliferation of images of "ass-kicking" women in popular culture, from *Buffy, the Vampire Slayer,* to the new *Charlie's Angels,* to the Quentin Tarantino film *Kill Bill I* and *II,* in which the female protagonist wreaks utter havoc (against a large group of Asian men in one instance) in her search for revenge.

18. See Anthony Giddens's (1991) discussion in "Ontological Security and Existential Anxiety."

19. See Baudrillard (2000) for a discussion of hyperreality and simulacra.

20. Vered Vinitzky-Seroussi (1998) makes a related point in her investigation of high school reunions. She examines how people manage the discrepancy between their biographical self and their social self, their past self and their present self, arguing that ultimately the most important audience for the performance of self is the self. This is a key point that Goffman (1959, 1963), in his investigations of impression management and the performance and presentation of the self, overlooked. I also argue that convincing the self of one's performance of self is especially important in the context of late modernity, given Anthony Giddens's arguments about the increased pressure to generate identity in a "reflexive" mode. In the posttraditional, demodernized period that characterizes late modernity, people are disengaged from social roles. Social roles have been replaced by a new individualism marked by the rise of anxiety and uncertainty as traditional anchors of identity become less secure. This has given rise to the idea of the self as a project for improvement, according to Giddens. See Giddens's (1991) discussion in "The Trajectory of the Self."

21. Giddens (1991): 75. Perhaps this explains why the feminist movements and the men's movement of the 1970s were able to publicly scrutinize masculinity in ways that were impossible at other historical moments.

22. The hypermasculine is increasingly antithetical to celebrated forms of masculinity, what R. W. Connell (1987, 1995) would regard as hegemonic masculinity because it is seen as inauthentic and unreflective.

23. The ultimate hypermasculine social type is almost always in the image of a white working-class guy. He can usually be seen drinking cans of domestic

beer, wearing flannel, his belly spilling over his jeans, espousing reactionary racist rhetoric. His wife, worn and beaten, is relegated to the kitchen, lest she be the subject of his wrath.

24. One might regard these acts and actions as "gender strategies," a term sociologist Arlie Hochschild uses to talk about the ways men attempt to solve the problem of achieving masculinity. See Hochschild (1984).

25. These passages posted to the bulletin boards appear as they appeared on the bulletin boards. I did not change typographical or grammatical errors.

26. I have placed in italics those portions of the text that I identify as particularly important to this masculine struggle.

27. See Goffman's (1963) classic examination of the interactional work involved in managing discredited and discreditable identities.

28. There is also a logic operating here about cultural boundaries and status hierarchies that is similar to the logic elites use to prevent the popularizing and massification of cultural practices. Presumably the scene was pure when it was restricted to those in the know. The opening or broadening of racer culture is seen to have spoiled or polluted the activity. See for example Lamont and Fournier (1992).

29. I draw here on boundary theory, which has explored the production and reproduction of social inequalities through the use of symbolic boundaries and status distinctions. Boundary theory often emphasizes the informal practices that constitute cultural boundaries, seeing these as central to the formation of cultural hierarchies. A particular emphasis has been placed on the connection between what Bourdieu first called "cultural capital," referring to types of "high-status" knowledge, and the reproduction of social and economic inequality. See Bourdieu (1977, 1984), Lamont (1992, 1995), Lamont and Fournier (1992). See DiMaggio (1982) for an examination of boundary distinctions and cultural capital in schooling. See Lareau (2003) for an examination of the distinctive class-based parenting logics that produce different kinds of cultural capital. See Carter (2003) for a discussion of dominant and nondominant forms of cultural capital (specifically black cultural capital) in educational contexts. See Vallas (2000) for an application of boundary theory to work organizations. Vallas explores the distinction between mental and manual labor and its role in creating new forms of social inequality at work as new technologies increasingly organize the workplace.

30. Boundary theory is particularly applicable to understanding the complex and subtle distinctions these young men draw between posers and fakes. "Symbolic capital" and "cultural capital" are both useful concepts here. See Bourdieu (1977, 1984); Vallas (2000). The refined knowledge about cars, car parts, and car engines held by many of these young men operates as a type of "cultural capital" that confers status on the knower, just as "symbolic capital," having a

particular kind of cars with particular kinds of modifications, confers prestige or status on or discredits the car owner.

31. Somewhere along the way, I realized that my ability to pass in this world as a woman who looks more like their teachers than like them is entirely dependent on the fact that my questions became an occasion for them to demonstrate their knowledge about cars. I found myself in situation after situation listening attentively to the breadth and depth of their knowledge about cars and car parts, which these boys were eager to share. Many of these young men relished the opportunity to teach me about this world of which they are so thoroughly a part.

32. These young men are engaged in a struggle over the relevance of what R. W. Connell has referred to as hegemonic masculinity. In a traditional Gramscian sense of hegemony, allegiance to this masculine construct is achieved largely through the consent of men, many of whom gain very little from this social arrangement, since it depends upon various subordinated forms of masculinity. For Connell (1987, 1995), the production of masculinity exists within a hierarchical order, so that some forms of masculinity are deployed to debase and discredit men. As Connell reminds us, it is the interplay among varying modes of masculinity that helps sustain a patriarchal social order, and thus active attempts at debasing and discrediting others are critical to masculine dominance. Relating to my points earlier, I argue that a hypermasculine type is one example of a subordinated masculinity that is used to gain men's allegiance to a hierarchy of masculinities and to a dominant type. For Connell, there is no hegemonic femininity that corresponds to a hegemonic masculinity, although a hierarchy of femininities is in operation. Forms of femininity, although always defined by their relation to hegemonic masculinity, uphold dominant masculine forms in varying degrees. He identifies "emphasized femininity" as a dominant form of femininity that works to secure masculine power, but he also recognizes that other forms of femininity subordinate to emphasized femininity threaten masculine dominance. See also Diaz (2002); Horowitz (2001); Mac An Ghaill (1994); Messner (1992); Meyer (2001); Shackleford (2001) for discussion of masculine identity construction in the context of social struggle.

33. There is a very large body of sociological literature that examines the social mechanics of status arising from Weber's work on status as a social good, but I see little reason to rehearse that here.

34. Thuy Vo's car discussed earlier in the chapter, though admired by many as "artwork" was also referred to as a "ricer" by some of the racers.

35. Goffman (1963): 107.

36. There is also a clear play on the meaning that circulates in commodity culture. I am reminded of the cleverly conceived and wildly successful marketing campaign "Got Milk?" launched by the American Dairy Association,

specifically targeting would-be young milk drinkers, that has appeared in a host of magazines for young readers, from *Rolling Stone* to *Seventeen*. The inscription *Got Rice?* as much as it reveals something about the racial order young people occupy, also provides clues about youths' immersion in a consumer world.

37. The import car culture emerged as a distinctly Asian American male youth culture within a broader context of hyperfeminization of Asian men. Cars became central to constructing masculine identity for young Asian men who had otherwise been excluded from the muscle car culture of the 1970s and 1980s, since cars are codified as masculine. Yet many of these Asian young men, as they forged alternative masculinities through the import car-racing scene, came to reject a "brutish" mode of masculinity epitomized in the muscle car of the 1970s and 1980s, distancing themselves from a masculinity rooted in white working-class culture, a form traditionally defined by one's physical strength and skill in working with one's hands (e.g., mechanics).

38. See Espiritu (1997): 90. See also Kondo (1998) and David Henry Hwang's *M. Butterfly*.

39. See O'Connell (1998).

40. During the conversation, as Brad talked, one of the guys, joking, said, "I am ricer." I was struck by how he embraced this. I raised the point of *ricer* being an anti-Asian slur, and the group fell silent. No one challenged me. While I cannot be sure if they too saw all this hubbub as expressing the anti-Asian and anti-immigrant nativist attacks that have intensified in post-9/11 America, they didn't attempt to teach me or correct me as they had at other times.

41. See Espiritu (1997); Rubin (2004); Wu (2002).

42. Within the context of Silicon Valley's economy, where Asian professionals play active roles in the tech sectors, the perception that Asian men on H1B visas are stealing jobs from skilled professional "American" workers (i.e., computer programmers and engineers) is widespread, fueled especially by the economic downturn that began in 2000. Thousands of professional workers were laid off as the tech bubble burst, among them were many South and Central Asians and Asian Americans. See also for historical discussions of this Anti-Asian pattern Takaki (1989); Nomura et al. (1989); Wu (2002).

43. Rubin (2004) argues that, although upper-middle-class whites have benefited from the influx of documented and undocumented immigrants because they provide a cheap source of domestic labor for the upper classes, the willingness of immigrants to work for cheap wages undercuts the demands for solid wages made by working-class unions. This point is also made by Fine and Weis (1998) in their examination of the eroding opportunities for young white working-class men who are part of the much maligned Generation X and in Weis's (1990) investigation of white working-class high-schoolers in deindustrialized Buffalo.

44. Thornton (1997): 201.

45. "Together but apart" is a statement Thorne (1993) used to describe the gender realities of elementary school playgrounds.

Notes to Chapter 4

1. Annual tuition at Bernards in 2003–2004 was just over $8,000.

2. However, he has not escaped the wrath of police officers on the road. In his interview he referenced the now-common phrase "driving while brown" and shared personal stories of routine and subtle harassment by police officers on the road that I discussed in chapter 1.

3. For an in-depth discussion of the increasing number of hours spent at work by American workers and the consequences, see Juliet Schor (1992). See also Hertz (1986) for a discussion of dual-earning couples, affluence, and the demands of work, and Hochschild (1997) for a discussion of home life as work.

4. See for example Annette Lareau (2003). Lareau demonstrates a relationship between social-class membership and parenting practices and the consequences of this relationship for the reproduction of social and economic inequalities. She identifies "concerted cultivation" as a distinctly middle-class parenting logic based on a commitment to developing or cultivating the child through a variety of organized activities. She contrasts this with "the accomplishment of natural growth," which she identifies as a working-class parenting practice that allows children significant freedom and less involvement in organized activities. Lareau argues that concerted cultivation instills a sense of entitlement in middle-class kids, while the accomplishment of natural growth instills an emerging sense of constraint in working-class kids. See also Amira Proweller (1998) for a compelling analysis of private schooling and social inequalities.

5. Parental anxiety is an enduring theme of the nineteenth century, as the historian Peter Stearns (2002) demonstrated. See also Kurz (2000a) for a discussion of parental concern for children's safety.

6. Beck (1998): 10. See also Giddens (1991); Furedi (2002).

7. Risk, once cast in positive terms, as in "one is willing to take risks," is now defined as a negative; thus, we are increasingly engaged in risk assessment, risk avoidance, risk analysis, and risk management. The limiting of risk has become big business, an ever-expanding and diversifying industry, argues Furedi (2002).

8. See Altheide (2002) for a discussion of children in a fear framework.

9. As a consequence, we continue to put in place more restrictive policies, further limiting the ways in which young people move in and through this world. Graduated Drivers Licensing, which places tighter restrictions on when youth may drive and with whom, is one such example. Fine, Espeland, and Rojek refer to laws like this as "symbolic fixes to complicated problems" (2001:

310). In this case, the complicated problems relate to larger transportation issues. Beyond Graduate Drivers Licensing laws, other means to control teens are in place. Surveillance and risk management have created lucrative business opportunities. "Track-A-Teen" is one of a number of companies offering teen driving surveillance. For a fee, the company provides a bumper sticker reading "HOW'S MY DRIVING? 1-877-711-Teen" to be placed on the teen's car. Drivers who witness errant driving may use the call-in number to report the teen, and parents are notified of the supposed misconduct. The "Teen Traffic Offender Program," in Santa Clarita County, California, is another such example. Several versions of "black boxes" are available on the market today (usually costing $300) that enable parents to closely monitor their children's driving. Black boxes installed in cars offer GPS systems (possibly even without the teen's knowledge) that enable parents to determine their child's exact location and the distance driven, as well as the speed and rates of acceleration. See Brottman (2001) for explorations of cars and danger and crash culture, and Garvey (2001) for a compelling discussion of driving and daring.

10. For example, the headline of an article in the *Washington Post* declared, "Teen Auto Fatalities Rise 5% in the U.S.: Studies Cite Speed, Alcohol as Factors." The article went on to report that "the number of people between 15–20 years old involved in fatal crashes rose 5% between 1993 and 2003." But what the article did not reveal is that the total number of drivers involved in fatal crashes also increased during that same period. In fact, young drivers between fifteen and twenty years old account for only 8 percent of the total increase. The article also fails to report that, while there was an increase in the number of traffic fatalities among teens, the number of licensed teen drivers rose by 7 percent, according to the National Center for Statistics and Analysis of the National Highway Traffic and Safety Administration; see www.nhtsa.dot.gov/people/ncsa. In 1992, almost 11.7 million licensed drivers were young drivers; in 2002, 12.5 million drivers in the United States were between the ages of fifteen and twenty. The rate of fatal crashes involving young drivers has declined, and young drivers are involved in a smaller percentage of the total number of fatal crashes than formerly; the rate went down from 14 percent in 1993 to 13.4 percent in 2003. Young drivers account for 6.4 percent of the 194.3 million licensed drivers in the United States, according to NHTSA. See Glassner (1999). Glassner demonstrates that many of our fears, especially around children—teen pregnancy, teen gambling, teen violence, teen drinking, child abduction—are social constructed, with little basis in reality. Glassner argues that we are worried about the wrong things. See Joseph Gusfield's (1981) discussion of drinking and driving as a public problem and the moral and legal framing of the problem. See also David Altheide (2002) for a thorough investigation of media and the discourse of fear. Children, Altheide argues, "are critical symbols in the entertainment-oriented fear perspective" (156).

11. Motor vehicle crashes are, in fact, the leading cause of death among fifteen- to twenty-year-olds. But they are also the leading cause of death for thirteen- and fourteen-year-olds, a group ineligible to drive. According to Child Trends' online databank, children are far more likely to die during their first year than at any other time during childhood. Available at http://www.child trendsdatabank.org. Mortality rates for men ages 15–19 are 95 per 100,000, but the rate is 800 per 100,000 for boys under the age of one. For black infants, the numbers are even higher, with an infant mortality rate of 1,506 per 100,000, whereas traffic fatalities among men ages 15–20 occurs at a rate of 66 per 100,000. In 2001, homicide was the second leading cause of death among young adults ages 15–24 overall, according to the Centers for Disease Control (www.saddonline.com).

12. One significant reason that teens are more likely to be involved in traffic accidents is that teens are more likely to travel in cars with other teens than are adults. Because most adults own their own cars and spend the majority of their time in cars either running errands or commuting to work, time spent in their cars is usually spent alone. Accidents involving teen drivers partly result in a higher number of injuries to teens because teenagers carry other teenage passengers in their cars. According to one report from the Insurance Institute for Highway Safety, 47 percent of teens between the ages of thirteen and nineteen who died in vehicle crashes were passengers. Forty percent of teens between the ages of sixteen and nineteen who died in vehicle crashes were passengers. It is important to note that 63 percent of passenger deaths for teens ages 13–19 occurred when another teen was driving.

Seventy-six percent of young drivers involved in fatal crashes involving alcohol in 2003 had a blood alcohol level of 0.00, according to the NHTSA. What this means is that 76 percent of teen drivers involved in alcohol-related fatal crashes were not drunk themselves. See www.nhtsa.dot.gov/people/ncsa.

13. See Hertz (1986); Hochschild (1997); Schor (1992).

14. I draw on a framework for understanding these interactional dynamics proposed by the family scholar Demie Kurz. Kurz (2002) emphasizes the collaborative dimensions of decision-making between parents and their adolescent children. Kurz calls for a framework that moves beyond the prevailing depiction in the social science literature of adolescents' relationship to their parents as "stormy." Kurz stresses "co-collaboration" as she analyzes the historically and contextually situated family negotiations and interactions that occur within families with teenagers.

15. The fact that parents are usually the ones who teach their children to drive provides one example of the way parents work, for better or worse, to control their children.

16. This also appeared gendered. As I discuss later in the chapter, girls are more closely monitored than boys by parents.

17. See Olsen (1997) for a discussion of this.

18. For others, public transit was simply inaccessible. Adriana explains, "The nearest bus stop is like five miles away, so either I'd just stay out and take the bus from one friend's house to the next or have a friend's parent pick me up."

19. See Kurz (2002).

20. See Tolman (1994).

21. See Brown (1999); Hudson (1984).

22. Further discussion of youth and the culture and meaning of risk are provided in chapter 3.

23. See Williams (2001). Young women represented 1,971 of the 53,401 drivers involved in fatal crashes in 1993, or 3.6 percent of all drivers involved in fatal crashes. In 2003, that number had increased slightly to 4 percent. These numbers are revealing when compared with those for young men, who represent a much larger percentage of drivers in fatal crashes than young women. In 1993, young men represented 10 percent of all drivers involved in fatal crashes; in 2003, they represented 9.5 percent of all drivers involved in such crashes, a significantly higher number than for their female counterparts.

24. While my analysis ultimately rests on the idea of "co-collaboration" within the context of ongoing family negotiations around teens and driving, this chapter also examines how parents continue to exercise control over their teen children, even in the context of more collaborative negotiations; see Gecas and Seff (1991). I define control primarily in terms of constraints on adolescents' physical freedoms through curfews, prohibitions on night driving, and so forth, in contrast to more internal forms of control through value transmission.

25. Olsen (1997), an ethnography on immigrant youth and schooling, makes this point.

26. Kincheloe (1997) provides an interesting discussion of these changes and their consequence for kids.

27. It is interesting that Jorge attributes time spent apart as a consequence of each family member's having his or her own car.

28. "Today's Image Conscious Youth Embraces Car Culture: Kids Head Back to School in Customized Rides," available at www.prnewswire.com, August 27, 2004.

29. Valerie Seckler, "Missing the Mark with Millennials: Fashion Industry Target Marketing Teenagers and College Students," *Women's Wear Daily*, February 19, 2003, available at www.lcourse.com.

30. R. J. Ignelz, "In the Lot of Luxury," *San Diego Union Tribune*, June 23, 2004, A1.

31. However, it is worth noting here the inverse relationship between youth labor force participation and socioeconomic status. That is, those youth who are least likely to need the wages from afterschool employment are actually

more likely to work, according to the 2000 U.S. Census Report on the Youth Labor Force. Sixty-eight percent of youth ages 16–19 are active in the labor force as either full-time or part-time workers.

32. See Bourdieu (1984); Halle (1993).

33. See Schor (1998).

34. According to the 2000 U.S. Census Report on the Youth Labor Force.

35. Parents are not the only adults who regularly threaten kids with losing "car privileges." Teachers, security guards on school campuses and other school monitors, court officials, and police officers regularly use the threat of the loss of car privileges to bring youth under their control.

36. See Ehrenreich (1985) for a discussion of education and the middle class.

37. See also Bourdieu (1984) and Lamont and Fournier (1992).

38. See Rank (2001), for example.

39. See Fine and Weis (1998); Hays (2004); Heath (1999) for discussions of family life in the context of poverty.

40. See Corsaro (1997) for a detailed discussion of scholarship focusing on children's contributions to family life.

41. For a discussion of the role of class in family life see DeVault (1991); Hertz (1986); Lareau (2003).

NOTES TO CHAPTER 5

1. Kunstler (1993): 86.

2. The issue of sexual safety is beyond the scope of my purposes here but is addressed in chapter 2 in greater depth.

3. Gitlin (2002): 39.

4. A number of scholars have noted changes in the conception of the self in late modernity or as a symptom of the postmodern condition. These scholars reject the humanist and totalizing notions of an enduring, presocial, unified self that were central to the Enlightenment view. Rather, the self in late modernity contains no essence, no solid inner core set against an outer world but is fluid, fragmented, and ever-changing in accordance with different space and time configurations. See Best and Kellner (1991); Jameson (2003); Kondo (1997); Harvey (1989).

5. Gitlin (2002): 53.

6. Gitlin is not the first to lament the isolation, atomization, and instrumental social ties associated with modernity. The German sociologist Georg Simmel, writing at the turn of the twentieth century, was also critical of the increasing social disconnection tied to the modern age and embodied in the metropolis, as was the sociologist Emile Durkheim. See Simmel (1950); Durkheim, *The Division of Labor in Society* ([1893] 1997) and *Suicide in Society* ([1897] 1997). See also Alexis de Tocqueville ([1853] 1969); Bellah (1985); Reisman (1950); Putnam (2002).

7. The average-price car in the United States in 2003 cost $25,523, and the average monthly car payment was $453. According to the Consumers Banker Association, the average loan for a new car in 2002 was $21,799 and for a used car, $16,542 (cited in "How Do You Stack Up?" October 7, 2003, available at http://money.cnn.com). Nearly 40 percent of new-car buyers carry car loans with terms that exceed sixty months. Thirty percent of new-car buyers carry seventy-two-month payment terms, according to an article in *Money* magazine ("Car Debt Getting Out of Hand," *Money* magazine, January 28, 2004, available at http://money.cnn.com). The consequence of this is that 30 percent of new-car buyers owe more money on their current cars than the cars are worth in trade. These buyers typically roll their outstanding debt ($3,700) into their next car. In California, 40 percent of new-car buyers roll over outstanding debt into their next car. The average debt is $4,700, according to *Money*.

8. Americans' mounting debt has led to staggering consumer bankruptcy rates. In 2000, 1,217,972 consumer bankrupcies were filed (www.debt.smart .com). Bankruptcy rates among those under the age of twenty-five have also grown. According to the Harvard Law School professor Elizabeth Warren, bankruptcies filed by those under the age of twenty-five grew 50 percent between 1991 and 1999; 100,000 youth were expected to file bankruptcy in 2000 according to *Consumer Reports* ("The New Rules of Borrowing," *Consumer Reports* 64[7]: 12). See also Stephen Broebeck and Jack Gillis, "Credit Card Debt Imposes Huge Costs on Many College Students," Consumer Federation of America, available at www.consumerfed.org.

9. Student debt is on the rise along with the cost of postsecondary education. In 1991, the average graduate carried $8,200 in debt, according to the National Center for Policy Analysis (www.ncpa.org). College students today are more likely to carry significant credit card debt than their counterparts ten years ago. An estimated 83 percent of college students carried at least one credit card in 2001. In 2000, the average undergraduate carried an average credit card balance of $2,748 (www.nelliemae.com). Significantly, in 1998, the average credit card balance was $1,879. Anxiety over mounting debt accounts for almost half of those who drop out of college, according to the 1998 National Student Loan Survey. See "Life after Debt," results of the National Loan Survey, available at http://www.nmfed.org/uimages/documents/Lifeafterdebt.pdf.

10. Life-course scholars have noted that longer periods of time spent living at home with parents are increasingly common among young adults. Researchers associate this pattern with what is called "emerging adulthood," which refers to the postponement of activities traditionally associated with adulthood: stable employment, home ownership, voting, and marriage. A number of scholars have tied this delay in assuming adult responsibility to changes in the economy since the 1970s, arguing that deindustrialization and the emergence of a centralized world economy have eroded the possibility of participat-

ing in these traditional markers of adulthood for a large number of young adults. See Arnett (2000).

11. Schor (2000): 447.

12. Ibid.: 448.

13. This point emerged in one of the focus group conversations and is discussed in chapter 2.

14. See Eder (1995); Eckert (1989).

15. Volkswagen is consistently ranked number one for its strong youth appeal by young adults in market research surveys.

16. Lipovetsky (1994): 155.

17. See Bauman (2000); Giddens (1991); Slater (1997).

18. Slater (1997): 30.

19. There are additional reasons why a car is part of the new essentials for youth. In chapter 4, I discuss the decision of parents to give their child a car as a way for parents to manage the changing demands of work.

20. William Julius Wilson (1996) makes a related argument in his book *When Work Disappears*. Wilson argues that lack of transportation imposes a significant limitation on black, low-income, and urban workers' ability to earn a living wage. Lack of car ownership among low-income urban dwellers, combined with the decentralization of employment (the decline of jobs in the urban core and their relocation to the suburbs), has created enormous difficulties, since the time and cost of travel without a car are so significant that they contribute overall to lower wages and lower rates and shorter periods of employment.

21. *Hooptie* is another word for jalopy.

22. Kotlowitz (2000): 255.

23. Lots of middle-class kids postpone getting a license for a variety of reasons, though that was generally not the case for the majority of the one hundred kids interviewed. Other middle-class kids go without a car because their parents are unwilling to help them purchase one, seeing it as largely unnecessary.

24. Recall C. Wright Mills's (1959) discussion of "public issue" and "personal troubles" in *The Sociological Imagination*. Those with resources use personal means to resolve the public problems of modern life. Having a country home outside the city as a way to escape the troubles of urban life is one example Mills provides.

25. Schor (1998): 39

26. The importance youth attach to cars is not specific to San Jose. Broader patterns of hyperconsumption exist across contexts. George Ritzer (2005), in his book *Enchanting a Disenchanted World*, identifies a "news means of consumption" as he discusses the ever-expanding role of consumption in our lives. Ritzer identifies the dual processes of rationalization and enchantment as defining features of the new means of consumption. The dual logic of enchantment

and rationalization organizes what Ritzer regards as "cathedrals of consumption": shopping malls, newly emerging town centers, amusements parks like Disney World, casinos, outlet shopping malls, electronic shopping malls, catalogues, superstores like Costco, and revamped cruise ships, where we spend much of our lives. Nevertheless, local economies, place, and community life play important roles shaping our relationship to the new means of consumption.

27. It is also meaningful to note here that people who live in and around Silicon Valley spend long hours in their cars commuting to work. Silicon Valley has high levels of traffic congestion in part because the influx of professional and wage workers to meet the demands of the expanding economy outpaced the rate of infrastructure development. The inadequacy of public transportation, for example, has been the subject of much debate in Silicon Valley and the larger Bay Area. BART (Bay Area Rapid Transit) and the VTA's (Valley Transportation Authority) Light Rail, two major mass transit projects, continue to provide limited services between various parts of the area.

28. According to the 2000 U.S. Census, only 4 percent of community residents regularly use public transit. Data available at www.sanjoseca.gov/Census_2000.

29. KIN (2001): vii.

30. See Jan English-Lueck (2002) for an insightful anthropological discussion of cultural, work, and community life among Silicon Valley's families. See also Benner (2002) for a discussion of the reorganization of work in Silicon Valley and the new economy.

31. Before World War II, San Jose, then known as the "Valley of Heart's Delight," boasted the largest concentration of fruit canneries in the world, according to the labor historian Glenna Matthews. With rapid economic expansion, resulting first from a series of military contracts and later from a growing demand for semiconductors, Silicon Valley emerged as the hub of information technology during the cold war. A burgeoning electronic industry followed, which led to eventual changes in the organization of production. Offshore production and outsourcing became increasingly common, and many community members who had held lifelong unionized jobs in the canneries watched those jobs disappear. These shifts in production have had serious consequences for employment, community, and the local economy. Most significant of all is a growing income gap between the professional classes and deskilled service workers. The explosion of electronics attracted laborers from outside the surrounding area, while changing the face of labor and productive work. Skilled immigrant laborers were among the new settlers, as were arriving refugees from Southeast Asia, many of whom were farmers before having to flee their homelands. A large number of immigrants were without the economic, cultural, and professional resources needed to occupy positions in the top tier and thus were

consigned to positions in the lower tier of the labor market. Though many newly arrived immigrants began small businesses in the service economy, helping to rebuild San Jose's downtown (Takaki [1989]), many others became service workers. Many workers moved into electronics, which, unlike cannery work, is typically not unionized and usually offers far lower wages because of the high levels of global competition in this industry, according to Matthews. See Matthews (2003) for an extensive discussion of work in Silicon Valley.

32. That millionaires were created daily was repeatedly broadcast in local and national news headlines, and the point permeated accounts of life in San Jose, among those who reside within the Valley and those outside it. This topic was the subject of numerous news hours and talk shows between 1997 and 2000, the height of the dot.com boom. Of course, most of these millionaires were "paper millionaires," whose fortunes were tied to tech stocks and employee IPO (initial public offerings) stock benefit packages for "startups," of which Silicon Valley was at the center. The economic downturn that gained force in the spring of 2001 and accelerated after September 11 left many of these paper millionaires without their fortunes and in many instances without their jobs and even their homes. National reports indicated, however, that the rates of housing foreclosures and unemployment in Silicon Valley surged after April 2001.

33. It is common in the United States for people to live beyond their means. In 1990, the average American paid more than $1,000 in interest and credit-card fees, according to Schor (1998, 2000).

34. Juliet Schor (1998, 2000) makes this point in her discussion of the new competitive consumerism. She identifies the decline of neighborhoods, which, she argues, once functioned as the primary consumer reference group for households, as partly responsible for the "upscaling of lifestyle norms." Schor identifies celebrities and the truly wealthy whose lives are made public by the media as a new reference group that has come to replace the neighbors down the street. Schor sees this group and our attempts to emulate their lifestyles as responsible for the upscaling of lifestyle norms. Certainly this is at work in San Jose, where the youth are avid consumers of media images. But the point I am making as I use Schor's concept is that even in areas like San Jose that have high levels of residential segregation, residents in the community will still see themselves as part of a community as a whole. The view of San Jose as wealthy is shared among the larger community, and the conspicuous display of wealth is pervasive.

35. Sassen (2000).

36. Communities of color experience the economic unevenness most dramatically. The median family income in San Jose reflects a significant ethno-racial hierarchy. In 2000, the median income for white families, with an average household size of 2.4 people, was $87,000. For Hispanic families, with an

average household size of 4.6, the median income was $52,000. For Asians, with an average family size of 3.6, the median income was $80,000. Statistics available at www.sanjoseca.gov/Census_2000. It is important to consider household size for two reasons. First a larger household size suggests more economic contributors. Second, household size affects the distribution of economic resources for the group. Individuals in large families receive fewer resources than individuals in smaller families. A disproportionate number of Latinos/as and Vietnamese are concentrated at the bottom end of the wage continuum and are overrepresented among members of Silicon Valley's working poor. They are concentrated geographically in low-income areas and attend underresourced schools. Theirs does not represent the whole of immigrant life in San Jose, however. Most transnational Asian families with considerable intellectual and economic capital live beside white professional families in the suburbs, where there are better schools, more spacious homes, and greater community resources, or have established their own professional, middle-class, suburban ethnic enclaves. There is also an expanding Latino/a suburban and professional middle class.

37. Matthews (2003): 258.

38. This has contributed to a situation where 18 percent of households live in overcrowded housing, according to 2000 U.S. Census. See www.sanjoseca.gov/Census_2000.

39. Sue McAllister, "Why Silicon Valley Housing Prices Are Still So High," *San Jose Mercury News,* August 1, 2004, p. 1A+.

40. According to the 2000 U.S. Census, 61 percent of residents dwell in owner-occupied housing, 7 percent below the national average.

41. In 1999, 68 percent of whites in Santa Clara County owned homes, as did 36 percent of Latinos, 55 percent of Asians, and 42 percent of black families. See Matthews (2003): 162.

42. Oliver and Shapiro (1995).

43. The more recent loss of tech jobs in the area following the economic downturn resulted in a decrease of 5 percent in the average wage in the San Jose area between 2001 and 2003. Sue McAllister, "Why Silicon Valley Housing Prices Are Still So High," *San Jose Mercury News,* August 1, 2004, p. 1A+.

44. In the late 1990s, San Jose began a coordinated effort to build more "affordable housing units" for teachers and civil servants such as fire and police department employees, since these groups were otherwise unable to live within the community.

45. See Markus and Nurius's (1986) discussion of "possible selves."

46. In fact, the responses quoted here represent a very small sample of a recurring response pattern.

47. For a critical examination of the relationship between aspiration and attainment that is attentive to a broader economic backdrop, see Jay MacLeod's (1994) classic ethnography, *Ain't No Making It.*

48. Sassen (2000) has argued that as demand for high-level professional services in finance, management, and information technology increases, the serving classes in urban centers will likewise expand. Since professional work in the global economy imposes heavy demands on time, an expanding number of household services are being provided by the market, usually by low-wage workers. This has been the case in Silicon Valley even though it is not a large global city as defined by Sassen. A series of articles in the *San Jose Mercury News* in the fall of 1999 addressed what was essentially experienced as a crisis in the service economy, stemming from a shortage of service workers. Because of the high rents and low wages in the area, the supply of service workers did not meet the demand for them.

49. The sociologist Carol Ray helped me to see this point through personal communication.

50. Of course, many were denied these securities, mostly notably black Americans. And thus it is important to resist the temptation to wallow in nostalgia.

51. Gilles Lipovestsky's (1994) remarks are especially useful for understanding the connection between the consumer market and postmodern individualism. He writes, "In a society of individuals committed to personal autonomy, it is clear why the new offers such a lively attraction: it is experienced as an instrument of personal 'liberation,' as an experience to be undertaken, an experience to be lived, a little adventure of the self" (155). For Lipovetsky, the postmodern individual is a product of the postmodern world of which she is a part, a world where social roles, norms, and social institutions have declined in importance and given way to alternative forms of social existence arranged in terms of the individual as consumer. The postmodern individual adjusts to a changing set of conditions by constructing himself, his social experience, and his social world through the market. For Lipovetsky, it is largely through the consumer market that individuals construct themselves as free. Lipovetsky seems to celebrate the adaptable individual who can respond to the imperatives of a new arrangement in social life where the market has largely replaced social institutions such as work, school and family. He sees this new individualism as vital to democracy; I take a slightly more pessimistic view.

Notes to the Conclusion

1. Much like other reality TV "makeover" shows, from *Swan* to *Extreme Makeover* to *The Biggest Loser*, *Pimp My Ride* focuses on the theme of transformation. There are several other reality makeover shows that deal with changes not only to the self and body but to objects that relate to the self, such as house or, in the instance of teens, bedrooms.

2. Unless, of course, they live a densely populated urban area like New York City where they can utilize an expansive public transit system.

3. McDonald (1999): 11.

4. The social theorist Alan Touraine has called this "demodernization," which he defines in terms of a decrease in the importance of social roles and social norms in organizing the behavior and action of individuals and the declining importance of social institutions in organizing and constructing social existence (cited in McDonald [1999]). See McDonald (1999) for an insightful discussion of demodernization as it organizes youth's social experiences

5. Slater (1997): 99.

6. This is a point made by many scholars. See Bauman (2000); Lipovetsky (1994); McDonald (1999); Slater (1997).

7. Slater (1997): 29.

8. I am drawing here on the language Juliet Schor uses in her book *The Overspent American* (1998).

9. See Best (2000); Giroux and Simon (1989); Graebner (1990); Fiske (1989a, 1989b); McRobbie (1991, 1993); Roman and Christian-Smith (1989); Willis (1977) for a discussion of the importance of studying youths' engagement with popular cultural forms.

10. This is a project to extend a line of inquiry developed by Dorothy Smith (1987, 1990a, 1990b, 1999) that is often called Institutional Ethnography. See Appendix for an elaboration of this methodological project.

11. Giddens (1991): 75.

12. Bauman (2000): 31.

13. I am reminded of Erving Goffman's (1959) point about the intensifying worship of the self as the resources to craft the self become increasingly elaborate in modern society. I am also reminded of Emile Durkheim's insights about the elaborate rituals that celebrate the individual in complex societies where solidarity and the mechanisms of social integration are largely instrumental. Members of society collectively worship the individual in celebration of the group because in complex societies members share little else.

14. See Anthony Giddens's (1991) discussion "Ontological Security and Existential Anxiety."

15. Import racers present a significant challenge to Anglo young men aligned with American Muscle as import cars claim a growing portion of market share in the commercial world and vie against American Muscle on the screen (see for example the films *The Fast and the Furious* and *2 Fast 2 Furious*), the track, and the street. Because of this, this struggle around masculine authenticity revolves around them.

16. This is a point Carol Ray helped me to see.

17. See Simmel (1950). I also draw here from Todd Gitlin's (2002) insightful discussion of the money economy, the blasé attitude, and the torrent of media images, as well as Calhoun, Cannon and Fisher's (1998) analysis of amateur stripping using Simmel's concepts.

18. I am thinking in particular of the prevailing developmental paradigms that have directed much research on youth over the past sixty years. I recognize developmental models as problematic for a number of reasons. First, developmental models often deny adolescents' social agency and presuppose that the socialization process ends upon entrance into adulthood, rather than seeing socialization as an ongoing process (Thorne [1993]). Developmental models tend to impose a false degree of linearity in accounting for how kids reach adulthood (Thorne [1993]). These models also tend to ignore structural factors and focus only on those internal and individual factors that shape kids' sense of themselves. For an excellent critique of developmental paradigms see also Corsaro (1997), Van Ausdale and Feagin (2001). Van Ausdale and Feagin mount a compelling critique of the embeddedness of Piaget's developmental stages in everyday thought on youth and the theory's limits for understanding the complex ways children as young as three and four use abstract racial constructs. Their ethnographic research on children's use of racial constructs to define the self and others, to dominate, to include and exclude others in the context of a Florida day care center, provides understanding of the sociocultural worlds young children construct with peers that (re)produce racial meanings.

19. Nancy Lesko (2001) has been instrumental in debunking conventional developmental discourses. She asks, "What are the systems of ideas that make possible the adolescence that we see, think, feel act upon?" (9) as she traces the discursive codes that produce "the fact" of adolescence and its effect: endless worries over normal developmental pathways, tightening controls over "at-risk" youth, and complex systems of self-discipline to govern all youth.

20. M. Males, "An Imaginary 'Youth Crisis' Spawns Dubious Teen-Control Panaceas," *Los Angeles Times,* June 11, 2000.

21. The San Jose Police Department conducted a yearlong voluntary study to document the prevalence of racial profiling. The research revealed that there are racial differences in who is likely to be pulled over. To counter these findings, SJPD argued that the greater likelihood that Latinos and blacks will be pulled over was better explained by economic inequalities than by race. Police officers are more likely to be concentrated in low-income areas designated as high-crime zones; people of color are also concentrated in these areas.

Notes to the Appendix

1. Smith (1987, 1990a, 1990b, 1999). See also DeVault (1999, 1992); McCoy (1995); Mueller (1995).

2. Smith does draw from theoretical approaches (and thinkers) within sociology, notably feminist thought, Marxism, poststructuralism, and ethnomethodology, as she develops her line of inquiry. She does not abandon sociology, nor do I.

3. Glaser and Strauss (1967).

4. In defining middle income, I exclude the income groups in the bottom 20 percent and top 20 percent of the U.S. population.

5. Best (2000); Brown (1999).

6. I was able to review the tapes and the transcripts of all the focus-group and individual interviews.

7. The reason the group was so large was that we had to combine two of the groups. Originally, I had intended to conduct one of the focus groups while Karen Ranier conducted the other. But we lost one of the rooms we had reserved to high school band practice, and so Karen assisted me in running the focus group, as she had with the first focus group.

8. Adler and Adler (1998).

9. See Best (2003).

10. I do not provide extensive information on the schools here because the focus of the research is not schooling or a comparison of schools. It therefore seems unnecessary to reveal the schools' identities.

References

Adler, P., and P. Adler. 1998. *Peer Power.* New Brunswick, NJ: Rutgers University Press.

Altheide, D. 2002. *Creating Fear: News and the Construction of Crisis.* New York: Aldine De Gruyter.

Alvord, K. 2000. *Divorce Your Car!: Ending the Love Affair with the Automobile.* Gabriola Island, B.C., Canada: New Society.

Anataki, C., and S. Widdicombe. 1998. *Identities in Talk.* London: Sage.

Anderson, B. 1983. *Imagined Communities: Reflections on the Origin and Spread of Nationalism.* London: Verso.

Anthias, F. 2001. "New Hybridities, Old Concepts: The Limits of 'Culture.'" *Ethnic and Racial Studies* 24(4): 619–641.

Anzaldua, G. 1987. *Borderlands La Frontera: The New Mestiza.* 2nd ed. San Francisco: Aunt Lute Books.

Arnett, J. 2000. "High Hopes in a Grim World: Emerging Adults' Views of Their Futures and Generation X." *Youth and Society* 3(3): 267–286.

Austin, J., and M. Willard. 1998. *Generations of Youth: Youth Cultures and History in Twentieth-Century America.* New York: NYU Press.

Baudrillard, J. 2000. "The Ideological Genesis of Needs." *The Consumer Society Reader,* ed. J. Schor and D. B. Holt. New York: New Press.

Bauman, Z. 2000. *Liquid Modernity.* Cambridge: Polity Press.

Beck, U. 2000. "Living Your Own Life in a Runaway World: Individualisation, Globalisation and Politics." *Global Capitalism,* ed. Will Hutton and Anthony Giddens. New York: New Press.

Beck, U. 1998. "Politics of Risk Society." *The Politics of Risk Society,* ed. Jane Franklin. Malden, MA: Polity Press.

Bellah, R. N., R. Madsen, W. Sullivan, A. Swidler, and S. M. Tipton. 1985. *Habits of the Heart: Individualism and Commitment in American Life.* Berkeley: University of California Press.

Benner, C. 2002. *Work in the New Economy: Flexible Labor Markets in Silicon Valley.* New York: Blackwell.

Best, A. 2003. "Doing Race in the Context of Feminist Interviewing: Constructing Whiteness through Talk." *Qualitative Inquiry* 9(6): 895–914.

Best, A. 2000. *Prom Night: Youth, Schooling and Popular Culture.* New York: Routledge.

Best, S., and D. Kellner. 1991. *Postmodern Theory: Critical Interrogations.* New York: Guilford.

Blackshaw, T. 2003. *Leisure Life: Myth, Masculinity, and Modernity.* London: Routledge.

Bordo, S. 1993. *Unbearable Weight: Feminism, Western Culture and the Body.* Berkeley: University of California Press.

Bose, M. 2003. "'Race' and Class in the 'Postsubcultural' Economy." *The Post-Subcultures Reader,* ed. David Muggleton and Rupert Weinzierl. Oxford: Berg.

Bourdieu, P. 1984. *Distinction: A Social Critique of the Judgment of Taste.* Cambridge, MA: Harvard University Press.

Bourdieu, P. 1977. *Outline of a Theory of Practice.* Cambridge: Cambridge University Press.

Bourgois, P. 1995. *In Search of Respect: Selling Crack in El Barrio.* New York: Columbia University Press.

Brake, M. 1985. *Comparative Youth Culture: The Sociology of Youth Culture and Youth Subculture in America, Britain and Canada.* London: Routledge & Kegan Paul.

Bright. B. J. 1998. "Nightmares in the New Metropolis: The Cinematic Poetics of Low Riders." *Generations of Youth: Youth Cultures and History in Twentieth-Century America,* ed. Joe Austin and Michael Nevin Willard. New York: NYU Press.

Brottman, M. 2001. *Car Crash Culture.* New York: Palgrave.

Brown, L. M. 2003. *Girlfighting: Betrayal and Rejection among Girls.* New York: NYU Press.

Brown, L. M. 1999. *Raising Their Voices: The Politics of Girls' Anger.* Cambridge, MA: Harvard University Press.

Brumberg, J. J. 1997. *The Body Project: An Intimate History of American Girls.* New York: Random House.

Butler, J. 1990. *Gender Trouble: Feminism and the Subversion of Identity.* New York: Routledge.

Cahill, S. 1990. "Childhood and Public Life: Reaffirming Biographical Divisions." *Social Problems* 37: 390–402.

Calhoun, T., J. Harms Cannon, and R. Fisher. 1998. "Explorations in Youth Culture: Amateur Stripping: What We Know and What We Don't." *Youth Culture: Identity in a Postmodern World,* ed. J. Epstein. Oxford: Blackwell.

Carter, P. 2003. "'Black' Cultural Capital, Status Positioning, and Schooling Conflicts for Low-Income African American Youth." *Social Problems* 50(1): 136–155.

Castellanos, T., et al. 2001. *KIN: Knowledge of Immigrant Nationalities in Santa Clara County.* San Jose, CA: Office of Human Relations of Santa Clara County and West Valley-Mission Community College District.

Chabram-Dernersesian, A. 1997. "On the Social Construction of Whiteness within Selected Chicana/o Discourses." *Displacing Whiteness: Essays in Social and Cultural Criticism,* ed. Ruth Frankenberg. Durham, NC: Duke University Press.

Chin, E. 2001. *Purchasing Power: Black Kids and American Consumer Culture.* Minneapolis: University of Minnesota Press.

Clarke, D. B., M. Doel, and K. L. Housiaux. 2003. *The Consumption Reader.* London: Routledge.

Cohen, S. 2002. *Folk Devils and Moral Panics.* 3rd ed. London: Routledge.

Cohen, S. 1997. "Symbols of Trouble." *The Subcultures Reader,* ed. Ken Gelder and Sarah Thornton. London: Routledge.

Collins, P. H. 1990. *Black Feminist Thought: Knowledge, Consciousness and The Politics of Empowerment.* New York: Routledge.

Connell, R. W. 1995. *Masculinities.* Berkeley: University of California Press.

Connell, R. W. 1987. *Gender and Power: Society, the Person and Sexual Politics.* Stanford: Stanford University Press.

Connolly, P. 1998. *Racism, Gender Identities and Young Children: Social Relations in a Multi-Ethnic, Inner-City Primary School.* London: Routledge.

Corrigan, P. 1975. "Doing Nothing." *Resistance through Rituals,* ed. S. Hall and T. Jefferson. London: Routledge.

Corsaro, W. 1997. *The Sociology of Childhood.* Thousand Oaks, CA: Pine Forge Press.

Cosgrove, S. 2002. "The Zoot-Suit and Style Warfare." *Cultural Resistance Reader,* ed. Stephen Duncombe. London: Verso.

Crossman, D. R., and R. M. Crossman. 2002. *Sixteen Is Too Young to Drive: Taking Control When Your Teen's Behind-the-Wheel.* Scotia, NY: Footnote.

Darder, A., R. D. Torres, and H. Gutierrez. 1997. *Latinos and Education: A Critical Reader.* New York: Routledge.

Davis, Mike. 2000. *Magical Urbanism: Latinos Reinvent the U.S. City.* New York: Verso.

Davis, Mike. 1990. *City of Quartz.* New York: Vintage.

de Graaf, J., D. Wann, and T. Naylor. 2002. *Affluenza: The All-Consuming Epidemic.* San Francisco: Berrett-Hoehler.

DeVault, M. 1999. *Liberating Method.* Philadelphia: Temple University Press.

DeVault, M. 1991. *Feeding the Family: The Social Organization of Caring as Gendered Work.* Chicago: University of Chicago Press.

Devlin, R. 1998. "Female Juvenile Delinquency and the Problem of Sexual Authority in America, 1945–1960." *Delinquents and Debutantes: Twentieth Century American Girls' Culture,* ed. Sherrie Inness. New York: NYU Press.

Deyhle, D. 1998. "From Break Dancing to Heavy Metal." *Youth and Society* 30(1): 3–31.

DiMaggio, P. 1982. "Cultural Capital and School Success: The Impact of Status Culture Participation on the Grades of U.S. High School Students." *American Sociological Review* 47 (April): 189–201.

Diaz, V. 2002. "'Fight Boys, 'til the Last': Island-style Football and the Remasculinization of the Indigeneity in the Militarized American Pacific Islands." *Pacific Diaspora,* ed. Paul Spickard, Joanne Rondilla, and Debbie Hippolite Wright. Honolulu: University of Hawaii Press.

Dimitriadis, G. 2001. *Performing Identity/Performing Culture: Hip Hop as Text, Pedagogy and Lived Practices.* New York: Peter Lang.

Douglas, M. 1992. *Risk and Blame: Essays in Cultural Theory.* London: Routledge.

Douglas, M. 1966. *Purity and Danger: An Analysis of Concepts of Pollution and Purity.* London: Routledge & Kegan Paul.

Duany, A., E. Plater-Zyberk, and J. Speck. 2000. *Suburban Nation: The Rise of Sprawl and the Decline of the American Dream.* New York: North Point Press.

DuGay, P., S. Hall, Linda Janes, H. Mackay, and K. Negus. 1997. *Doing Cultural Studies: The Story of the Sony Walkman.* London: Sage.

Duncombe, S. (ed.). 2002. *Cultural Resistance Reader.* London: Verso.

Durkheim, E. (1897) 1997. *Suicide* (reissue edition). New York: Free Press.

Durkheim, E. (1893) 1997. *The Division of Labor in Society* (reissue edition with Lewis Coser). New York: Free Press.

Durkheim, E. 1965. *Elementary Forms of Religious Life.* New York: Free Press.

Dwyer, C. 1998. "Contested Identities: Challenging Dominant Representations of Young British Muslim Women." *Cool Places: Geographies of Youth Culture,* ed. Tracey Skelton and Gill Valentine. London: Routledge.

Eckert, P. 1989. *Jocks and Burnouts: Social Categories and Identity in High School.* New York: Teacher's College Press.

Eder, D., C. Evans, and S. Parker. 1995. *School Talk: Gender and Adolescent Culture.* New Jersey: Rutgers University Press.

Ehrenreich, B. 2001. *Nickel and Dimed: On (Not) Getting By in America.* New York: Holt.

Ehrenreich, B. 1985. *Fear of Falling: The Inner Life of the Middle Class.* New York: HarperCollins.

English-Lueck, J. A. 2002. *Culture@Silicon Valley.* Palo Alto: Stanford University Press.

Epstein, J. 1998. *Youth Culture: Identity in a Postmodern World.* Oxford: Blackwell.

Espiritu, Y. L. 1997. *Asian American Women and Men: Labor, Laws and Love.* Thousand Oaks, CA: Sage.

Escobar, E. 1999. *Race, Police and the Making of a Political Identity: Mexican Americans and the Los Angeles Police Department, 1900–1945*. Berkeley: University of California Press.

Etzioni, Amitai, and Jared Bloom. 2004. *We Are What We Celebrate: Understanding Holidays and Rituals*. New York: NYU Press.

Fass, P. 1977. *The Damned and The Beautiful: American Youth in the 1920s*. Oxford: Oxford University Press.

Fine, M. 1991. *Framing Dropouts: Notes on the Politics of an Urban Public High School*. Albany: State University of New York Press.

Fine, M., and L. Weis. 1998. *The Unknown City: The Lives of Poor and Working-Class Young Adults*. Boston: Beacon Press.

Fine, G. A. 1987. *With the Boys: Little League Baseball and Preadolescent Culture*. Chicago: University of Chicago Press.

Fine, G. A., W. Espeland, and D. Rojek. 2001. "Young Citizens: The Position of Children in Communitarian Theory." *Sociological Studies of Children and Youth*, ed. David A. Kinney. Vol. 8. 299–318.

Fish, S. 1980. *Is There a Text in This Class? The Authority of Interpretive Communities*. Cambridge, MA: Harvard University Press.

Fiske, J. 1989a. *Understanding Popular Culture*. Boston: Unwin Hyman.

Fiske, J. 1989b. *Reading the Popular*. Boston: Unwin Hyman.

Flink, J. J. 1988. *The Automobile Age*. Cambridge, MA: MIT Press.

Frank, T. 2000. "Advertising as Cultural Criticism: Bill Bernbach versus the Mass Society." *The Consumer Society Reader*, ed. J. Schor and D. B. Holt. New York: New Press.

Furedi, F. 2002. *Culture of Fear*. London: Continuum.

Gaines, D. 1990. *Teenage Wasteland: Suburbia's Dead End Kids*. Chicago: University of Chicago Press.

Gans, H. J. 1967. *The Levittowners: Ways of Life and Politics in a New Suburban Community*. New York: Vintage Books.

Garcia, A. 1990. "The Development of Chicana Feminist Discourse, 1970–1980." *Unequal Sisters: A Multicultural Reader in U.S. Women's History*, ed. E. Dubois and V. Ruiz. New York: Routledge.

Garvey, P. 2001. "Driving, Drinking and Daring in Norway." *Car Culture: Materializing Culture*, ed. Daniel Miller. Oxford: Berg.

Gecas, V., and M. Seff. 1991. "Families and Adolescents: A Review of the 1980s." *Contemporary Families: Looking Forward, Looking Back*, ed. A. Booth. Minneapolis, MN: National Council on Family Relations. 208–223.

Gelder, K., and S. Thornton (eds.). 1997. *The Subcultures Reader*. London: Routledge.

Gettis, V. 1998. "Experts and Juvenile Delinquency, 1900–1935." *Generations of Youth: Youth Cultures and History in Twentieth-Century America*, ed. Joe Austin and Michael Nevin Willard. New York: NYU Press.

Giddens, A. 1998. "Risk Society: the Context of British Politics." *The Politics of Risk Society,* ed. Jane Franklin. Malden, MA: Polity Press.

Giddens, A. 1991. *Modernity and Self-Identity: Self and Society in the Late Modern Age.* Stanford: Stanford University Press.

Gilroy, P. 2001. "Driving while Black." *Car Culture: Materializing Culture,* ed. Daniel Miller. Oxford: Berg.

Gilroy, P. 1993. *The Black Atlantic: Modernity and Double Consciousness.* London: Verso.

Giroux, H. 1995. *Fugitive Cultures: Race, Violence and Youth.* New York: Routledge.

Giroux, Henry, and Roger Simon (eds.). 1989. *Popular Culture, Schooling and Everyday Life.* Granby, MA: Bergin & Garvey.

Gitlin, T. 2002. *Media Unlimited: How the Torrent of Images and Sounds Overwhelms Our Lives.* New York: Metropolitan/Owl Books.

Glaser, B., and A. Strauss. 1967. *The Discovery of Grounded Theory.* Chicago: Aldine.

Glassner, B. 1999. *The Culture of Fear: Why American Are Afraid of the Wrong Things.* New York: Basic Books.

Goffman, E. 1967. *Interaction Ritual: Essays on Face-to-Face Behavior.* New York: Pantheon.

Goffman, E. 1963. *Stigma: Notes on the Management of Spoiled Identity.* New York: Simon & Schuster.

Goffman, E. 1959. *The Presentation of Self in Everyday Life.* New York: Doubleday.

Goldman, R., and S. Papson. 2000. "Advertising in the Age of Accelerated Meaning." *The Consumer Society Reader,* ed. J. Schor and D. B. Holt. New York: New Press.

Graebner, W. 1990. *Coming of Age in Buffalo: Youth and Authority in the Postwar Era.* Philadelphia: Temple University Press.

Gudis, C. 2004. *Buyways: Billboards, Automobiles, and the American Landscape.* New York: Routledge.

Guillamine, C. 1995. *Racism, Sexism, Power and Ideology.* London: Routledge.

Gusfield, J. R. 1981. *The Culture of Public Problems: Drinking, Driving and the Symbolic Order.* Chicago: University of Chicago Press.

Hall, S., and T. Jefferson (eds.). 1975. *Resistance through Rituals.* London: Routledge.

Halle, D. 1993. *Inside Culture: Art and Class in the American Home.* Chicago: University of Chicago Press.

Halter, M. 2000. *Shopping for Identity: The Marketing of Ethnicity.* New York: Schocken.

Handel, W. 1982. *Ethnomethodology: How People Make Sense.* Englewood Cliffs, NJ: Prentice-Hall.

Harris, A. 2004a. *Future Girl: Young Women in the Twenty-first Century*. New York: Routledge.

Harris, A. 2004b. *All about the Girl: Culture, Power and Identity*. New York: Routledge.

Harvey, D. 1989. *The Condition of Post-Modernity: An Inquiry into the Origins of Culture*. Cambridge: Blackwell.

Hays, S. 2004. *Flat Broke with Children: Women in the Age of Welfare Reform*. Oxford: Oxford University Press.

Heath, D. T. 1999. "Single Mother, Single Fathers: The Intersection of Gender, Work and Family." *Journal of Family Issues* 20(4): 429–431.

Hebdige, D. 2000. "Object as Image: The Italian Scooter Cycle." *The Consumer Society Reader*, ed. J. Schor and D. B. Holt. New York: New Press.

Hebdige, D. 1997. "Posing . . . Threats, Striking . . . Poses: Youth, Surveillance, and Display." *The Subcultures Reader*, ed. Ken Gelder and Sarah Thornton. London: Routledge.

Hebdige, D. 1979. *Subculture: The Meaning of Style*. London: Routledge.

Hertz, R. 1986. *More Equal Than Other: Women and Men in Dual-Career Marriages*. Chicago: University of Chicago Press.

Hochschild, A. R. 1997. *The Time Bind: When Work Becomes Home and Home Becomes Work*. New York: Metropolitan Books.

Hochschild, A. 1989. *The Second Shift*. New York: Avon.

Hollander, J. 2002. "Resisting Vulnerability: The Social Reconstruction of Gender in Interaction." *Social Problems* 49(4): 474–496.

Holtz, J. M. 1975. The Low Riders: Portrait of an Urban Subculture. *Youth and Society* 6(4): 495–508.

Horowitz, R. 2001. *Boys and Their Toys? Masculinity, Class, and Technology in America*. New York: Routledge.

Horowitz, R. 1983. *Honor and the American Dream: Culture and Identity in a Chicano Community*. New Brunswick, NJ: Rutgers University Press.

Horrocks, R. 1994. *Masculinity in Crisis: Myths, Fantasies and Realities*. New York: St. Martin's Press.

Hudson, B. 1984. "Femininity and Adolescence." *Gender and Generation*, ed. Angela McRobbie and Mica Nava. London: Macmillan.

Hutton, W., and A. Giddens (eds.). 2000. *Global Capitalism*. New York: New Press.

Inness, S. (ed.). 1998. *Delinquents and Debutantes: Twentieth-Century American Girls' Cultures*. New York: NYU Press.

Jameson, F. 2003. *Postmodernism or the Cultural Logic of Late Capitalism*. Durham, NC: Duke University Press.

Jones, G. W. 2002. "Rural Girls and Cars: The Phenomena of 'Blockies.'" *Rural Society* 2(3): 1–15.

Kahani-Hopkins, V., and N. Hopkins. 2002. "'Representing' British Muslims:

The Strategic Dimension to Identity Construction." *Ethnic and Racial Studies* 25(2): 288–309.

Katz, C. 1998. "Disintegrating Developments: Global Economic Restructuring and the Eroding of Ecologies of Youth" *Cool Places: Geographies of Youth Culture*, ed. Tracey Skelton and Gill Valentine. London: Routledge.

Kay, J. H. 1997. *Asphalt Nation: How the Automobile Took Over America and How We Can Take It Back*. Berkeley: University of California Press.

Kellner, D. 1997. "Beavis and Butthead: No Future for Postmodern Youth." *Kinder Culture: The Corporate Construction of Childhood*, ed. S. R. Steinberg and J. L. Kincheloe. Boulder, CO: Westview Press.

Kennedy, L. (ed.). 2000. *Race and Urban Space in Contemporary American Culture*. Edinburgh: Edinburgh University Press.

Kimmel, M. 1997. "The Contemporary 'Crisis' of Masculinity in Historical Perspective." *The Making of Masculinities: The New Men's Studies,* ed. H. Brod. Boston: Allen & Unwin.

KIN: Knowledge of Immigrant Nationalities in Santa Clara County 2001. A Publication of the Immigrant Action Network. Office of Human Relations of Santa Clara County.

Kincheloe, J. 1997. "'Home Alone' and 'Bad to the Bone': The Advent of Postmodern Childhood." *Kinder Culture: The Corporate Construction of Childhood,* ed. S. Steinberg and J. Kincheloe. Boulder, CO: Westview Press.

Klein, N. 2002. *No Logo*. New York: Picador.

Kondo, D. 1998. *About Face: Performing Race in Fashion and Theater*. New York: Routledge.

Kotlowitz, A. 2000. "False Connections." *The Consumer Society Reader*, ed. J. Schor and D. B. Holt. New York: New Press.

Kunstler, J. 1993. *The Geography of Nowhere: The Rise and Decline of America's Man-Made Landscape*. New York: Simon & Schuster.

Kurz, D. 2002a. "Caring for Teenage Children." *Journal of Family Issues* 23(6): 748–767.

Kurz, D. 2002b. "Adding 'Generation' to Family Studies: Studying Families with Teenagers." Unpublished paper presented at the 97th Annual American Sociological Association's special session "Theorizing Families: New Currents and Shifting Frameworks." Atlanta, GA.

Laguerre, M. 1999. *Minoritized Space: An Inquiry into the Spatial Order of Things*. Berkeley, CA: Institute of Governmental Studies Press.

Lamont, M. (ed.) 1999. *The Cultural Territories of Race: Black and White Boundaries*. Chicago: University of Chicago Press.

Lamont, M. 1992. *Money, Morals, and Manners: The Culture of the French and American Upper Middle Classes*. Chicago: University of Chicago Press.

Lamont, M., and M. Fournier. 1992. *Cultivating Differences: Symbolic Boundaries and the Making of Inequality*. Chicago: University of Chicago Press.

Lareau, A. 2003. *Unequal Childhoods: Class, Race, and Family Life.* Berkeley: University of California Press.

Leahy, T. 1994. "Taking Up a Position: Discourse of Femininity and Adolescence in the Context of Man/Girl Relationships." *Gender and Society* 8(1): 48–72.

Lesko, N. 2001. *Act Your Age: The Social Construction of Youth.* New York: Routledge.

Lesko, N. 1996. "Denaturalizing Adolescence: The Politics of Contemporary Representation." *Youth and Society* 28(2): 139–161.

Lightfoot, C. 1997. *The Culture of Adolescent Risk-Taking.* New York: Guilford Press.

Lim, S. J. 2004. "'Hell's a Poppin': Asian American Women's Youth Consumer Culture." *Asian American Youth: Culture, Identity, and Ethnicity,* ed. Jennifer Lee and Min Zhou. New York: Routledge.

Lipovetsky, G. 1994. *The Empire of Fashion: Dressing Modern Democracy.* Translated by Catherine Porter. Princeton, NJ: Princeton University Press.

Lipsitz, G. 1997. "Cruising Around the Historical Bloc: Postmodernism and Popular Music in East Lost Angeles." *The Subcultures Reader,* ed. Ken Gelder and Sarah Thornton. London: Routledge.

Lipsitz, G. 1994. "We Know What Time It Is: Race, Class and Youth Culture in The Nineties." *Microphone Fiends: Youth Music and Youth Culture,* ed. Andrew Ross and Tricia Rose. New York: Routledge.

Logan, J., and H. Molotch. 1988. *Urban Fortunes: The Political Economy of Place.* Berkeley: University of California Press.

Lopez, N. 2003. *Hopeful Girls, Troubled Boys: Race and Gender Disparity in Urban Education.* New York: Routledge.

Lucas, T. 1998. "Youth Gangs and Moral Panics in Santa Cruz, California." *Cool Places: Geographies of Youth Culture,* ed. Tracey Skelton and Gill Valentine. London: Routledge.

Mac An Ghaill, M. 1994. *The Making of Men: Masculinities, Sexualities and Schooling.* Buckingham, UK: Open University Press.

Macdonald, N. 2001. *The Graffiti Subculture: Youth, Masculinity and Identity.* London: Palgrave Macmillan.

MacLeod, J. 1995. *Ain't No Making It: Aspirations and Attainment in a Low-Income Neighborhood.* Boulder, CO: Westview Press.

Malbon, B. 1998. "*The Club*: Clubbing, Consumption, Identity and the Spatial Practices of Every-Night Life." *Cool Places: Geographies of Youth Culture,* ed. Tracey Skelton and Gill Valentine. London: Routledge.

Males, M. 1999. *Framing Youth: 10 Myths about the Next Generation.* Monroe, ME: Common Courage Press.

Markus, H., and P. Nurius. 1986. "Possible Selves." *American Psychologist* 41: 154–169.

Marquez, B. 2001. "Choosing Issues, Choosing Sides: Constructing Identities in

Mexican-American Social Movement Organizations." *Ethnic and Racial Studies* 24(2): 218–235.

Martinez, J. 2000. *The Phenomenology of Chicana Experience: Identity, Communication and Transformation in Praxis.* New York: Rowan & Littlefield.

Massey, D. 1998. "The Spatial Construction of Youth Cultures." *Cool Places: Geographies of Youth Culture,* ed. Tracey Skelton and Gill Valentine. London: Routledge.

Matthews, G. 2003. *Silicon Valley, Women, and the California Dream: Gender, Class and Opportunity in the Twentieth Century.* Stanford: Stanford University Press.

Maxwell, S. 2001. "Negotiating Car Use in Everyday Life." *Car Culture: Materializing Culture,* ed. Daniel Miller. Oxford: Berg

McCoy, L. 1995. "Activating the Photographic Text." *Knowledge, Experience and Ruling Relations: Studies in the Social Organization of Knowledge,* ed. Marie Campbell and Ann Manicom. Toronto: University of Toronto Press. 181–193.

McDonald, K. 1999. *Struggle for Subjectivity: Identity, Action and Youth Experience.* Cambridge: Cambridge University Press.

McDowell, L. 1999. *Gender, Identity and Place: Understanding Feminist Geographies.* Minneapolis: University of Minnesota Press.

McRobbie, A. 1993. "Shut Up and Dance: Youth Culture and Changing Modes of Femininity." *Cultural Studies* 7: 406–426.

McRobbie, Angela. 1991. *Feminism and Youth Culture: From Jackie to Just Seventeen.* Boston: Unwin Hyman.

Mead, G. H. 1934. *Mind, Self & Society: From the Standpoint of a Social Behaviorist.* Chicago: University of Chicago Press.

Messner, M. 1992. *Power at Play: Sports and the Problem of Masculinity.* Boston: Beacon Press.

Meyer, S. 2001. "Work, Play, and Power: Masculine Culture on the Automotive Shop Floor, 1930–1960." *Boys and Their Toys? Masculinity, Class, and Technology in America,* ed. Roger Horowitz. New York: Routledge.

Miller, D. 2001a. "Driven Societies." *Car Culture: Materializing Culture,* ed. Daniel Miller. Oxford: Berg.

Miller, D. (ed.). 2001b. *Car Culture: Materializing Culture.* Oxford: Berg.

Mills, C. W. 1959. *The Sociological Imagination.* Oxford: Oxford University Press.

Min, P. G., and R. Kim. 1999. *Struggles for Ethnic Identity: Narratives by Asian American Professionals.* Walnut Creek, CA: AltaMira Press.

Mirande, A. 1998. *Hombres y Machos: Masculinity and Latino Culture.* Boulder, CO: Westview Press.

Miron L. F., and J. X. Inda. 2000. "Race as a Kind of Speech Act." *Cultural Studies: A Research Annual* 5: 85–107.

Moll, L., and R. Ruiz. 2002. "The Schooling of Latino Children." *Latinos: Remaking America,* ed. Marcelo M. Suarez-Orozco and Mariela M. Paez. Berkeley: University of California Press.

Molnar, A. 1996. *Giving Kids the Business: The Commercialization of America's Schools.* Boulder, CO: Westview Press.

Montero-Sieburth, M., and F. Villarruel (eds.). 2000. *Making Invisible Latino Adolescents Visible: A Critical Approach to Latino Diversity.* New York: Falmer Press.

Moore, D. 1997. "Remapping Resistance: 'Ground for Struggle' and the Politics of Place." *Geographies of Resistance,* ed. Steve Pile and Michael Keith. London: Routledge.

Mueller, A. 1995. "Beginning in the Standpoint of Women: An Investigation of the Gap between Cholas and 'Women in Peru.'" *Knowledge, Experience and Ruling Relations: Studies in the Social Organization of Knowledge,* ed. Marie Campbell and Ann Manicom. Toronto: University of Toronto Press. 96–105.

Muggleton, D., and R. Weinzierl (eds.). 2003. *The Post-Subcultures Reader.* Oxford: Berg.

Mukerji, C., and M. Schudson. 1991. *Rethinking Popular Culture: Contemporary Perspectives in Cultural Studies.* Berkeley: University of California Press.

Namkung, V. 2004. "Reinventing the Wheel: Import Car Racing in Southern California." *Asian American Youth: Culture, Identity, and Ethnicity,* ed. Jennifer Lee and Min Zhou. New York: Routledge.

Nava, M. 1991. "Consumerism Reconsidered: Buying and Power." *Cultural Studies* 51: 57–172.

Nava, M. 1987. "Consumerism and Its Contradictions." *Cultural Studies* 1: 204–210.

Nishioka, J. 2001 "Rice Rockets: Inside the Import Car Phenom." *Asian Week* 22(44): 18–20.

Nomura, G., R. Endo, S. Sumida, and R. Leong (eds.). 1989. *Frontiers of Asian American Studies: Writing, Research and Commentary.* Pullman: Washington State University Press.

O'Connell, S. 1998. *The Car in British Society: Class, Gender and Motoring, 1896–1939.* Manchester: Manchester University Press.

Odem, M. 1998. "Teenage Girls, Sexuality, and Working Class Parents in Early Twentieth Century California." *Generations of Youth: Youth Cultures and History in Twentieth-Century America,* ed. Joe Austin and Michael Nevin Willard. New York: NYU Press.

Odem, Mary E. 1995. *Delinquent Daughters: Protecting and Policing Adolescent Female Sexuality in the United States, 1885–1920.* Chapel Hill: University of North Carolina Press.

Oliver, M., and T. Shapiro. 1995. *Black Wealth/White Wealth*. New York: Routledge.

Olsen, L. 1997. *Made in America: Immigrant Students in Our Public Schools*. New York: New Press.

Omi, M., and H. Winant. 1986. *Racial Formation in the United States*. New York: Routledge.

Palladino, G. 1996. *Teenagers: An American History*. New York: Basic Books.

Pile, S., and M. Keith (eds.). 1997. *Geographies of Resistance*. London: Routledge.

Poster, M. 1988. *Jean Baudrillard: Selected Writings*. Stanford: Stanford University Press.

Presdee, M. 2000. *Cultural Criminology and the Carnival of Crime*. New York: Routledge.

Proweller, A. 1998. *Constructing Female Identities: Meaning Making in an Upper Middle Class Youth Culture*. Albany: State University of New York Press.

Putnam, Robert. 2000. *Bowling Alone: The Collapse and Revival of American Community*. New York: Simon & Schuster.

Quart, Alissa. 2003. *Branded: The Buying and Selling of Teenagers*. New York: Basic Books.

Raby, R. 2002. "A Tangle of Discourses: Girls Negotiating Adolescence." *Journal of Youth Studies* 5(4): 425–448.

Radway, J. 1984. *Reading the Romance: Women, Patriarchy and Popular Literature*. Chapel Hill: University of North Carolina Press.

Rank, M. 2001. "The Effect of Poverty on America's Families: Assessing Our Research Knowledge." *Journal of Family Issues* 22(7): 882–903.

Reisman, D. 1950. *The Lonely Crowd: A Study of the Changing Character*. New Haven: Yale University Press.

Ritzer, G. 2005. *Enchanting a Disenchanting World: Revolutionizing the Means of Consumption*. 2nd ed. Thousand Oaks, CA: Pine Forge Press.

Roberts, I. 2003. *Adbusters* 11(4): 7.

Roman, L., and L. Christian-Smith (eds.). 1988. *Becoming Feminine: The Politics of Popular Culture*. London: Falmer Press.

Ross, A., and T. Rose (eds.). 1994. *Microphone Fiends: Youth Music and Youth Culture*. New York: Routledge.

Rubin, L. 2004. *Families on the Fault Line: America's Working Class Speaks about the Family, the Economy and Race and Ethnicity*. New York: HarperCollins.

Sandoval, D. 2003. "Bajito y Suavecito/Low and Slow: Cruising through Lowrider Culture." Unpublished Ph.D. diss., University of California at Los Angeles.

Sassen, S. 2000. *The Global City: New York, London, Tokyo*. Princeton, NJ: Princeton University Press.

Sassen, S. 1998. *Globalization and Its Discontents*. New York: New Press.

Sato, R. S. 1998. "What Are Girls Made Of? Exploring the Symbolic Boundaries of Femininity in Two Cultures." *Millennium Girls,* ed. Sherrie Inness. New York: Rowan & Littlefield.

Scharff, V. 1991. *Taking the Wheel: Women and the Coming of the Motor Age.* Albuquerque: University of New Mexico Press.

Schippers, M. 2002. *Rockin' Out of the Box: Gender Maneuvering in Alternative Hard Rock.* New Brunswick, NJ: Rutgers University Press.

Schlesinger, A. 1992. *The Disuniting of America.* New York: Norton.

Schor, J. 2000. "Towards a New Politics of Consumption." *The Consumer Society Reader,* ed. J. Schor and D. B. Holt. New York: New Press.

Schor, J. 1998. *The Overspent American: Why We Want What We Don't Need.* New York: Harper Perennial.

Schor, J. 1992. *The Overworked American: The Unexpected Decline of Leisure.* New York: Basic Books.

Schor, J., and D. B. Holt (eds.). 2000. *The Consumer Society Reader.* New York: New Press.

Shackleford, B. 2001. "Masculinity, the Auto Racing Fraternity, and the Technological Sublime: The Pit Stop as a Celebration of Social Roles." *Boys and Their Toys? Masculinity, Class, and Technology in America,* ed. Roger Horowitz. New York: Routledge.

Sharpe, M. 2003. "The Logo as Fetish: Marxist Themes in Naomi Klein's *No Logo.*" Available at eserver.org/clogic/2003/Sharpe.html.

Shrum, W., and J. Kilburn. 1996. "Ritual Disrobement at Mardi Gras: Ceremonial Exchange and Moral Order." *Social Forces* 75(2): 423–458.

Silverstone, R. (ed.). 1997. *Visions of Suburbia.* New York: Routledge.

Simmel G. (1903) 1950. "The Metropolis and Mental Life." *The Sociology of Georg Simmel,* ed. K. Wolff. New York: Free Press.

Skelton, T., and G. Valentine (eds.). 1998. *Cool Places: Geographies of Youth Culture.* London: Routledge.

Slater, D. 1997. *Consumer Culture and Modernity.* Oxford: Polity Press.

Smith, D. 1999. *Writing the Social: Critique, Theory and Investigations.* Toronto: University of Toronto Press.

Smith, D. 1990a. *Texts, Facts and Femininity: Exploring the Relations of Ruling.* New York: Routledge.

Smith, D. 1990b. *The Conceptual Practices of Power: A Feminist Sociology of Knowledge.* Boston: Northeastern University Press.

Smith, D. 1987. *The Everyday World as Problematic: A Feminist Method.* Boston: Northeastern University Press.

Smith, R. 2002. "Gender, Ethnicity, and Race in School and Work Outcomes of Second-Generation Mexican Americans." *Latinos: Remaking America,* ed. Marcelo M. Suarez-Orozco and Mariela M. Paez. Berkeley: University of California Press.

Sommers, L. 1985. "Symbols and Style in Cinco de Mayo." *Journal of American Folklore* 390: 478.

Stearns, P. 2003. *Anxious Parents: A History of Modern Childrearing in America.* New York: NYU Press.

Steinberg, S., and J. Kincheloe (eds.). 1997. *Kinder-Culture: The Corporate Construction of Childhood.* Boulder, CO: Westview Press.

Sterngold, J. 2000. "How Lowriding Evolved from Chicano Revolt to Art Form" (February 19). Available at NYTimes.com.

Suarez-Orozco, M., and M. Paez (eds.). 2002. *Latinos: Remaking America.* Berkeley: University of California Press.

Takaki, R. 1989. *Strangers from a Different Shore: A History of Asian Americans.* Boston: Little, Brown.

Taylor, C. 2004. *Modern Social Imaginaries.* Durham, NC: Duke University Press.

Thorne, B. 1993. *Gender Play: Girls and Boys in School.* New Brunswick, NJ: Rutgers University Press.

Thornton, S. 1997. "The Social Logic of Subcultural Capital." *The Subcultures Reader,* ed. Ken Gelder and Sarah Thornton. London: Routledge.

Tienda, M., and W. J. Wilson. 2002. *Youth in Cities: A Cross-National Perspective.* Cambridge: Cambridge University Press.

Tolman, D. L. 1994. "Doing Desire: Adolescent Girls' Struggle for/with Sexuality." *Gender and Society* 8(3): 324–342.

Tocqueville, A. de. (1853) 1969. *Democracy in America.* Ed. J. P. Mayer. Garden City, NY: Doubleday.

Tsuda, T. (Gaku). 2001. "When Identities Become Modern: Japanese Emigration to Brazil and the Global Contextualization of Identity." *Ethnic and Racial Studies* 24(3): 412–432.

Valdivia, A. 2003. "Radical Hybridity: Latinas/os as the Paradigmatic Transnational Post-subculture. *The Post-Subcultures Reader,* ed. David Muggleton and Rupert Weinzierl. Oxford: Berg.

Vallas, S. 2000. "Symbolic Boundaries and the New Division of Labor: Engineers, Workers and the Restructuring of Factory Life." *Social Stratification and Mobility* 18: 3–37.

Van Ausdale, D., and J. R. Reagin. 2001. *The First R: How Children Learn Race and Racism.* Lanham: Rowan & Littlefield.

Vigil, D. 2002. "Community Dynamics and the Rise of Street Gangs." *Latinos: Remaking America,* ed. Marcelo M. Suarez-Orozco and Mariela M. Paez. Berkeley: University of California Press.

Vigil, D. 1997. *Persona Mexicanas: Chicano High Schoolers in a Changing Los Angeles.* Fort Worth, TX: Harcourt Brace.

Vigil, D. 1988. *Barrio Gangs: Street Life and Identity in Southern California.* Austin: University of Texas Press.

Vinitzky-Seroussi, V. 1998. *After Pomp and Circumstance: High School Reunion as an Autobiographical Occasion.* Chicago: University of Chicago Press.

Walker, J. C. 1987. *Louts and Legends: Male Youth Culture in an Inner-City School.* London: Allen & Unwin.

Watt, P., and K. Stenson. 1998. "The Street: 'It's a Bit Dodgy Around There': Safety, Danger, Ethnicity and Young People's Use of Public Space." *Cool Places: Geographies of Youth Culture,* ed. Tracey Skelton and Gill Valentine. London: Routledge.

Weis, L. 1990. *Working Class without Work: High School Students in a De-industrializing Economy.* New York: Routledge.

West, C. 1994. *Race Matters.* Boston: Beacon Press.

West, C., and S. Fenstermaker. 2002. *Doing Gender: Doing Difference.* New York: Routledge

West, C., and D. Zimmerman. 1987. "Doing Gender." *Gender and Society* 1: 125–151.

Whyte, William Foote. 1955. *Street Corner Society.* Chicago: University of Chicago Press.

Williams, A. 2001. "Teenage Passengers in Motor Vehicle Crashes: A Summary of Current Research." Insurance Institute for Highway Safety. Available at http://www/highwaysafety.org.

Williams, S. 2002. "Trying on Gender, Gender Regimes, and the Process of Becoming Women." *Gender and Society* 16(1): 29–52.

Williams, S., S. Alvarez, and K. Andrade Hauck. 2002. "My Name Is Not Maria: Young Latinas Seeking Home in the Heartland." *Social Problems* 49(4): 563–584.

Willis, P. 1977. *Learning to Labour.* Aldershot, UK: Saxon House.

Wilson, W. J. 1996. *When Work Disappears.* New York: Knopf.

Witzel, K., and K. Bash. 1997. *Cruisin': Car Culture in America.* Osceola, WI: MBI.

Wollen, P., and J. Kerr (eds.). 2002. *Autopia: Cars and Culture.* London: Reaktion Books.

Wu, F. 2002. *Yellow: Race in America beyond Black and White.* New York: Basic Books.

Yaeger, P. 1996. *The Geography of Identity.* Ann Arbor: University of Michigan Press.

Young, J. 1997. "The Subterranean World of Play." *The Subcultures Reader,* ed. Ken Gelder and Sarah Thornton. London: Routledge.

Zukin, Sharon. 2003. "Urban Lifestyles: Diversity and Standardisation in Spaces of Consumption." *The Consumption Reader,* ed. D. B. Clarke, M. Doel, and K. L. Housiaux. London: Routledge.

Zukin, Sharon. 1995. *The Culture of Cities.* Oxford: Blackwell.

Index

About the Author

Amy Best is Associate Professor of Sociology at George Mason University. She is the author of *Prom Night: Youth, Schools, and Popular Culture,* winner of the 2002 American Educational Studies Association Critics Choice Award.